"The caring aspects of medicine have been lost in [the] shuffle, so that many Americans have good reason to question the quality of the advice and care they receive. One of this book's strengths is that it tells us why. [It] deserves to be read by all who care about the nation's health—or their own."

—*Washington Post*

"An important book. [Dr. Hiatt] illustrates each step of his argument using actual case histories, which are easy to identify with and therefore compelling to read. He surveys the latest developments in medical technology, managing simultaneously to impress us with their wonders and to make us realize the impracticality of their mass application. For a book on such a depressing subject, [this] is surprisingly engaging."   —*New York Times*

"The United States spends nearly 11% of gross national product on health care—three times more per head than Britain—but the health outcomes produced by this vast expenditure are less than impressive in terms of infant mortality, life expectancy, and access to care. This book is an excellent review of the problems and it offers some stimulating solutions. Essential reading for doctors and policy makers."   —*The Lancet*

"[Dr. Hiatt] has the happy—and all too rare—facility for illuminating and clarifying a complicated and controversial subject. This makes for a book that should be read carefully by physicians, politicians and present and potential patients—in other words, all of us."   —*Kirkus Reviews*

"(A) clear and persuasive book."   —*New York Times Book Review*

"A perceptive, hopeful new book."   —*Baltimore Sun*

"Others have pointed out [the American health care system's] inequities, its inflated cost, and its preoccupation with high technology, but few have done it with the balanced approach of the author of this readable book, and I suspect that is because of Dr. Hiatt's personal experiences as a bedside physician, as a biomedical investigator, as an administrator of a major medical school of public health and, perhaps most important of all, as a teacher."   —*Squibbline*

"This important and readable book is recommended for administrative and policy collections as well as public libraries."   —*Library Journal*

"Hiatt is no young ideologue out to change the system. He has been part of it for years and knows of what he speaks."   —*Cope Magazine*

"In a quietly factual way, Hiatt describes in detail a medical system whose inequities should inspire in us a rage for action."   —*Harvard Magazine*

MEDICAL LIFEBOAT

Will There Be Room for *You*
in the Health Care System?

HOWARD H. HIATT, M.D.

 A Cornelia and Michael Bessie Book

PERENNIAL LIBRARY
Harper & Row, Publishers, New York
Cambridge, Philadelphia, San Francisco
London, Mexico City, São Paulo, Singapore, Sydney

Designer: Sidney Feinberg

Library of Congress Cataloging-in-Publication Data
Hiatt, Howard H.
  Medical lifeboat
  "A Cornelia and Michael Bessie book."
  ("Perennial Library.")
  Includes index.
  1. Medical care—United States. 2. Public health—
United States.   I. Title.
RA395.A3H53   1989   362.1'0973   86-45661
ISBN 0-06-091560-9

89 90 91 92 93 CC/FG 10 9 8 7 6 5 4 3 2 1

To Doris

Contents

Introduction to the Paperback Edition

I welcome the opportunity to reintroduce and retitle the book I first called *America's Health in the Balance: Choice or Chance?* The original title now seems to me too academic, too detached. It suggests that since there are practical—if not perfect—solutions to the problems of our health care system, they will be embraced if only they are laid out. I hope that the new title, drawn from a metaphor in the text, is alarmist enough. The problem certainly is that bad. How much worse must it get before we confront it seriously? "Lifeboat"? Passengers don't "take to boats" unless their ship is wrecked or foundering. The American ship of health is not yet on the rocks, at least not for most Americans, but it is headed that way, and in this last year alone it picked up speed.

Certainly notice is being taken that our jerry-built "system" of health care and health care delivery is improperly provisioned, unseaworthy, and inadequate to hold us all. In the last year, there have been several initiatives to improve it, most notably a bill in Massachusetts to provide health insurance for all. But most have been tinkering. And when efforts are made to seal one leak, for example, to insure the elderly against catastrophic illness, another results, usually in the form of higher costs. Yet most proposals, like catastrophic insurance, are so crucial to the nation's health that we can't afford to ignore them. Many changes must be made, but as part of fundamental reform of the system.

America's health remains in the balance. Its fate will continue to be determined by chance if we don't make choices. And increasingly the question will be whether there will be a place for all of us in America's health care system.

· · · · ·

Every day we hear of health care costs out of control, of tragedy born of limited resources, of failure to use resources wisely. The nation is experiencing a crisis in health care today. The crisis has long been here for the more than 35 million Americans without health insurance who, as a result, risk being refused lifesaving measures when their lives are threatened; for the thousands of families in every American city whose infants die before their first birthday (at a higher rate than do those in many Third World countries); and for the sick elderly who have to exhaust their meager savings in order to become eligible for nursing home coverage. The crisis is more recent for the more than 80,000 Americans who had contracted AIDS by early 1989, and it is here now, if not yet perceived, for the more than 200,000 more already infected with the AIDS virus who will have the disease in the next three years.

AIDS and high infant mortality rates may not seem to be personal threats to many readers of this book. In the eyes of some they threaten mainly what is coming to be called "the permanent underclass," that growing stratum of Americans too poor to cope, too illiterate to learn how to cope, too hopeless even to try. But let the complacent majority take notice: The AIDS problem is a threat to us all, and the ills of those now trapped by medical tragedy of all kinds already cost the rest of us dearly. The sick seek and often, but not always, get places in the health care system, places many need only because society permitted the social conditions that helped produce their medical problems.

Crisis may seem too strong a word for many more fortunate, but frustrated, others who can afford to get into the system, but who often have difficulty in finding care appropriate to their needs. The general sense of crisis will deepen as taxpayers find that they are diminishing in proportion to the ever-growing number of dependents. These include not only the poor—and the poor are much sicker than the affluent—but also the aged, who are much sicker than the young. Medical care for an old person costs three times what it does for someone young or middle-aged, and medical advances have greatly prolonged those costly dependent periods.

In Great Britain, crisis has long been present for some in need of certain lifesaving procedures. There the general population is about as healthy as ours at less than one-third the per capita cost, but some measures (kidney dialysis, for instance) are routinely denied to older people; that is, elderly kidney patients are simply allowed to die. That's triage by choice. In our country, inner-city babies are allowed to die, and the uninsured 15 percent of our population is allowed to die. That's triage by chance. We never deliberately *chose* to abandon these millions of Americans; it just happened. Not to choose is a choice. But America is already experiencing explicit, if haphazard, triage—as an Oregon mother recently told a television audience after her seven-year-old had died of leukemia. She said that her child might have been saved by a bone marrow transplant, but that her request for state money to pay for it had been turned down when the state legislature decided that public funds were inadequate to pay for marrow and other organ transplants.

The necessity for triage and the prospect of more make even more scandalous the wasteful use of the system—the useless (and potentially harmful) antibiotic for a cold, the often unnecessary (and risky and painful, as well as costly) hysterectomy or prostate or gall bladder operation. And the wasteful deployment of resources is a scandal, too—the four hospitals in the same city equipped for complex heart surgery, when one would often do better, or the almost 40 percent of the nation's hospital beds that are empty while many areas with excess hospitals have too few nursing homes. And the use of resources for problems that could have been avoided is a quieter scandal, but equally wasteful—the (usually unsuccessful) operation for the lung cancer that would not have occurred had the victim not smoked cigarettes, or the costly (and often only partly effective) rescue procedures in the neonatal intensive care unit for the low-weight infant who would have been of normal weight had his mother had proper prenatal care. All of this avoidable or useless spending was part of last year's $500-billion bill.

For my insistence that "health policy is social policy," for my advocacy of broad-gauge, "social" approaches to our health problem, I have been accused of favoring "socialized medicine"—whatever that is. Hardly. I reply that government is often more meddlesome with respect to how doctors manage their patients in our country than in, say, Great Britain or Canada. I doubt that British doctors would tolerate what we American doctors must: a government agency telling *them* the proper length of hospital stay for a patient with a heart attack. Such intrusions demean the doctor, devalue his judgment, sap his pride; caring, and the powerful drive to do one's best for the patient, are the root and branch of honorable medicine.

I recognize, of course, that doctors vary in their values, as do any other group of Americans. I winced when I read of an eye surgeon who received $5.6 million from Medicare last year. I felt humiliated when a patient I referred to a specialist was told (by form letter) that she would be seen only if she brought a check or a credit card with her. I am saddened when a sick friend tells me that he waited in a doctor's office for three hours, and another a longer period in an emergency unit of a prominent hospital, and that neither heard a word of apology for the delay. I am pained when medical negligence is uncovered in the local newspaper, but not by the hospital where it took place.

Crisis may be too strong a word to describe the outlook for many doctors, but not for the obstetricians who have given up medical practice because of the litigious climate surrounding issues of malpractice. Perhaps not yet for the family doctor in a nearby rural area who is wondering how he can continue unless he can increase his income above its present level of $35,000. (He is aware that some of his medical school classmates in heart and eye surgery and other specialties have incomes of six and seven figures; they up the average physician incomes that appear in the newspapers but only make his situation more difficult for people to understand.) And perhaps not yet for the medical student I know who gave up her nurse-practitioner job working with migrant farm workers to train as a physician to work in the Third World. Now, with the prospect of having to pay off the more than $100,000 she will have borrowed for her medical training, she wonders how she will be able to afford to care for the poor.

The crisis cries for public attention and for leadership at federal, state, and local levels. The tragedy is greater because the United States *can*—for no more than we spent on health care last year—have a medical care system that provides every man, woman, and child with comprehensive health insurance; with immediate access to hospitals without crippling bills when the stay is over; with nursing homes and home care programs when the illness does not require the facilities of the hospital; and, above all, with a family doctor. The doctor would see patients in the office or clinic, in the hospital, or at home, depending on the condition of the patient and nothing else. She would take preventive measures, like immunization against polio and measles for kids, and against the flu for adults. She would advise the patient on how to avoid preventable diseases like AIDS, lung cancer, and coronary heart conditions. She would keep a complete medical record that would be computerized and available—with the patient's permission—anywhere in the country where the patient might get sick. She would refer the patient in need of complex surgery to a specialist in a hospital equipped for that surgery. She would recognize early cancer of the uterus and early heart failure and treat them while they were still curable, or while damage could be minimized. She would see that patients disabled by a stroke, mental illness, or Alzheimer's Disease received the same compassionate and skillful care that her alert patients with acute illnesses took for granted.

We can be a country that looks on the health of our children as crucial to our security. That understands that our educational system may mean as much to the future of America's health as the amount of penicillin that is available. That continues to give high priority to biological research to advance the understanding of today's medical enigmas like AIDS, schizophrenia, and Alzheimer's Disease and then applies that understanding to the control of those devastating problems. That recognizes that the health of children in Third World countries is essential for international security.

This book suggests specific ways to reduce waste, risk, and inefficiency while providing universal access to care. To do so would require a broad perspective, a general shakeup, and a hard look at our priorities, so many of which have been graven into legislation apparently at random. (Why, for instance, should every American with kidney trouble be guaranteed enormously expensive care at every other American's expense, while most with heart, liver, and lung disease take pot luck?)

Let's not refuse places in the health care system to those whose lives could be saved, at least not while many places are occupied by people who don't need them. Some choices should be easy—the infant dying of a preventable disease, for example, should be there, but not the elderly man whose life is prolonged by life support systems against his earlier expressed wishes. But many other choices will be very tough. They will grow tougher as our capabilities and our needs grow. Their outcomes will be tougher still if we continue just to let them happen.

· · · · ·

This book emphasizes that the system's deficiencies are many and complicated. No single reform measure will cure its problems. And few of the changes that are necessary can be implemented at once. These realities are arguments not for inaction, but rather for long-range planning starting now. Simultaneously, the most urgent defects can be attacked, but in the framework of an overall approach. In that way, we can hope to minimize our traditional tendency to fix today's most pressing problem in ways that create several more tomorrow.

Several states are addressing the problems they consider most pressing in ways they consider most appropriate. That is encouraging, for the problems and the perceptions of the problems vary from one region of the country to another, and no single solution to any of them exists. Therefore, competition among the creative spirits throughout the nation could bring rich dividends. All of this can best take place with a federal government that assumes ultimate responsibility for the health of all citizens everywhere, including those regions that cannot or do not give the health care system the attention it merits.

Reform of our health care system might be higher on the nation's political agenda if people understood how much more we could get for our present investment in health. It would likely be higher if people knew how bad things are now for many Americans. It would likely be higher if people knew how much worse things will be for many more of us if we don't undertake systemic change at once. It would likely be higher if politicians knew how demoralized many doctors are with the existing system and how receptive they might be to change. It would likely be higher if people recognized that magic bullets don't exist, and that in any event *the* answer can't emerge from Washington.

Most important is that we understand that our health problems, as formidable as they are, can be understood by all of us, and that the health care systems from one part of the country to another can be changed to our taste. Then the American ship of health could be refitted and redirected to the open seas again, and the medical lifeboats could be stowed away.

Acknowledgments

I am indebted to many people for their suggestions and support. Several read portions of the manuscript and offered very helpful comments. These included Len Ackland, Donald Berwick, Sir Douglas Black, Theresa Brady, John Bunker, John Cairns, Daniel Creasey, James Dickson, Howard Eder, Leon Eisenberg, Harvey Fineberg, Howard Frazier, Sir George Godber, Irving Goldberg, Lee Goldman, William Hsiao, Penny Janeway, Brian Jarman, Anthony Komaroff, Felicia Lamport, Cyrus Levinthal, Harry Marks, Robert Maxwell, Thomas J. Murray, H. Richard Nesson, Dwight Perkins, Thomas Pyle, Brooke Drysdale Samuels, Donald Shepard, the late Herbert Sherman, Barbara Stocking, Paul Weiler, Milton Weinstein, and Karl Yordy.

Peter Braun, Doris Hiatt, Tom Lee, Fred Mosteller, Elizabeth Vorenberg, and James Vorenberg read most of the manuscript and offered not only extraordinary insights, but continuing encouragement.

The Alfred P. Sloan Foundation provided financial support to faculty of the Harvard School of Public Health for studies of the allocation of health resources. That work increased my awareness of a need for this kind of book. Arthur Singer of the Foundation encouraged both those studies and my decision to write the book. The Klingenstein Fund provided financial help for the book.

I began the book during a sabbatical year away from Harvard, first at the Institute of Medicine of the National Academy of Sciences in Washington, and subsequently at the King's Fund in London and the Collège de France, Paris. Frederick Robbins, then president of the Institute of Medicine, Robert Maxwell, secretary of the King's Fund, Jacques Ruffié, professor at the Collège, and Guy de Thé all extended great hospitality to me during that period.

My publisher, S. Michael Bessie, forced me to continue at moments when I was prepared to abandon the whole project as a bad idea. Above all, my debt to E. S. Yntema is boundless. She served as editor, critic, and friend. The book is a far better one because of her. Mrs. Yntema and the others listed are not responsible for any of the book's deficiencies, but have added greatly to its strengths.

Introduction:
Taking Control

By most yardsticks the United States should be the healthiest nation in the world. No country spends more on health than we do—more than $2,000 per year for every one of us—man, woman, and child. Medical science is nowhere better developed and applied than in America's many superb hospitals. A focus on health issues—on healthy patterns of living, eating, drinking, exercise, personal hygiene—is to be found in virtually every newspaper every day. We have more doctors per capita than most other industrialized societies. Yet medical tragedy stalks our nation: Many citizens, rich and poor, are not benefiting from medicine's achievements when they need them. We are seventeenth among the world's nations with respect to infant mortality, and in fifteen countries life expectancy is equal to, or greater than, ours. (Both are measures commonly used to assess the health of a population.) We and South Africa are the only industrialized countries to lack medical insurance for all, and the number of uninsured Americans has grown by almost 50 percent since 1977. Every day lives are lost that could be saved. Millions have disease, disability, pain, and anguish that could be prevented or relieved. Our children, unforgivably, are most affected, and our elderly next. The poor are more affected than other income groups. The mentally ill and the mentally handicapped are more affected than the mentally fit.

But no group is spared. Americans of all ages in all economic classes have trouble getting appropriate care. Many people don't know where to turn when illness strikes. More are baffled when they try to judge the quality of their care. Some have too many tests, medications, operations; billions of dollars are wasted on efforts that don't help anyone.

Alarms are sounded frequently, particularly as costs mount. And programs aimed at cost containment have become so widespread that some ask whether the primary goal of America's health care system is to save money rather than to promote health. Unnecessary costs must be contained, and some efforts today are effectively addressing that problem. But they are largely random and not part of a comprehensive program with sensible goals and methods designed to correct existing deficiencies. Most are having adverse effects on the most vulnerable members of our society. It is little wonder that many critics consider the system to be not only out of control, but uncontrollable.

It is uncontrollable if enough people think it is. I don't.

This book will examine developments that contribute to the strengths and weaknesses of American medicine. It will argue that some developments in both biomedical science and social policy simultaneously promote strengths and weaknesses. Medical advances, for example, that make it possible to save the lives of patients with heart disease in their seventies mean that there will be more people in their eighties, with all of *their* medical problems. We should not slow down the medical advances; many will improve the health of Americans, including that of the new octogenarians. We should not set aside social changes; we need many more. But in our world of growing medical capabilities and of scarce resources, every program we choose means we have to pass over other useful activities. Therefore, we should know what each option promises before we make choices.

Many analyses of health policy by economists and other social scientists are criticized because they do not pay enough attention to the nature of the doctor-patient relationship. On the other hand, descriptions of the world of health care by physicians are often faulted because they seem not to recognize that resources are limited, that society cannot afford to do everything for everybody. But the primary concern of personal-care physicians is the well-being of their patients, and society should not want it any other way.

Both perspectives—the one that recognizes the importance of the doctor-patient relationship, the other concerned with the overall needs of society—are essential in the development of rational and humane public policy in the health field. I have attempted to look from both perspectives at the issues dealt with here.

Both perspectives were evident in the health care system I saw during a sabbatical year away from my post as head of a medical service in a Boston teaching hospital.

I spent the academic year 1969–70 in London as Visiting Scientist at the Imperial Cancer Research Fund Laboratories. I did so primarily to catch up with the rapidly progressing field of cancer viruses, an area that had been of special interest to me. I chose to work that year in London rather than at several equally exciting laboratories in the United States, where similar research was going on, so that I could spend some time out of the lab observing the British health system firsthand. "Wonderful," I had heard. "Not up to American standards" . . . "Free medical care" . . . "Socialized medicine," and often so dismissed, as though *that* told me all I needed to know.

The year was exhilarating. The laboratory was first-rate, and I did experiments directed at learning more about how viruses convert normal cells to a cancerous state. But I left the lab often enough to see how the NHS—the National Health Service—worked. Professors of medicine from excellent English medical schools showed me that complex medical care was delivered extremely well in the teaching hospitals—as well as in the American teaching hospitals that I knew and worked in. No surprises there.

I also saw the NHS with the help of a few GPs—general practitioners. That was eye-opening. I made house calls; I spent time with social workers preparing people about to retire for new activities; and I saw GPs working with "home health visitors" to keep people out of hospitals. I saw medical and social services linked, so that the GP could readily mobilize nursing services to ensure that antibiotics and other medications were taken on time, meals on wheels, housekeeping arrangements, and a volunteer group that arranged for a neighbor to come in to help at bedtime. All of this with the GP's daily visit meant that an elderly person with pneumonia could be treated and convalesce at home. I learned that GP, hospital, and nursing services are distributed throughout the country, that everybody, independent of geography, income, or family status, has access to medical care, and that even prolonged illness bankrupts nobody.

Two seeds were planted that year, unknown to me. The first germinated, two years later, in my entering the field of public health; the second, fourteen years later, in my deciding to write this book. I returned home still persuaded that, at its best, American high technology medicine is unsurpassed. But I also saw social aspects of medicine to which as a professor of medicine I had paid inadequate attention. Perhaps the most vivid lesson I took away from that year was that medical care, however crucial, is only one approach to health problems.

Not long after my return from England to my post at the teaching hospital, the head of surgery sought my support for a proposal that the surgical service begin a kidney transplant program. Since the medical service would be responsible for referring most patients in need of transplants and for helping to care for those patients, its support was crucial if the surgical program was to do well. I consulted my medical colleagues, particularly those in charge of patients with kidney disease. We knew that at least four other hospitals in the city had kidney transplant units. We also knew that a new unit might mean less money for other programs in the hospital, although in those days new resources could generally be readily obtained for worthwhile programs. However, we were aware that the costs of health care in our area and in the nation were mounting rapidly. Here was an opportunity to demonstrate that we were prepared to take leadership on the issue. If we decided against the proposal and stated publicly that enough kidney transplant programs already existed in the area, it would be an important signal that we were aware of the problem of duplication of facilities and were willing to forgo having our own program.

The chief of surgery was sympathetic to our concerns. He pointed out, however, that the absence of a transplant unit hindered the program in surgery. It was true that the Department of Surgery had a very strong program in surgical care, teaching, and research. It was attracting extremely capable graduates for its training program and very able young surgeons for its faculty. All of the hospital's patients, staff, and students benefited.

Comprehensive training and research in surgery now required a transplant unit. We felt confident that the proposed program would help make important contributions to the field of transplant surgery. Even more decisive was our conviction that the maintenance of the surgical service's standards was essential to the quality of patient care throughout the hospital. The chief of surgery had made strenuous efforts to set up an exchange program with other local hospitals with transplant units, but for a variety of reasons beyond his control, his efforts had failed.

Once I learned this, I knew I had no choice. I had major reservations about starting yet another transplant program. I was greatly concerned about the rising costs of medical care. I was aware that many other needs both within and outside the health area might be judged—at a societal level—to be more important. But my first loyalty had to be to the patients for whom I was responsible. Therefore, I agreed to support the new program.

That experience provided evidence of another fact of which I was becoming increasingly aware: A conflict of interest existed in my two roles. As a doctor, I was ultimately responsible both for the personal care of all of the patients on a busy medical service and for the related education and research programs. As a citizen, I was concerned with health issues of society in general, particularly the need to find ways to set priorities among our multiple—often unmet—health needs. Focusing on the conflict helped me realize that if I was to concern myself *primarily* with health policy, I could not do so from my current position. Shortly thereafter, I resigned as chief of medicine to become dean of a school of public health.

The range of activities of my public health colleagues—statisticians, decision scientists, epidemiologists, policy analysts, economists, political scientists, management experts, biologists, behavioral scientists, and others—all have helped me appreciate the complexities of our health care system and the importance of nonmedical factors as determinants of health. I learned from my students, one quarter of whom were physicians from abroad, much about how other countries manage their health problems. I also learned from them of the enormous burden of illness in less developed countries and of opportunities for Americans to work with people from those countries in dealing with their concerns. This background complements the insights into the powers of modern medicine and the natural sciences that I owe to my earlier experiences as a physician concerned with the care of patients and as a laboratory scientist. I trust that my respect for each will be evident in what follows.

I will first examine medical care—the good and the bad—within our own country. I will pay close attention to the caring function of the physician, a role often overlooked when the outcome of medical encounters is measured in terms of such yardsticks as life expectancy and infant mortality, but a role I consider to be essential.

I will then consider issues of cost, access, quality, and organization of medical services. I will point out that at present, however inadvertently, we are rationing basic medical care. Changes are taking place so quickly that much written today will be obsolescent tomorrow. What is now going on, however, is not, in my view, likely to solve many of our most serious problems. The grave problem of medical neglect, for example, is getting steadily worse.

In the second section I will consider how some other countries, particularly Britain and Canada, have dealt with problems similar or related to those that confront us, and what we can learn from their experiences. The British have a tax-supported, government-operated health service that provides care—without direct charge—to all residents throughout the nation. Canadian physicians, nurses, and health care institutions retain their independence, but all are compensated by a government-operated insurance program that covers all residents—also without direct charge for services.

The third section of the book will propose specific ways in which we can make our system more efficient and effective. That could stretch our resources considerably and help us deliver good medical care to the millions of Americans who now get poor care or none.

In the last section, I will touch on values within the health field that can affect the rationing of medical care. I shall argue that we could eliminate the de facto rationing of basic medical services that more than 37 million Americans now know. We could probably do so, without committing more money to the health field, by using today's funds more prudently. Indeed, who would not give up unnecessary tests and operations, duplications of facilities, and other inefficiencies in return for basic health care for citizens now without it—and often for better care for themselves in the bargain? Such tradeoffs should arouse no controversy. But as increasing medical technology and the health needs of an aging population put more pressure on the system, the tradeoffs will become harsh. Thus, we cannot avoid coming to grips with the reality that we shall never be able to provide everybody with everything that medical care could make possible.

One way to deal with the dilemma would be to designate those elements of health care that we believe essential for everybody and ensure their universal availability before committing large sums of money to less crucial programs. In other words, we could recognize that we are making tradeoffs in the health field, even if by default, and be discriminating in the way we make them. A next step could be to examine more carefully the tradeoffs we are now making from one sector to another—for example, in favor of unnecessary and ineffective military programs, rather than for health measures that many Americans now lack. All of this takes on greater importance if we keep in mind that it is within our power to change our present priorities if we find they are not serving us well. In considering priorities it will be necessary to go beyond health to broader issues that confront our society and that are crucial to the awesome and very real questions: Who shall live? Who shall die?

Most of the writing I have done previously has been directed at colleagues in medicine, science, or public health. This book is addressed to my fellow citizens—including colleagues, of course. The involvement of all Americans is required if our nation is to find the best solutions to the formidable problems involved in minimizing health care rationing today and tomorrow. *Best,* not perfect, solutions. Perfect solutions don't exist, but we can aspire to sound, well-informed, and, I hope, fair ones.

Most people and institutions presented in this book have been given fictitious names and characteristics to respect their privacy. But, with one exception (Jack Washington in Chapter 9), the case histories describe either my own experiences or those of medical colleagues or patients I have known or read about.

I

HEALTH CARE
IN AMERICA

1 Rationing by Default

Visitors to the United States sometimes depart with wondrous stories about the health of its citizens and their medical care. Infant mortality—the fraction of newborns who die in the first year of life—has decreased by 50 percent in the past thirty years. Advances in medical science have led to the prevention of polio and the cure of children with leukemia. Surgical triumphs occur daily in the transfer of blood vessels within the same individual and of kidneys, livers, and hearts from one to another. Deaths from heart disease—the nation's leading killer—are down by 30 percent, and from stroke—third on the list of causes of death—by over 40 percent in the past two decades. Cancer of the stomach, first on the list of fatal cancers forty years ago, has fallen to seventh position now and is still going down. Drugs have been discovered that ease the burden of many people with mental and emotional disease. Awareness among Americans is growing that cigarette smoking is responsible for one third of all fatal cancers and one quarter of all deaths. As a result, per capita cigarette consumption is decreasing, and so are illness and deaths from cigarette-related diseases. At the same time, changes in social policy now make available to the poor and the elderly health insurance programs that did not exist in the early 1960s. An amendment to the Social Security legislation in 1972 abolished the means test for life-saving treatment for victims of kidney disease. Since then, everybody in need has access to kidney dialysis or kidney transplant at no personal cost.

Our visitors are, of course, told that medical costs have risen at a rate far in excess of the cost of living—from 6 percent of the gross national product twenty-five years ago to almost 11 percent now. This year the nation will spend more than $450 billion on health, over $2,000 per person. But why not invest more in health, they might ask, for returns so worthwhile?

A Two-Class System

Only if their tour has been highly restricted, however, do those visitors go away feeling that all is well. It does not take long to learn that in the health realm, we have two kinds of citizens. Despite steady increases in health expenditures and the availability of the most sophisticated technology to perhaps 85 percent of our population, in 1986, nearly 37 million Americans had neither private health insurance nor government health benefits. Some with potentially curable medical problems are permitted to die because they are unable to pay for treatment. Disparities are great between the health of the poor and the nonpoor. Infant mortality rates for black babies are twice those for whites; poor people have more early deaths from cancer and heart disease and other illnesses.

Even the 85 percent with health insurance includes many second-class citizens. Some are subjected to unproved tests and treatments, which may involve great risk and great cost. Many don't have a primary-care doctor, who serves as the overseer of their health. As a result, they often don't get to the right specialist when they need one and sometimes find their way to specialists, tests, and even operations and other treatments that they don't need. This is particularly troublesome, because *every* procedure carries a risk. Many people have little way to evaluate the medical advice they are given or the quality of their advisers. Elderly citizens from all economic groups live in terror of catastrophic illness. One third of today's over-eighty-fives are senile, over 35 percent have heart disease, and 25 percent are in nursing homes. Appropriate health facilities for them are inadequate in number and in quality.

And the situation is worsening. Access to medical services has deteriorated in the 1980s, largely because of reductions in government funding for important health programs. Those particularly affected are poor children and poor older citizens. Medicaid, for example, covered 65 percent of the poor in 1976, but less than 40 percent ten years later. In some states as few as 20 percent of poor people have health coverage. Only one third of poor children nationwide are now covered. Out-of-pocket payments by the elderly for hospital costs in 1985 were twice what they were in 1981. The average out-of-pocket cost of health care for the elderly in 1984 was over $1,700. Americans with incomes below $3,000 paid 10.2 percent of their income in health care in 1977, while those with incomes over $15,000 paid 1.7 percent. Community health centers, the only source of medical care for many poor people, are known to have important benefits to health.

But in 1982 alone, cutbacks closed more than 250 centers, and more than 1 million people lost their access to care.

Some preventable conditions like lead poisoning and the complications of untreated high blood pressure are on the rise. Nationwide, infant mortality, which had been falling by 4.6 percent per year from 1965 to 1982, fell by only 2.7 percent from 1982 to 1983, and by 2 percent from 1983 to 1984. And actual increases in mortality have been reported in twenty states. It rose by 40 percent in Boston's inner city after cuts in government funding of maternal and child health programs. The number of pregnant women who receive inadequate care or no care during pregnancy has increased in some cities by as much as 40 percent. Such women are twice as likely as others to have very premature babies who need intensive care— a very expensive medical technology used for what in this instance are often preventable problems. Moreover, such babies often have lifelong disabilities.

The "savings" the budget cuts were intended to achieve are likely to prove shortsighted in economic as well as in human terms. No one yet knows the cost of care for the medical problems that more government support could have prevented. How many of tomorrow's special educational programs for today's very premature babies might have been avoided?

It is true that the figures reflect in part the present administration's insensitivity to the needs of our most vulnerable people. But they also speak to the reality that our nation, like every other, cannot do all that it would like to. Although we don't use the term, we are now rationing even the most basic medical services and thus not discharging our often stated responsibility to provide them to all our citizens. And because we have not as a nation confronted the problem explicitly, we are rationing by default.

In the absence of major changes in our health care system, the gulf between our two medical classes will continue to widen in the years ahead; the number of Americans receiving inadequate or inappropriate care will grow. One reason is the increase in more effective technology. Some of the new technology will save money. Most will add to medical bills.

Growing Demand

Simultaneously the number of potential beneficiaries is increasing. When today's ten-year-olds join the over-sixty-fives, the group generally labeled "the elderly," they will constitute 20 percent of the population, a marked increase over today's 11 percent. More than 13 million Americans will be over eighty-five in 2040, more than five times the number in that category today. Older people tend to have more illness that is complicated, chronic, and resistant to treatment. If today's health spending patterns continue, when the present ten-year-olds become elderly, they and the other over-sixty-fives will consume 45 percent of health dollars, as compared with just under 30 percent today.

Other demographic trends are ominous too. We have fewer children (one-third fewer in the 1980s than in the 1960s), and more of them live below the poverty line (in 1969, 14.1 percent, in 1983, 22.2 percent). More of them are born to single mothers of racial minorities. And we are doing less and less for their support. Across the country, Aid to Families with Dependent Children (AFDC) and food stamps (reckoned for a family of one adult and three children having no income) went down by over a third between 1965 and 1981. A population like this is likely to grow up with disproportionately numerous and serious medical needs.

Once the large "baby boom" generation begins to go into retirement, and the working-age population declines in proportion to the elderly, the burden of old people's health care costs will increase at an even faster rate. At present, annual health expenditures for the elderly are less than $500 for every American of working age. By the time today's ten-year-olds have begun to collect Social Security payments, that figure will be almost $1,000.

These statistics and projections signal a growing crisis in health. That crisis is putting increasing pressure on government, doctors, hospitals, the business community, and the insurance industry. Most affected are patients, particularly the elderly and the young. Their numbers will grow larger, and their lot will grow worse in the years ahead, unless there are fundamental changes in the behavior of all the other groups.

Until perhaps fifty years ago, what medicine had to offer was almost as limited as the nation's resources. Therefore, it was realistic to visualize providing everybody with access to the medical interventions then available. Throughout the years many political and some medical leaders proposed that the nation do so. Although a universal health insurance bill was never passed, the 1965 Medicare and Medicaid amendments to the Social Security legislation were intended to ensure access to health services for all of our elderly and our poor. Those laws have brought great benefit in the years since.

But now, the increasing costs of health care, the steady advance of medical science, and the growing demand for medical services have made the goal of universal access seem increasingly remote. The severe cutbacks since 1980 in government support for medical services for the elderly and the poor now focus attention more explicitly than ever on the need to use medical resources more equitably and sensibly.

De Facto Rationing

In fact, rationing has been part of medical practice since its beginnings, even though it is generally not so labeled. One familiar example is the long wait in the hospital emergency room for the patient with a less serious problem, while doctors and nurses look after the critically ill first. A harsh form of rationing in military or civilian disaster situations is called triage. Under circumstances where, for example, the number of battle casualties exceeds medical capabilities, those in charge decide who will be treated first, who later, and sometimes who not at all. It often means neglect of the severely wounded who have less chance of recovery than do others and of those who need more resources than are available.

Sometimes circumstances require that resources be rationed by design and on a continuing basis. That happened in 1981, when a shortage of nurses at the Massachusetts General Hospital in Boston led hospital authorities to close a portion of the medical intensive care–coronary care unit. To preserve what was considered a necessary ratio of nurses to patients, between four and ten of the total of eighteen beds were closed for several months. Many seriously ill patients who would have been hospitalized on the unit were cared for elsewhere in the hospital. Further, patients were transferred from the unit to regular hospital facilities after periods that were, on average, shorter than in 1980. A careful study comparing outcomes during 1980 and 1981 indicated no changes in survival figures for comparable groups of patients throughout the hospital in the two periods.

However, not all triage decisions have such relatively happy outcomes. When the facility being rationed can be used to save one life, and two or more are at risk, tough choices must be made. Faced with this dilemma, the head of one of the country's first kidney programs put the decisions in the hands of what became known there and in other cities as "God committees." At that time the number of kidney dialysis machines was limited. A group of people from the hospital and the outside community were told that the patients whose lives could be saved this week by the one available place in the program included, let's say, a twenty-eight-year-old mother of three children, a sixty-seven-year-old retired person without dependents, and a twenty-two-year-old college senior. The choice had to be made on other than medical grounds, and the committee set the rules. Whatever the guidelines, a review in later years demonstrated that men were chosen over women in a ratio of 2 to 1, and the rejects included disproportionate numbers of the old and the mentally ill.

Many American physicians, as well as government, business, and other leaders, have publicly rejected explicit rationing. And the argument is persuasive that rationing is unconscionable as long as so much money is squandered in the health field and outside, as is presently the case. This increases the urgency of reducing the waste, for the billions of dollars recovered could likely pay for basic medical care for all of those now being rationed because they are unable to pay. It may be unrealistic to believe that enough resources for health will ever be available to cover the nation's rapidly growing medical needs and its rapidly growing medical capabilities and opportunities. But if we are to come as close as possible to handling this problem in accord with our traditional values, we must address it. We can do much better than we are doing at present, when often we do poorly *because* we refuse to acknowledge the existence of the problem.

Who Should Set Priorities?

In the absence of a government policy, society sometimes turns to physicians to set priorities. That poses a conflict for the doctor concerned with the care of the individual patient.* Mark Heller learned that lesson early in his medical career.

Mark was a medical student in the early 1970s. Warm and sensitive, but superficially appearing tough and even gruff, he had been an "activist" group leader in college in the late 1960s and had come to medical school determined to address the health problems of the inner city. For his first course in clinical medicine he had chosen the hospital where I was physician-in-chief. On the evening of the day on which he had been assigned his first patient, I happened to be on the unit where he had just completed his examination. He was sitting in a staff room attempting to record his findings, but so emotionally disturbed that he could not write. At my invitation he accompanied me to my office, where we talked. His patient, a woman in her eighties, had suffered what seemed to have been a massive brain hemorrhage that had left her unconscious and paralyzed on one side of her body. Prior to this catastrophe she had been ailing, but with an

---

* I am not referring to medical doctors working with others in the field of health policy, of course. Resource allocation *is* their business.

active interest in life around her. She would now require skilled nursing care and extensive examinations to determine the precise nature of her medical problem. Decisions concerning definitive treatment had, of course, to await the results.

I had seen Mark some weeks before at a student reception, where he raised, as he often had previously, a subject of great concern to him. How could I justify, he asked, the expenditure of huge sums of money and the commitment of so many skilled people to the care of the elderly (over half of the patients on our medical service were over sixty-five), many with incurable illness, in a city in which thousands of people living nearby had inadequate medical care, nutrition, and housing? Now, for the first time, he was personally responsible for the care of just that kind of patient. As deputy to that patient's personal physician, he had no choice but to recommend the use of all the resources available to him that might help. At this early moment in her hospitalization, her prognosis was uncertain. Recovery was very much a goal and still a realistic possibility.

Mark's interest in the needs of the underserved was no less, but that interest clearly had to be set aside while he addressed himself to his immediate responsibility, the care of his patient. The virtually instinctive way in which he resolved the apparent conflict in favor of the individual patient startled him. He realized, perhaps for the first time, where his first loyalty must lie if resource constraints threaten medical services for the person whose care is entrusted to him.

Mark Heller's lessons are surely among the most important in the area of health resource allocation. First, resource decisions that would compromise optimal patient care must be made in the abstract. Further, they generally cannot be made objectively by those responsible for the care of the patients who might be affected. On the other hand, let's suppose that government agencies had earlier decided that more resources were to be used to provide food and shelter for the impoverished and less for high technology hospitals in the city where Mark worked. He and the staff of his hospital would then have been prepared to use whatever was available to them to meet—as best they could—the needs of the patient with the brain hemorrhage. Whatever their personal reactions to the wisdom of the allocation decision, they would have had a framework in which to place the problems presented to them. That framework would have included doing everything they could possibly do within set limits to promote the interests of their patient. If one result of the allocation decision made by society had meant less money for hungry children in the inner city, Mark and the doctors—*as citizens*—would have been concerned. But their actions *as doctors,* nonetheless, would have been influenced only by what was best for their patient. (One can, of course, visualize circumstances in which it might have been in the interests of Mark's patient to withhold life-saving measures. That is another problem and will be dealt with in Chapter 2.)

This is not to say that doctors are oblivious to the financial problems that surround the health care area at present. They have growing interest in what are called cost-effectiveness issues. Physicians are deciding more and more often that it is not justifiable to do one more laboratory test when the chances are minimal of learning more that would be useful to the patient. They are sending patients home from the hospital a day earlier if it seems very likely that little would be achieved from prolonging the stay. (But they are conscious that the premature discharges of the sick elderly that have resulted from new Medicare regulations can be both cruel and shortsighted, since many such patients need to be sent back to hospitals.)

In the absence of a preexisting, well-publicized, and generally accepted policy, the politician is sometimes placed in a position similar to that of the physician responsible for the care of the individual patient. This may have been the case in 1984, when the governor of Maryland was asked to authorize the use of state Medicaid funds for a heart transplant for one of his constituents. The patient, a fifty-year-old gospel singer, had been told that he would die soon unless his own hopelessly damaged heart was replaced with a normal one. He was also told that the Virginia teaching hospital where such heart operations are performed would not admit him without a deposit of $30,000.

The governor surely knew that existing Medicaid funds did not cover many of the needs of Maryland's poorer citizens, who were totally dependent on those funds for all their basic medical services. But knowing also that refusal of the request before him would be a death sentence for the singer, he had little choice. (The fact that his decision was being made in the full glare of newspaper and television attention further narrowed his options.) He ordered that money be made available. The operation was performed a few days later, and the patient's life was saved. The issue of tradeoffs had been laid aside, as it almost had to have been, in the face of an urgent need to make a decision concerning the life of a dying person.

The Trade-Off Issue

The trade-off issue is not much considered by Americans, for we have not been accustomed to thinking in terms of what economists call opportunity costs—that is, what might be done with the resources saved, if a given decision were made differently. For example, in July 1984, the governor of Illinois signed a bill passed by his state's legislature entitling every citizen up to $200,000 in state funds to cover the costs of any organ transplantation procedure not covered from other sources. One wonders whether anyone mentioned at that time the fact that more than 30 percent of Chicago's children were living in poverty. Or that in the previous two years an increase of 21 percent had occurred in the number of children admitted to the emergency room of Chicago's municipal hospital because of diarrhea and dehydration or what is called "failure to thrive," conditions that are associated with poverty and inadequate child care. Or that 60 percent of black preschoolers are not immunized against polio. What was surely an act of compassion and generosity on the part of the Illinois governor and legislators inadvertently helped make worse or at least prolong health problems for a much larger, if less visible, number of the state's citizens, including children in the inner city, the elderly, the mentally ill, and other disadvantaged groups with less "newsworthy" health needs.

The officials in Illinois were expressing their view that inability to pay should not penalize citizens in need of a life-saving procedure that modern technology has made possible. But the very act of ensuring that the citizens with the condition in question were not discriminated against led to discrimination against a much larger group of sick people unable to pay for even basic medical services.

The connections may not have been made in the public mind. In the Maryland example, it meant discrimination in favor of the gospel singer, but against all other citizens with unmet medical needs. In Illinois those discriminated against were all who required medical care other than an organ transplant. The Social Security amendment of 1972 made possible life-saving measures for all Americans with kidney failure, and in voting for it, the Congress—however well motivated its action—discriminated against all uninsured Americans with any other medical condition. Priorities were thereby set, and until additional legislation is passed, they remain.

It is only at the level of setting policy that opportunities exist for making objective judgments about the priorities that best serve the nation as a whole. In the absence of explicit rules that dictate otherwise, physicians must give first priority to their patients' welfare. In my judgment it is essential that society protect them from conflicts in this realm, for it is in the public interest that their primary consideration continue to be caring for their patients.

2   Caring

The secret of the care of the patient
is in caring for the patient.

—Francis W. Peabody, 1930

When the contributions of modern medicine are added up, the caring function is sometimes forgotten. But it is critical, always has been, and always will be. No good doctor, nurse, social worker, or other health professional responsible for the health of the individual patient neglects it. For convenience I will often refer to "the doctor," although many generalizations also apply to the others. Caring is impossible to quantify in today's cost-benefit analysis, but wise practitioners of that new science don't try. Clearly, knowledge of what modern medical technology can and cannot do and of how to use the technology is essential to the practice of medicine. But for every condition in every patient, caring is also necessary. And for many patients, particularly those with chronic illnesses, that function may be the only one that makes a difference.

Caring—listening to the patient, identifying and relieving anxiety, recognizing and managing pain and other symptoms, compassionately attending to the general and specific needs of patient and family—remains one of the doctor's supreme responsibilities. The woman who has lain awake at night racked with worry about a lump in the breast needs support even if the lump proves to be harmless; she needs it much more if it is found to be cancerous. It is never justified for a doctor to say that nothing can be done—not for the patient with advanced heart disease, nor for the person who has been paralyzed by a stroke or an accident, nor for the elderly person immobilized by chronic disease, nor for the person who is mentally subnormal, nor for the countless people of all ages with emotional or mental disease.

13

Something Can Always Be Done

The victim of a cancer that resists specific treatment is almost without exception in urgent need of a doctor who recognizes that meaningful action is still possible. Daniel Beck is such a doctor. He was available to Jonathan Carlyle and his family whenever they needed him.

Mr. Carlyle, a fifty-one-year-old lawyer, consulted Dr. Beck about a month after he began to have upper abdominal pain after meals and loss of appetite. In that period he lost ten pounds. The doctor arranged extensive testing, including X rays, which showed a mass near his stomach. Mr. Carlyle was hospitalized, and a surgeon recommended by Dr. Beck found what appeared to be a large cancer of the pancreas, which seemed to have spread to several areas in his liver. Biopsies of the mass and of the liver nodules bore out the surgeon's impression. He knew that since the cancer had already spread to the liver, it was incurable. Because it was not obstructing any normal functions, no surgical steps could be helpful. He therefore terminated the operation.

Dr. Beck, who had known the patient for many years, had from the time of the X rays shared with him his concern that the problem was probably very serious. They had had a long conversation after the X rays, during which Mr. Carlyle had asked a range of questions. Thus, when Dr. Beck told him of the diagnosis, it confirmed his fears but did not come as a complete surprise.

Dr. Beck had also investigated and supported his own impressions that chemotherapy for this disease, after it had spread to the liver, offered no benefit, and could well lead to serious side effects. He presented the available facts to Mr. Carlyle, but recommended that he see an oncologist whose judgment Dr. Beck greatly respected. The oncologist said that cure of pancreatic cancer at this stage is impossible and that very few patients with this condition benefit in any way from chemotherapy. Even in the exceptional patient whose response seems to be favorable, it is for weeks or, at most, a few months, whereas toxic reactions occur in most patients. For these reasons, he advised against chemotherapy.

Dr. Beck then discussed the outlook in some detail with Mr. Carlyle and his wife—such matters as the course of the disease in most patients, the symptoms that could arise and how they are managed, and average survival time. He stressed the difficulties in drawing conclusions from statistics. For example, it might be crucial—given his family and outside responsibilities—for Mr. Carlyle to know that the disease is fatal within one year for 90 percent of those afflicted. On the other hand, that figure would be only a statistic if he happened to fall in the other 10 percent. Further, the doctor could think of no symptom that might arise that modern drugs could not control. He predicted that Mr. Carlyle would likely hear from a variety of friends, eager to be helpful, who would tell of *their* friends who had had "identical" problems and had been greatly benefited, perhaps even cured. Dr. Beck said that he believed that he, the oncologist, and the surgeon had access to the latest information, but that it was important to chase down anything that Mr. or Mrs. Carlyle felt might be worth pursuing. He urged that he be permitted to help them evaluate such reports. If additional consultants were recommended, he would gladly help arrange appointments. But he warned that people in their situation are sometimes exploited, occasionally by those who are unscrupulous, more often by those who are overenthusiastic and well-meaning. Therefore, he urged them to protect themselves from spending too much of their time and energy pursuing leads that could make useless and painful incursions on their lives.

Dr. Beck was able to have so direct a talk with the Carlyles relatively soon after the medical facts were known because of his long and close relationship with them. With patients he knows less well, Dr. Beck usually finds it necessary to spend even more time sharing information of this kind and discussing the outlook.

Mr. Carlyle did ask for material to read about pancreatic cancer. He also wanted to see another oncologist, who had been described to him as particularly experienced with the disease. The second consultant confirmed the facts that had been given to Carlyle earlier and said that he sometimes used chemotherapy for such patients, but "not with enthusiasm." The Carlyles decided not to pursue this further.

The next few months were difficult but full. They set their priorities according to guidelines that they had earlier talked about in the abstract— such as spending more time together and with their children and making no social engagements except those with close friends. Mr. Carlyle's abdominal pain continued, but it was controlled by medication.

Four months after the diagnosis, control of his pain required periodic injections, and increasing weakness confined him to bed and chair. Dr. Beck recommended a social worker, who helped Mrs. Carlyle arrange for practical nurses during the day and taught her how to give him injections at night. Dr. Beck visited Mr. Carlyle most days and was in touch with the family by telephone when he could not drop by. The Carlyles and Dr. Beck had agreed from the first that Mr. Carlyle would not be hospitalized if it could in any way be avoided, and that no heroic measures would be taken to keep him alive when the end approached. Three weeks after he became housebound, about six months after his symptoms began, he died in his sleep.

Primary Care, Then and Now

Dr. Beck, who comes from a long line of doctors, harked back in this case to his father, John Beck, who practiced in a small farming town in Pennsylvania. There was little the senior Dr. Beck could do for most of his sick patients except, literally, to "care for" them. But because he could do no more, the caring role was the more important. Indeed, in the late 1920s, John Beck could find, in the first edition of the medical textbook his son now frequently consults in its seventeenth edition, instructions as to how to cure his pediatric patients of rickets with cod liver oil (and even better, how to prevent the problem). But such curable conditions were exceptional; only 2 percent of the medical problems described in the first edition could be cured.

Many people look longingly at the well-known painting of the physician of an earlier era sitting on the bed and tenderly holding the hand of the desperately ill child whose anguished parents hover in the background. They yearn for the compassion that scene conveys, but sometimes forget that compassion and the other elements of caring were all of value that the doctor could offer for most illnesses. In fact, some of the "treatments" recommended in the senior Dr. Beck's medical textbooks, like potassium iodide for mumps and angina pectoris, are now known to be worthless. And others, like violent purges with castor oil for hemorrhage from the lung, were harmful.

As a progressive country doctor, John Beck kept in contact with specialists at the city hospital thirty miles distant, to whom (like Daniel Beck with Mr. Carlyle) he could refer his more complicated cases—those of them, that is, who could afford treatment. Like his son, John Beck educated his patients. "Always wash your hands before milking," he told the farmers. "Boil drinking water; keep the privies distant from the well; wear shoes in the pasture and the barn." Health, not just medicine, was his concern. He advised the local high school about hygiene classes, he saw to it that the children in the community were vaccinated against smallpox, and he tacked up quarantine signs when mumps, measles, or whooping cough struck. Like his son, who found a social worker to help Mrs. Carlyle, the senior

Dr. Beck could be expected to know of a neighbor willing to help in the house of an invalid.

Daniel Beck feels little nostalgia for his father's era. A lot of his father's patients died young or lived crippled and in pain. There was little money for medical technology then, and less technology. His father found it gratifying to provide emotional support for his patients, who were generally his neighbors and friends. And he found particularly frustrating his inability to save his young patients from fatal or debilitating sicknesses.

Daniel Beck was trained as a specialist in internal medicine. He is widely respected by his physician colleagues for his medical acuity, and they often ask him as a consultant to see a patient with a particularly baffling medical problem. Dr. Beck offers his opinion regarding diagnosis and treatment, and the patient then continues under the primary care of the doctor who consulted him.

Gatekeeping

But most of Beck's patients are like the Carlyles—people who regard him as "our doctor." For twenty years he has been, in today's parlance, their primary-care doctor; that is, they turn first to him for any medical problem they consider significant. When the need has arisen, they have discussed with him the merits of various consultants, hospitals, and other kinds of facilities. Indeed, they never see a specialist except on his advice. When Mrs. Carlyle was found to have high blood pressure during her second pregnancy, Dr. Beck teamed up with the obstetrician to treat it. When she developed the symptoms of what proved to be acute appendicitis, he was called at 4 A.M. He made the diagnosis, suggested the surgeon to be called, and saw her while she recuperated in the hospital. Their confidence in his judgment gave them a sense of security about these and other issues that they would not have had without him. As a result of his involvement, his records contain comprehensive summaries of their adult medical histories. But he has been even more than their doctor in a strictly medical sense. His role as counselor and friend, both Carlyles felt, helped save their marriage at an earlier period when it had been under great stress. Dr. Beck was their medical "gatekeeper."*

---

* The word "gatekeeper" is used in a variety of ways in medical journals. Occasionally it is given a pejorative tone: the person who keeps patients *away from* needed medical care. I use it to refer to the crucial function of providing patients with access to appropriate care.

Communication

Dr. Beck is on the teaching staff of Memorial Hospital, which belongs to the medical school in his city and is near his office. Periodically, in one of his self-effacing moods, he finds himself wondering whether his messages to medical students and residents are worth their time, particularly when that same time might be used for them to have additional teaching by some of the eminent researchers on the faculty. But the professor in charge holds Dr. Beck's teaching contributions in very high esteem and considers him the model of a caring physician. Nobody can better demonstrate to doctors in training how to communicate with patients.

Dr. Beck tells his beginning students that when they accept the privilege of caring for a patient, they assume a burden that is awesome, unreasonable, and sometimes even impossible. Not only are they responsible for what they say when they speak to their patients, he says, and for what they mean when they speak, but they are also accountable for what their patients *think* they said and *think* they meant. To discharge this responsibility properly requires sensitivity and skill, of course. But it also requires time. Lots of it. That is especially true when the facts the doctor has to share are unpleasant, unwelcome, or difficult to understand.

Few students forget his lesson on *how* to be candid with the patient. He shares his view that—with rare exceptions—*all* information concerning a patient belongs to the patient. When the patient so desires, it also belongs to the family, but to *nobody* else. He believes that the doctor is generally obliged to tell a patient, for example, that he has cancer. But the doctor has a prior obligation to assure himself that the patient has the resources to hear, to understand, and to integrate such information and all of its implications. No formula exists for "giving the facts," for the facts differ greatly from one patient to another. The ways in which the facts are received and perceived differ even more. Thus, the doctor must know not only the medical facts in painstaking detail, but equally intimately, the patient to whom those facts pertain and to whom they belong. That means that important information cannot be imparted in a spare moment by a doctor whose waiting room or schedule is full of other patients with concerns that are often of equal importance. That's not to say, of course, that the waiting room or the doctor's schedule must be cleared before such discussions can take place. But it does mean that people with crucial business to transact with their doctor can expect to be treated as though the waiting room and the schedule were empty.

Dr. Beck had received Jonathan Carlyle's permission to have a medical student and a resident in the room when he told Mr. Carlyle that his biopsy showed cancer. His patients have all heard him say that he learned from his teachers much of what they value in him. They generally welcome the opportunity to help him pass on those benefits to tomorrow's doctors. The student and resident listened while Beck and Carlyle spent more than forty minutes discussing the disease and some of its implications. They later learned that many more aspects would be discussed in subsequent days and weeks. They also discovered that before he leaves patients who have been given new information, particularly information with unhappy or uncertain implications, Beck usually asks them to summarize their impressions of what he has said. These lessons cannot be learned from textbooks. They are among the most important messages that are taken away by the students and residents who know Dr. Beck as a teacher.

Practice in a Changing World

Daniel Beck loves the practice of medicine now no less than when he first began. His formal scientific and medical education took place in the late 1940s and early 1950s, when nature was beginning to yield some of its secrets to the probes of modern biology. He has followed with excitement and fascination the application of the rapidly unfolding knowledge to the problems of human health. It has meant that he is practicing medicine in a world that is changing far more rapidly than did his father's and much more rapidly now than it did early in his career. He keeps up by reading medical journals and new textbooks, remaining in close touch with his colleagues, attending teaching conferences at his hospital, and going to refresher courses at least once a year. He has no illusions that this permits him to stay on top of all of the developments that are relevant to all the medical problems of his patients. Medicine has become far too complex for that. But he does feel competent to identify the problems he can solve, those that can be solved by specialists, and those which, like Mr. Carlyle's pancreatic cancer, remain resistant to treatment. Thus, he remains aware of what medicine can do and its limitations, and what he can do and his own limitations. He finds it an ever-greater challenge to keep abreast of new medical knowledge, but a stimulating and invigorating one. Continuing education has always been a crucial element of medical practice, and Daniel Beck relishes it. The increasing intellectual content and capabilities of modern medicine make him feel fortunate that he followed in his father's footsteps, and more fortunate that his world is so different. But the changes taking place in today's medical world involve far more than advances in medical science, and some Dr. Beck finds disconcerting and even frustrating. Many reflect the growing complexity of the health scene; some arise from unrealistic expectations of medicine on the part of his patients; others are rooted in a popular misconception that medicine and health are synonymous.

Daniel Beck's practice includes people from very different backgrounds. Janie Peters is the twenty-two-year-old daughter of a housekeeper who once worked for the Beck family. Janie ran away from home when she was fourteen years old and returned four years later, a single parent with two infants. Because she had severe headaches and had not been helped by the doctors she had seen in the emergency unit of a local hospital where she had gone for help, her mother consulted Dr. Beck, who—at Janie Peters' request—took her on as his patient. He found her to have severe high blood pressure and started her on treatment. Dr. Beck helped her get Medicaid support for herself and the babies. But despite the fact that the babies have been treated in the emergency unit of the local hospital repeatedly for respiratory infections and twice for rat bites, he has been completely unable to do anything about getting them out of the appalling slum housing in which they live.

Dr. Beck regards the Peters story as symptomatic of a widespread failure to appreciate that medicine is only one of many ways to deal with health problems, and that it is often ineffective. He knows that poor people not only may have rat bites, but also have more heart disease, cancer, strokes, mental disease, and many other health problems than people with higher incomes. In this day of ever more impressive medical technology, many of his friends in the community, including those who are well educated and in influential positions, have a sense that virtually all health problems can somehow be managed by modern medicine. It is what he calls "magic bullet thinking." Even when medicine can work "miracles," he tells his patients, it's far more miraculous to identify cause and then prevent the problems. Wendy Bates, a younger doctor who now shares Dr. Beck's office suite, learned this lesson on the job.

Poverty and Illness

Dr. Bates worked in Rosehill, an inner city health clinic, in the early 1970s, just after she finished her clinical training. She had gone to medical school because of her desire to work with the medically underserved. She

completed four years of residency in internal medicine and then took a
position as physician at Rosehill.

Dr. Bates was quickly exposed to people with medical problems that
were often far advanced because they had been neglected: lead poisoning
in children; unrecognized tuberculosis; gangrene of the feet and serious
kidney disease in patients with diabetes that had not been diagnosed or
adequately treated; strokes and coronary attacks in people with untreated
high blood pressure; and many more.

Initially, this was all of great clinical interest to Bates. (Among the
mainly nonpoor population for whom she had cared previously, many
such conditions were prevented or recognized in an early state and arrested.)
Her success in diagnosing and treating a range of medical conditions was
gratifying. She soon became attached to, and was revered by, a large group
of enormously grateful patients. She, the nurses, and the aides from the
neighborhood who worked in the clinic organized a home care program
that brought medical, nursing, and home help to people who were housebound because of chronic illness. Particularly rewarding to her was the
readiness to learn about health programs and the dedication of some of
the residents of the community, who welcomed the opportunity to become
health aides. They often saved the need for hospitalization or nursing home
placement of their sick neighbors by taking responsibility for dropping in
on them regularly, for household chores and marketing, for seeing that
medications were taken on time, and for assuring that a nurse or doctor
was called when the need arose.

Dr. Bates's female patients learned the importance of reporting their
pregnancies early and then of regular medical visits, of proper diet, of
giving up smoking and alcohol, of getting proper rest, and of learning
about child care. Dr. Bates helped launch educational programs at the
Rosehill center, and her patients began to realize how much they could do
for their own health and the health of their families.

Early in her work at Rosehill, she did not understand why so many
patients came back repeatedly with the same or related complications. The
answers were soon apparent—even a concerned and informed mother could
not constantly guard her two-year-old from chewing the paint on the win-
dow sills. And the failure of the landlord to remove the lead-based paint
meant that episodes of lead poisoning recurred. Dr. Bates got nowhere in
her pleas to the local authorities that this made no sense in humanitarian
terms—the abdominal pains of lead poisoning can be dreadful and the
brain damage can be permanent—nor in economic terms—the cost to
society of treating lead poisoning is greater than of deleading the neigh-

borhoods where most lead poisoning is found.

The proper treatment of diabetes required a diet that many of her poor patients could not afford. She could do little for many patients with tuberculosis, who were homeless and who stopped taking their medication. As a result, many were out on the streets with a disease that was curable, but that was becoming progressively worse and that was being spread to others. Her promise that stopping cigarette smoking could prevent heart disease and lung cancer twenty years on and would lead to longer life evoked little response (hardly a surprise!) from most of her young patients, who enjoyed cigarettes and had little reason to look forward to what their lives would hold two decades later. In later years Wendy Bates would have greater insight than many people as to why the reduction in smoking occurred so much more often among the more affluent. Even her most persuasive heart-to-heart talks seemed to have little effect in preventing the hepatitis of drug addicts and the liver and brain damage of alcoholics. And her periodic letters to the editor of the local newspaper brought congratulations from her friends who shared her views, but had little effect in promoting the social change that she became convinced was essential if most of the medical problems were to be prevented or effectively dealt with.

After two years of what were at the start exhilarating, and later on frustrating, experiences, Wendy Bates resigned from the center. She suffered from the burnout that many of her similarly motivated medical colleagues also went through after working in similar settings. She left with little doubt that the medical approach to solving health problems was very important. But even more important was that it be accompanied by identifying the major social causes and controlling as many as possible. The lesson and her decision to leave were painful for her. That lesson was well known to her patients in the inner city, and her decision to go was far more painful for them. Their feelings about their doctor differed little from those of Daniel Beck's about *theirs.*

For two years Wendy Bates's patients had their own gatekeeper, one who was skillful and who cared. Each group—Bates's patients and Beck's—would be hard put to find a carbon copy of their doctor. But if forced to do so, there was little doubt as to which would be more likely to succeed. Some of Dr. Bates's patients knew her departure might be followed by the arrival of a successor. But most assumed—unhappily rightly—that they would more likely be forced to resume waiting in long lines in hospital emergency units. And many would find themselves forced to ignore many of the symptoms that Dr. Bates had taught them to tend to early.

Professional Frustrations

A Career Deflected

At the time of Dr. Bates's decision, Daniel Beck was considering moving into a new suite of offices with more space than he needed. They knew each other, for Bates had trained at Memorial Hospital. Beck offered to rent space to Bates and help in launching her practice. In return, they agreed that they would take calls for each other on nights and weekends. A few years later, they were joined by a third doctor, Dr. Steven Kantor, who, as a college volunteer, had worked with Wendy Bates at the Rosehill health center. Indeed, Wendy had been the role model that led Steve Kantor to enter medical school in 1973. Steve, however, was deflected from his original goal early in his medical career.

Like his classmates, Steve spent the first two years in medical school studying the natural sciences. They provided background important to understand the biology of disease, but some seemed only remotely related to his original goal in medicine. The exposure he had to clinical medicine was mainly in Memorial Hospital, where the most visible role models were experts in the high technology that was used to deal with complicated medical problems. The achievements in that setting were often awesome, and Steve's attention was steadily diverted from medical care in underserved areas toward the pressing and challenging medical problems that continually confronted him. He and his classmates had little exposure to the problems that he had known in Rosehill or to people who were addressing those problems.

During his third year in medical school, Steve accepted an invitation to participate in the research of one of his teachers, a prominent professor of cardiology, who studied the effects of certain drugs on patients who had had heart attacks. The exposure to scientific method not only was exciting, but also led to a kind of discipline in his thinking that proved invaluable. He became increasingly interested in cardiology and, following a three-year residency in internal medicine in Memorial Hospital, was selected for a two-year clinical fellowship in cardiology.

Steve emerged from his nine years of medical training at age thirty-three, a very promising cardiologist. He was conscious that his education had had major gaps. The social problems of medical care that originally attracted him to medicine had long since been displaced. He had not developed the historical perspective that would permit him to compare the role of social change with that of medical care in promoting human health. He was well aware of the widespread dissatisfaction with the nation's system of medical care delivery, but he had few insights into how its defects might be repaired. He was aware of ethical dilemmas in the management of many of the very ill patients with whom he had been involved, but he had spent little time considering how these might be resolved. Finally, he knew that other professionals were involved in considering health problems, but he had had no opportunity to work with such people. As a physician about to begin medical practice, he felt confident of his ability to care for very sick patients, but he had had little background for dealing with people in the community.

Another factor was crucial to his career planning: Dr. Kantor emerged from his training with a wife and two young children and with a personal debt of over $50,000. Like the majority of his medical school classmates, he had been forced to borrow money in order to cover his medical education. He had then borrowed additional funds when his wife gave up her job to have their first baby. As a result, he had to find a position that would assure him enough money to support his family and to begin to pay off his debt. Thus, by virtue of both his training and his financial needs, he had long since ceased to be a candidate for a Rosehill health center. But he had heard from Wendy Bates that she and Dr. Beck were looking for a third doctor to share their office space and to rotate night and weekend calls. Steve Kantor greatly admired them both, considered himself lucky for the opportunity to associate with them, and seized it.

Drs. Beck and Bates had originally planned to seek a doctor trained in primary care for the third slot in their informal association. But they liked and respected Steve Kantor so much that they chose him instead. Growing numbers of primary-care doctors are now entering medical practice. This is partly the result of recent changes in medical school and hospital educational programs, many of which are placing more emphasis on primary care. These are changes that Daniel Beck and Wendy Bates applaud, and they have served on the faculty of some of Memorial Hospital's primary-care teaching programs. However, the increasing costs of medical education put pressure on recent graduates to turn away from Rosehill-type positions. Of Harvard Medical School's class of 1985, for example, 77 percent graduated with indebtedness ranging from $5,000 to $100,000. The average debt was $39,000, and the majority of borrowers owed over $30,000.

It doesn't require a background like Wendy Bates's to realize that if the nation is to deal effectively with the health problems of underserved urban areas like that around Rosehill and similar rural ones, the financing of medical education requires urgent attention. At the present time, medical education is more and more the privilege of the affluent. Loans constituted 21 percent of student aid in 1975 and 61 percent in 1983. Those from less well-to-do families who are prepared to borrow to become doctors find themselves heavily encumbered when they finish. As a result, those doctors who want to return home after their training, to practice in areas like Rosehill, can't afford to do so. Meanwhile, the black and Hispanic communities are rapidly increasing, the Hispanic by 61 percent from 1970 to 1980, as compared to 9 percent for the non-Hispanic. Blacks were about 14 percent of the population in 1982; that fraction is expected to reach 24 percent in the next century. That means that the Rosehills in our society with their major medical needs will increase in size and in misery. Meanwhile, the federal programs that were created to address those needs are disappearing. Federal money for community health centers like that at Rosehill has been cut back. The U.S. Public Health Service National Health Service Corps was set up in the late 1960s and through the 1970s financed medical education. In return, after their training was complete, many graduates who had been supported in medical school by the Corps served for two years in urban or rural areas of medical need. This program has also been drastically reduced by the Reagan Administration. Such reductions in federal support mean that it is virtually impossible for many doctors who are motivated to address some of our society's most urgent medical needs to do so. Their indebtedness forces them to seek positions with relatively high starting incomes.

Medicine for Profit

The irony of the situation is compounded, because increasing numbers of well-paid positions are being offered by for-profit medical institutions, most of which refuse care to patients who are unable to pay. This has led to expressions of frustration by some physicians. One such doctor, a North Carolina primary-care practitioner, recently wrote to a medical journal of his own "disappointment, anger and degradation" over what a for-profit hospital did to a patient of his. She was a thirty-five-year-old woman who had sustained grave head injuries in an automobile accident. Because she did not have insurance, she was refused care by a neurosurgeon at a private hospital with emergency facilities to which she was taken. The neurosurgeon told the primary-care doctor that he had previously been criticized by the hospital administration for having agreed earlier to accept an uninsured patient. The primary-care doctor wrote in the journal that ". . . business managers should not have the final say in determining who gets health care because the less fortunate will always suffer." Other physicians working in some for-profit institutions have also complained that they are constrained from making the patient's welfare their primary concern.

Technology, Overspecialization, and Waste

Daniel Beck recognizes that the high cost of medical education and all that implies are among the conditions in today's medical world that need change. The economic rewards that society has attached to medical high technology are another source of concern to him. In his view, they discourage the caring medicine that he thinks is needed, and they encourage cost inflation. He cites as an example a patient who recently came to see him because she had had gradual loss of eyesight over recent years. He did a complete examination, in the course of which he identified cataracts as the likely source of her failing vision. His inquiries led to her disclosing and discussing a range of problems at home. He arranged for her to see an eye specialist and recommended a social worker who helped her get her house problems in order. The patient had Blue Shield insurance, which paid Dr. Beck $63.65 for what proved to be more than an hour of office time, plus additional time on the telephone. The specialist confirmed Dr. Beck's diagnosis and subsequently removed the lens with the larger cataract. The operation was done without hospitalizing the patient and required about thirty minutes. The specialist saw the patient, who had a splendid result, in a follow-up visit that took about twenty minutes. Blue Shield paid the specialist $1,300 for a total time commitment about equal to Dr. Beck's.

Dr. Beck's own style of practice has not been, and will not be, influenced by such inappropriate incentives. But he does worry that they help discourage young doctors who are motivated to pursue neglected paths in medicine. He knows that while an interest in primary care is growing, the medical and surgical specialties continue to attract many more medical graduates, despite the fact that they are overcrowded in most parts of the country, and the need for primary-care doctors is still very great in many. Until very recently, few of the residents leaving the training program at Memorial Hospital wanted to practice primary-care medicine. But at the same time he knows that in his own state there appears to be an excess of many kinds of specialists: ten times more neurosurgeons per capita, for example, than in Great Britain. He knows that diseases of the brain and the rest of the nervous system requiring surgery are no more frequent here, and there is no evidence that British patients with neurosurgical problems are neglected. He has read studies that indicate that more procedures— tests and treatments—than necessary are carried out in areas where there appears to be an excess of specialists. He also worries whether, given the limited number of neurosurgical problems, all the local neurosurgeons can maintain their skills.

He has been told that in the past the disparity in numbers between specialists and general practitioners in the United Kingdom was similar to that here. However, in recent years more than half of British medical graduates opt for general practice. The reasons are many, but among them is the fact that salaries for general practitioners are now approximately the same as for specialists in medicine and surgery.

Dr. Beck is conscious of the great benefits of new technology. The CT scanner recently helped identify an unsuspected blood clot on the brain of one of his patients, who had become increasingly unsteady on his feet. The patient was then operated on and cured. In the pre–CT scan era, methods for making such a diagnosis were far more painful and dangerous for the patient. But Dr. Beck is conscious too of the risks of much new technology and of its expense, not only in dollars, but in the time it can consume. When the technology leads to cure or other important help for the patient, he is, of course, delighted with the investment. But he feels that too often it is used when the available evidence gives no reason to anticipate benefit— as, for example, the CT scan for headaches, which an unhurried interview might have revealed began when a patient lost her job. Dr. Beck recognizes the time that is required to communicate with patients, and he resents the incursion on that time that is one cost of technology overuse.

Dr. Beck knows that proved and relatively inexpensive technology can also be costly if used inappropriately. For example, it used to be routine to take chest X rays of all patients admitted to the hospital for surgery. It is now recognized that such X rays rarely offer useful information, but in the aggregate they add more than $1.5 billion to the nation's annual health bill. Indeed, unless the reasons for this or any other test are carefully considered—which includes using imagination and foresight about possible outcomes and their implication—the consequence of a "routine" test can be harmful in more ways than its cost in dollars. The family of William French, a cousin of Dr. Beck's, learned this lesson the hard way.

Technology Versus Human Judgment: A "Routine" Test

Mr. French was an eighty-five-year-old retired Los Angeles lawyer, who had experienced periods of confusion and forgetfulness and depression since a stroke three years earlier. He saw his physician at intervals of a few months, complaining of unsteadiness and poor memory. On one occasion the doctor suggested that, since he hadn't had a chest X ray in more than two years, that be done "just to make sure we're not overlooking anything." Had Dr. Beck been consulted at this point, he would have advised against looking for trouble that was unlikely in the first place. At any rate, trouble was found. The chest X ray demonstrated an abnormal shadow in his right lung that was believed almost surely to be cancer. (Mr. French had smoked more than a package of cigarettes daily for forty years.)

However, it was possible, even if remote, that a tuberculosis infection that had occurred earlier in his life might have been reactivated and caused the shadow. If that proved to be the case, drug treatment would be appropriate. Therefore, he was subjected to extensive further tests to explore that possibility. All were negative.

During the course of the investigations, the French family asked that the almost certain diagnosis of cancer not be discussed with the patient, because they felt it would be devastating to him. His wife, however, found it very hard to live with. When tuberculosis was finally ruled out and the doctors recommended a biopsy, Mrs. French called Daniel Beck. Even if cancer was found, she told him, the doctors thought him much too fragile to survive lung surgery, so what was the point? Dr. Beck agreed.

In actual fact, Mr. French lived more than two years longer. During the last month of his life he developed a cough. When he died of a heart attack just after his eighty-seventh birthday, the cancer, as it proved to be, had increased in size, but except for the recent cough, it had had no apparent physical effect on his life. *Mrs.* French, however, had found the last two years devastating. As she put it, "I was certain that cancer and all of its terrible effects would take over at any time and destroy his little remaining spirit and a good deal of mine."

Medicare and a supplemental private insurance policy paid for all of the doctors' and laboratory bills. Mrs. French paid with two years of anxiety and suffering for knowledge that was of no use to anyone.

In a world of unlimited resources, Mr. French's "routine" chest X ray and all the studies it led to would have no effect of economic consequence, but the suffering it caused his wife would be no less. Therefore, it would not be allowed. In today's real world, the resources used unnecessarily for Mr. French's chest X ray and all the medical procedures that followed would not have brought needed help directly to others. But Dr. Beck is aware that money so spent contributes to the inflation of medical costs and thereby is harmful to the many in our society with major unanswered medical needs. Dr. Beck also resents the degree to which he and other doctors feel constrained to use much technology as part of what is called "defensive medicine"—that is, to carry out procedures without regard to expense or even appropriateness, because of concern that failure to do so would lead to a courtroom.

Technology and the Malpractice Issue

Dr. Beck recognizes the complexities of the malpractice problem and is impatient with those who proffer simplistic solutions. He does not deny incompetence within his profession—one large study by the California Medical Association showed that 5 percent of patients hospitalized in California hospitals in the 1970s had unexpected complications, and one fifth of these probably resulted from negligence by hospital personnel. He knows too that his profession has not done a good job in policing itself against inadequate performance and problems like alcoholism and drug addiction. He has read, for example, that in some states the boards that control licenses to practice medicine take more than ten times as many disciplinary actions against doctors as do those of other states.*

Yet while doctors differ in their capabilities, just as lawyers, taxi drivers, and professors do, there is no reason to think that the overall performance of doctors varies from state to state. Dr. Beck feels that all of these factors and more put all doctors at risk.

But many problems that lead to litigation are reflections not of malpractice, but rather of the complexities of human biology, complexities that today's knowledge cannot unravel. The tragedies of birth defects and birth injuries are the basis for many lawsuits against obstetricians. When defects or injuries may be the result of drugs inappropriately prescribed during pregnancy or of medical incompetence during delivery, Dr. Beck

---

* In 1983 there were only 563 disciplinary actions against the nation's more than 389,000 doctors, in New York State, twenty-one actions against 42,000 doctors. From 1975 to 1984, the number of malpractice suits rose from 5 to 16 per 100 doctors. Very few such suits are successful, but awards made as a result of out-of-court settlements in 1984 averaged $120,000, awards in trials $962,000. Victims receive, on the average, about 30 percent of the awards. The rest goes for investigation, administration, and lawyers' fees.

would never attempt to defend the doctors involved. He is aware, however, that the causes of most birth defects are now unknown. This does not diminish the suffering for the family, but he resents deeply the self-seeking lawyers who exploit the aggrieved by persuading them to seek "justice" by suing the doctor.

Technology and Ethical Issues

Dr. Beck is troubled too by the number of other medical problems that are now referred to the courts for decisions. Often these arise when doctor and patient or family are unable to agree on ethical issues that modern technology has created. A growing number concern the use of life-sustaining machines in patients who a few years ago could not have been kept alive. Dr. Beck knows that some of his colleagues are more likely to use life-sustaining technology in situations where he would not do so. But he also knows the tremendous burden involved in giving the order to discontinue life-preserving measures. He sometimes refers his students to articles on the subject by Dr. Bryan Jennett, a British neurosurgeon. Dr. Jennett describes an emotional problem that often afflicts doctors involved in "rescue" medicine, which he calls the vicious cycle of commitment. To illustrate he cites a seventy-five-year-old patient who is in deep coma after a head injury and is referred to the intensive care unit. On examination the patient is found to have several neurological signs that signify to experts that he cannot recover. But the doctor orders a CT scan before making a final decision not to intervene. The scan shows a large blood clot on the brain. Although the patient cannot be saved, the doctors find themselves unable to ignore what is—at least in some patients, even if they differ from this one—a "treatable" condition. They operate, but afterwards the patient cannot breathe without a respirator. He is returned to the intensive care unit, where the next day he can breathe a bit, but his overall condition is not improved. He lingers in the unit for several days before he dies.

Dr. Beck knows that the availability of life-saving technology is often the basis for its automatic use. In most instances its automatic use is very beneficial. On occasion, however, it can prolong tragedy. That was the case for Gilbert Madden, whose medical history was reported to Dr. Beck by one of his colleagues.

Mr. Madden was a retired mathematician of eighty-one, who suffered from heart and brain disease that resulted from atherosclerosis. Over a period of three years he gradually lapsed into a semicomatose condition. His elderly wife cared for him at home, feeding, washing, and nursing him. Her daughters who lived nearby, neighbors, and occasionally visiting nurses sometimes came in to help her hoist him onto bedpans and to turn him. On one occasion he became completely unresponsive, and she called the police. The emergency service arrived, found that his heart had stopped, and resuscitated him. He was taken to the hospital, where over a period of two weeks he was restored to the condition he had been in before the cardiac arrest. He was then returned home, where the previous pattern of life continued for the Maddens until his death eighteen months later.

To minimize such outcomes, Memorial Hospital's policy is to attempt to identify patients who are admitted with far-advanced, incurable illness and who are, therefore, more likely than others to have sudden, potentially terminal events like stoppage of the heart or inability to breathe without assistance. When that happens, and with the explicit guidance of those patients—when they are competent—their families, the doctors responsible for their care, and a specially designated committee including people from the hospital and the community, so-called DNR decisions may be made. These instruct the resuscitation teams, in case of what may be a fatal event, Do Not Resuscitate.

Dr. Beck finds few decisions in medicine as troubling as these. Modern technology has put in the hands of doctors the power to sustain people who could not previously have been kept alive. Many feel it unethical not to use that power. One study of resuscitation procedures in a Massachusetts hospital indicated that most physicians had not discussed the issue in advance with their patients. Further, in several instances where patients had expressly asked not to be resuscitated, their wishes were ignored. The reasons for ambivalence of doctors (and nurses) about this issue are many. First, except in extreme situations—the patient who has been paralyzed and in coma for months or years following a stroke is an example—one cannot predict with certainty what the patient's quality of life will be following resuscitation and recovery, even when the recovery is only partial. Second, many patients in the condition described are depressed. Whether their attitudes toward resuscitation might change at a later time cannot be known. Some doctors have difficulty separating their own religious and ethical attitudes in their decision making about the lives of their patients. Finally, doctors are concerned about the possibility of legal action. Many were sensitized by the Barber case in California. There, the doctors complied with the request of the family of a seriously brain-damaged man in a coma to disconnect the respirator and stop other life-support activities. After the patient died, the doctors were indicted for murder. Although the indictment was subsequently dismissed, it has left its mark on the medical community. Most doctors are unwilling to expose themselves to the emotional distress, the unpleasant publicity, and the enormous demands on their time such cases can generate.

For all of these reasons, questions of withholding treatment are receiving public notice, and more are being decided in the courts. One such decision was made by a court of appeals in California and was reported in a medical journal in early 1985.

The patient was a seventy-year-old man with a long history of serious medical problems, including lung cancer, atherosclerosis with an aneurysm of the main blood vessel in his abdomen, and emphysema, a lung disease that can lead to serious breathing problems and death from suffocation. For some months he had been kept alive by mechanical devices. He wanted these withdrawn, but the hospital and the doctors refused. They did not question his competence, but felt that it would not be ethical for them to comply with his request and that it was their responsibility to preserve life. In a first trial the court upheld the position of the hospital's lawyers that medical ethics outweighed the patient's rights. The Appeals Court, however, overturned the lower court. It stated that "If the right of the patient to self-determination as to his own medical treatment is to have any meaning at all, it must be paramount to the interests of the patient's hospital and doctors. The right of a competent adult patient to refuse medical treatment is a constitutionally guaranteed right which must not be abridged." The patient died before the decision was rendered. However, it sets a precedent that will undoubtedly be called upon for similar cases in the future.

Malpractice suits were unknown to Dr. Beck's father, and Dr. Beck himself has not (or, as he sometimes says, not yet) been sued. But a growing number of his colleagues have been, and many, in specialties like obstetrics, surgery, and radiology, are paying malpractice premiums in excess of $25,000 per year; in some states premiums are three and more times higher. These costs are passed on to patients, and thereby increase health care bills.

Dr. Beck ascribes the malpractice problem in part to unrealistic expectations on the part of some patients. Some do not accept that every procedure in medicine (and in life) carries a risk, no matter how well it is carried out. Several years earlier, one of Dr. Beck's patients recovering—

seemingly uneventfully—from treatment for heart failure had a near-fatal blood clot in a lung on the day he was scheduled to be discharged from the hospital. Patients with chronic illness, particularly involving the heart, are more subject to the formation of clots, which may then migrate to the lungs. In this instance, the near-catastrophe could not have been predicted. Recovery required several extra days in the hospital. Fortunately, the patient was insured and the additional hospitalization did not lead to much out-of-pocket expense. Fortunately, too, he had a salaried position in a firm that continued his pay during the additional three weeks of his disability. The patient understood that nobody was "at fault." But Dr. Beck says that if that patient had been uninsured or had he lost wages, he might have been tempted to seek some way to be compensated for the unanticipated losses. In Canada and Britain, where everyone is covered, no patient risks financial ruin as a result of additional expenses that follow unexpected complications. Perhaps this explains in part why there is so much less medical malpractice litigation in those countries.

Malpractice suits are one more unpleasant aspect of today's medical practice about which Dr. Beck feels helpless. But there are elements that he could change. He feels that much of his paperwork—insurance forms, records, correspondence, and the administrative aspects of maintaining his office facilities—could be better managed if he were part of a larger group of doctors. And he sees this aspect of medicine becoming more burdensome in the years ahead. His shared office arrangement with Wendy Bates and Steve Kantor suits him well, but if he were starting out today, he would consider seriously joining a group, rather than doing solo practice. However, since he plans to retire in a few years, he does not want to subject his patients to change.

Dr. Beck's patients often refer to their relationship with him as the reason they would not want any other form of medical practice than his solo arrangement. With the rapid changes in medical practice forms now taking place, however, many people are finding that the nature of a doctor's caring is a reflection of the doctor rather than of the way the practice is organized. The next chapter will consider some of the ways in which Americans find medical care today.

3 Finding Care

Many Americans from all walks of life have no Dr. Daniel Beck to turn to when their need for a gatekeeper asserts itself, often in the form of an emergency situation. John Nichols was among them.

A Gatekeeper Keeps the Record

Mr. Nichols is a fifty-year-old business executive who had recently been transferred to the Boston area. He had been free of medical complaints most of his adult life, except for two episodes of infection of his prostate in the previous year. These had been treated in the emergency room of a nearby hospital, which he and his wife had used for their relatively infrequent medical needs. He had developed a skin rash during his second course of treatment. He had returned to the emergency room, where one of the doctors ascribed it to the antibiotic Mr. Nichols was taking and substituted another. The rash had disappeared, and the infection cleared. Since their move, they had not "bothered" to look for a physician who would be responsible for their care. Therefore, when Nichols awoke at 2 A.M. with a shaking chill and a fever of 104 degrees, he had his wife drive him to the emergency room of Forest Hospital, a small hospital in the Boston suburb where he lives. (He said later that he chose Forest because it was closest and would be convenient for his wife to visit him there, should he have to stay.)

Mr. Nichols reported to the doctor in charge that he had had a few days of urinary symptoms, including pain on urination and frequency, similar to what he had experienced a year earlier when he had the prostatic infections. The doctor found that his prostate was enlarged and very tender. He prescribed an antibiotic to be taken for ten days and sent him home.

The fever and the urinary symptoms diminished over the next two days, and Mr. Nichols then returned to work. Three days later, while at work, he developed a shaking chill and was taken back to Forest. On admission, his temperature was found to be 105 degrees. Shortly thereafter, his blood pressure dropped precipitously, and he went into a state of shock. He was believed to have septic shock, a potentially fatal complication of some severe infections. He was taken to the intensive care unit, where the doctor in charge started him on intravenous antibiotics and successfully treated the shock. However, the doctors found no ready explanation for the fever, which by this time had disappeared. However, they began a search for a possible hidden infection. His temperature rapidly fell to normal, as a result, the doctors assumed, of the intravenous antibiotic, which they had continued. His prostate was much less tender than a week earlier and therefore almost surely not the source of his fever. Therefore, the doctors turned their attention elsewhere, looking first for possible sites of infection in his kidneys, in his lungs, or on a heart valve. Extensive x-ray examinations and blood tests, including cultures for infecting bacteria, were all negative. After ten days of normal temperature and the absence of any signs of infection, he was discharged home, having by then had two weeks of intravenous antibiotic treatment. As a precaution, the doctor in charge prescribed antibiotic tablets for an additional two weeks.

Three days after his discharge, Mr. Nichols' temperature began to rise, and a day later it was 104 degrees. He returned to the hospital, where he was admitted at once. A day later, at the recommendation of one of Mr. Nichols' business associates, a friend of mine, Mrs. Nichols called me for advice. I suggested that she ask the doctor in charge to call in as consultant a specialist in infectious diseases, and I gave her the names of two whom I knew well. She hesitated, wondering whether the doctors at Forest might be reluctant to do so, and whether they might, as a result, be "prejudiced" against Mr. Nichols. I reassured her that such a request would be considered entirely appropriate by any good doctor. Indeed, given the complexity of the situation, the doctors at Forest would surely welcome help. If their request offended the doctors, then the Nicholses would have real reason to worry about them.

The doctor in charge at Forest responded very positively to the Nicholses' request. He promptly consulted Dr. Marilyn Fields, one of the specialists I had named. She saw Mr. Nichols later that day. He had again been started on intravenous antibiotics on admission to the hospital, and by the time of her visit, his temperature had dropped. She found no obvious explanation for the fever on her examination and on reviewing all of the studies that had been carried out previously. It was possible, she agreed, that he had a hidden focus of infection on a heart valve. A tumor can sometimes produce fever. But Mr. Nichols' general condition seemed surprisingly good for someone who might be harboring so serious a condition as either of those, or other possibilities that had occurred to the doctors at Forest and to her.

She questioned Mr. Nichols further, particularly about the antibiotic that had caused the skin rash a year earlier. He didn't recall what the drug was, but a telephone call to the hospital in the city where he had previously lived established that it was the same form of penicillin that he had taken by mouth during both of the periods at home following his visits to Forest. In the hospital, the penicillin tablets had been stopped, and he had been given different antibiotics intravenously.

Dr. Fields pointed out that in some sensitive individuals certain antibiotics, though rarely, cause what is called drug fever. She then offered one possible solution to the medical mystery that was causing him so much grief. At the time of his first visit to Forest Hospital, Mr. Nichols had a prostatic infection, which caused fever and the urinary symptoms. Dr. Fields suggested that the infection was cured during the first few days of penicillin treatment. Mr. Nichols (properly) had been instructed to continue the penicillin tablets for several days after the infection seemed to have been controlled. The fever he had then developed, which led to his first admission to the inpatient service of the hospital, was not, as the doctors quite reasonably assumed, a return of his prostatic infection, but a reaction to penicillin. The fever disappeared during his first hospitalization not because he was given a more powerful intravenous antibiotic, as had been (again reasonably) assumed, but because the penicillin tablets had been stopped. He resumed the penicillin tablets after his discharge from the hospital, and they caused the second episode of fever. Their discontinuation after the present admission to the hospital was again followed by disappearance of his fever. The only way to establish this beyond doubt was to give him a very small amount of the drug, while he was carefully observed for any other serious toxic reactions. Even suspected sensitivity to penicillin is generally reason not to take the drug again, because a second reaction can be catastrophic. However, in this instance, it was essential to establish with certainty the cause of his fever. If it was not the penicillin, it would be essential to find out what the cause was and then to remove it. A renewed search for a hidden infection would involve risk-laden procedures and prolonged hospitalization.

All of this was explained to the Nicholses. With Mr. Nichols' agreement, a small dose of penicillin was given under close observation. Within an hour his temperature started to rise, and several hours later, it returned to normal.

The mystery was solved, and Mr. Nichols' ordeal was over.

I met the Nicholses shortly thereafter and took the liberty of volunteering one additional bit of advice. I suggested they establish a continuing relationship with a physician who would serve as their primary-care doctor and who, in that capacity, would keep their medical records, educate them about what they could do to promote their own health (including the importance of remembering any drugs to which they are sensitive), and in other ways to be the gatekeeper they urgently needed. In the absence of such a person, they might not be so lucky the next time. Mr. Nichols, in turn, as a computer expert, mused about what his field could do for medical record keeping. He mentioned that the airlines keep careful records of who is booked for what seat going to what city—and even with what kind of special diet—for months in advance. If the nation considered it a matter of priority, it would not be all that difficult to put in place a computerized medical data system. Consider the virtues of providing patients and doctors access to the kind of information that would have saved society the more than $7,000 in hospital bills that Mr. Nichols' insurance plan paid, and would have spared him the discomfort and risks of his illness and the anguish it brought him and his family.

A Gatekeeper Makes Referrals

Until serious illness strikes, the absence of a gatekeeper is often not perceived to be a problem. It is not now an issue high on Edward Katz's agenda.

Mr. Katz is a forty-five-year-old lawyer who lives in a Boston suburb. He, his wife, and his children have been in generally good health. He has Blue Cross–Blue Shield insurance, which is completely paid by his firm. The last doctor he saw on a regular basis was "my pediatrician, thirty years ago." Four years ago he injured his Achilles tendon while playing tennis and consulted his next-door neighbor, an orthopedic surgeon, who is "a lovely guy and a good friend." The surgeon suggested that he be hospitalized so that the tendon could be repaired. Mr. Katz readily agreed, and the operation was carried out in a nearby suburban hospital. All went well, he was discharged after a week, and he resumed playing tennis in less than three months.

In discussing the procedure now, he says that he was lucky to have had a good orthopedic surgeon as his neighbor. He has since learned that tendons sometimes heal without surgery when they are immobilized. Even if he had been aware of it at the time of his accident, however, he would "probably not have raised the question" with the doctor. Besides, the operation entailed "little expense" for him. Most of the cost was covered by his insurance; the $500 balance he paid for himself. From time to time he has thought about finding a primary-care doctor, but he hasn't known where to turn.

How do lay people pick a primary-care doctor, specialists, hospitals, nursing homes, and other medical facilities and personnel? Once the choices have been made, how do they evaluate performance? The latter question is serious not only for members of the public concerned with personal medical care. It is also important for government, insurance firms, and large companies that seek ways to measure what they get for the fees they pay. Directors of hospitals and clinics that deliver medical services wonder how to determine objectively the quality of the product that their institutions deliver. For example, the head of one of the nation's most respected health maintenance organizations (HMOs) recently expressed his own sense of frustration. He is ultimately responsible, he said, for the health of more than 200,000 people. His HMO employs more than 275 doctors, twice that number of nurses, and a total of 800 employees. Its annual income is almost $200 million. But he has only very crude instruments available to measure the quality of medical care that his organization delivers because refined ones don't exist.

Medical Competence: Skill, Judgment, Efficiency, Compassion

The problem of choosing among doctors and the institutions in which they serve is complicated by the fact that at least four levels of competence are involved. The first relates to technical skills. How good is the doctor at diagnosing heart failure or gallstones and then at prescribing the proper drugs or surgery? The Nicholses needed advice in finding a consultant who could help make a diagnosis. Mr. Katz, the tennis player, acknowledges now that his confidence in his surgeon's orthopedic skills was based on grounds that he would not accept in evaluating the legal competence of a colleague.

Medical licensing procedures that exist from state to state cover minimal qualifications. Some states now ask for periodic evidence that doctors are

keeping abreast of their field as a condition of relicensing. Doctors themselves, through specialty organizations like the American Board of Internal
Medicine and the American Board of Surgery, and the hospitals where
they practice have a variety of approaches to the problems of assessment
of medical performance. For example, surgeons must have four years of
training and pass special examinations in order to qualify as specialists
certified in their field. Doctors in hospitals participate in a peer-review
process that asks such questions as whether the patients of Surgeon X have
the same number of deaths and complications as those of other surgeons
doing the same kind of operations? Do pathology tests on materials from
his patients confirm his diagnoses? How long do his patients remain in the
hospital, as compared with others? Similar information is collected in hospitals about the comparative performances of other members of their
staffs—primary-care doctors and specialists in other branches of medicine
such as internal medicine, obstetrics, and ear, nose, and throat surgery.
The issue of technical skill is one that can generally be readily dealt with,
although more could be done toward making available to the public the
results of the assessments.

The second level of medical competence is far more difficult to evaluate:
the matter of judgment. How good is the doctor at evaluating the usefulness
of the drugs that are prescribed for the heart failure? Is removal of the
gallbladder in a particular patient the best, or even appropriate, treatment
for the gallstones? Would it be better to do nothing? How does one decide?
How many appendectomies does a surgeon do relative to his colleagues?
If the answer is many more, then what fraction of the appendices removed
are normal? And if he is removing more normal appendices, does this
mean that he is performing unnecessary surgery, or that fewer of his patients
run the risk of having an inflamed appendix perforate? If highly competent
orthopedic surgeons themselves disagree about whether surgery is the best
way to deal with ruptured Achilles tendons, how is Mr. Katz himself to
make a decision?

These are very complicated questions, and they are currently the topic
not only of intense debate within the medical profession but also, fortunately, of investigation. Dr. John Wennberg is a leader in this field of
research. He has focused on the marked variations in medical practice
from one area to another, even those very close to each other. For example,
he found that the chances of a child in Vermont having a tonsillectomy
by age sixteen range from 8 percent to 65 percent, apparently depending
only on place of residence. Among women in Maine, the likelihood of
hysterectomy varies from 20 percent to 70 percent. And the chances of a

male in Iowa aged eighty-five having had his prostate removed vary from 15 percent to 60 percent from one part of the state to another.

No scientific explanations can be found for such variations. Some people blame them on the desire of some doctors to increase their incomes by doing unnecessary procedures. While that does happen, much evidence says that it accounts for only a very small part of the problem. For example, we know that doctors generally don't charge other doctors and members of their families. If greed were the explanation, one might expect that doctors' families would have less surgery than the families of others. In fact, the evidence says that relatives of doctors have more. Whatever the causes, a growing number of people agree with Dr. John Bunker, a professor at Stanford University Medical School, who recently wrote that "much of current medical practice may be ineffective."

As a result, medical pioneers like Wennberg and Bunker are promoting the relatively new field of medical technology assessment. Working with statisticians and other nonmedical specialists, they and a growing number of other doctors with similar interests are attempting to develop objective criteria by which doctors and patients can make decisions about which medical interventions are appropriate and which are not. Meanwhile, the knowledge that such questions are unanswered should encourage all patients to ask questions of their doctors and to insist on answers that seem reasonable. A doctor's response to a patient's question about these issues is one way to judge whether that doctor has qualities that they might want in the person to whom they entrust their medical care. (The area of medical technology assessment will be discussed in detail in Chapter 11.)

Thirdly, patients need reassurance that primary-care doctors can manage the multiple details of medical practice. Can they readily arrange for proper consultants, for hospitalization, for social services, for around-the-clock coverage for patients when they themselves are not available?

As if judgment and technical and managerial skills are not sufficiently severe tests of competence, a fourth attribute is at least as important to many people in their search for a personal doctor. I speak of the doctor's sensitivity and compassion. Is the patient uppermost in the doctor's mind? Does the doctor know how to listen? Does the doctor encourage a sense of trust? Is the doctor available around the clock either directly or, since this is not humanly possible, via a surrogate in whom the patient has confidence? In other words, does the doctor care?

Are these impossible or unreasonable demands to make of the person to whom you entrust your health? The answer is clearly no, for many doctors presently fill this role. Some such doctors, like Dr. Beck, are in solo medical practice; others work as part of larger groups. But it is increasingly true that many doctors with the inclination and the ability to fill this role cannot do so because of competing demands made on them by existing organizational arrangements.

How Health Care Is Delivered

No arrangement that I know is ideal. None will suit all patients or all doctors. The strengths and weaknesses of each are determined not only by the people involved, but also in part by local conditions, such as geography and population density. Roberta Samuels is pleased with a health maintenance organization, where she now receives health services. Dr. Joan Rubin finds it a rewarding place in which to practice medicine.

The HMO: Benefits for the Patient

Mrs. Samuels is a thirty-seven-year-old married secretary who has been in generally good health. Eight years ago she, her husband, and their two children, aged twelve and nine, moved to Boston from St. Louis. On the few occasions she had medical problems in St. Louis, she and her husband consulted a doctor, an internist who specializes in cardiology. She saw the doctor no more than five or six times during the sixteen years she lived in St. Louis. The first time was for severe pain in her belly, which proved to be appendicitis. Up to that time she had had no doctor, and a business friend of her husband's had recommended *his* family's doctor. The doctor referred her to a surgeon, who agreed with the diagnosis, hospitalized her, and removed an inflamed appendix. At the time of her first pregnancy, she chose the obstetrician used by two of her close friends. The obstetrician, in turn, recommended a pediatrician, who looked after her child and the one who followed. Most of the Samuels family's hospital expenses were covered by Blue Cross–Blue Shield, and they paid out of pocket for their visits to doctors and for drugs. The family's general health had been good, and they counted themselves fortunate for that, for the relationships they had with their doctors, and for the fact that their out-of-pocket medical expenses had been modest over the years.

In Boston, at the suggestion of Mrs. Samuels' employer, the family joined the Boston Family Health Program, a health maintenance organization. In return for an annual fee, the BFHP offers members comprehensive medical care, ranging from such preventive services as immunizations through diagnosis and treatment of sore throats, psychotherapy, hospitalization, and prescription drugs. There is a charge of $2 for each visit and of $1 for each prescription. The doctors associated with BFHP are salaried employees. Other HMOs use doctors who are members of group practices that contract to offer medical services to HMO members. A third kind of arrangement is to contract with independent physicians, who provide their services to the HMO members. In all of these plans, agreed-upon services are provided to members in return for the annual membership fee. In other words, the HMO does not charge a fee for each service, only a nominal fee for each visit.

Patients must choose their doctors from those associated with the HMO. It is, of course, in the HMO's interests to present a roster of good doctors, with the attributes described earlier. For persons who want a specific doctor not associated with the HMO, or who want to pick their doctor from the community as a whole, the restricted choice the HMO permits may be unacceptable. On the other hand, people who feel insecure about selecting a personal doctor can assume that much of the screening process has been done for them by the HMO.

At BFHP, the Samuelses were given a list of primary-care doctors on the staff, with some biographical information about each. Their first choice, the doctor who looked after Mrs. Samuels' employer, had a full complement of patients and could not take them on. He suggested Dr. Joan Rubin, who had recently joined the staff. Mr. and Mrs. Samuels met Dr. Rubin. They discussed with her what they were seeking in their doctor. They liked her and soon thereafter chose her as their primary-care doctor. Dr. Rubin introduced them to the nurse, Ruth Frankel, who worked side by side with her. Dr. Rubin also discussed with them the pediatricians on the staff, and from that group they and their children picked Dr. Mark Fallon.

Shortly after their arrival, one of their children broke his wrist when he fell from his bicycle. Mrs. Samuels brought him to the emergency unit of BFHP, where he was examined and x-rayed. The orthopedic surgeon on duty that day set the wrist and put the arm in a cast. Healing was uneventful. No other medical problem since they have been in Boston has required consultation. But the Samuels family has been pleased with the sense of security they have about what to do if they become ill. Mrs. Samuels says that of great importance to her is a telephone number she can call twenty-four hours a day that connects her with someone who has ready access to the medical records for her and her family.

The HMO: Benefits for the Doctor

Joan Rubin is a graduate of Stanford University Medical School. After three years of medical residency and one year of training in cardiology at a Harvard teaching hospital, she joined another doctor in the practice of internal medicine in a Boston suburb. She found the patient contact gratifying, but not some of the other aspects of private practice. She did not care at all for the paperwork that was necessary in conjunction with insurance programs. She missed the opportunity to consult easily with other doctors when she found problems that were puzzling or of special interest. She found herself doing tasks such as responding to telephone calls about routine symptoms that could as well have been handled by nurses or other well-trained people working closely with her. Finally, she wanted to be certain that her patients were adequately covered around the clock, but she did not see how she could continue to make herself available every other night and every other weekend, particularly since she and her husband were eager to start a family. As a result, when she heard of an opening for an internist at the BFHP, she applied for it.

At BFHP the practice is arranged so that each doctor works closely with a nurse and a nurse's aide. Dr. Rubin's assistant, Ms. Frankel, is a competent, compassionate, and pleasant nurse, whose patients quickly come to know and to trust her. Ms. Frankel deals readily with most of the problems that lead them to phone during the day. When they want to speak to Dr. Rubin, or when Ms. Frankel feels herself unequal to the question presented, Dr. Rubin calls back.

BFHP takes pride in the fact that it has grown in each of the fifteen years since it was started. When its members are asked what features keep them loyal, a frequent answer is that of Mrs. Samuels—confidence that they have a person who has access to their records available to them around the clock. They are also confident that personal medical care is available to them whenever they have a need. They believe they will get an informed response to their question, whether it comes in the middle of the day or at midnight. The advice might be to take aspirin and call back in the morning if things are no better. It might be to come in at once to the special facility set up to deal with emergency or urgent problems. It might be to stay where they are, and the doctor will come to see them. But, as is true for Mrs. Samuels, most feel secure.

As a member of the medical group, Dr. Rubin receives a printout each month, comparing aspects of her practice with those of her colleagues. The printout tells how many prescriptions each doctor has written and for what drugs, how many patients each has hospitalized, how many and which kinds of laboratory tests and X rays each has ordered. Dr. Rubin thereby learns that she has prescribed many more, or fewer, tranquilizers than her colleagues, that she ordered the same number of, or more, or fewer thyroid function tests than average, that her patients with heart attacks spent more (or fewer) days in the hospital than the patients with the same diagnosis hospitalized by others. The only doctor's number on the list she recognizes is her own, but the comparisons help alert her to her own practice patterns that merit her special attention.

The PPO

Many other attempts to integrate medical services and make them more efficient are under way in the United States. Some began in response to a widespread effort on the part of American industry and government to control medical costs. Some have built on preexisting organizational arrangements. Bill Sweeney chose one such plan because it meant less disruption in medical services for his family.

Mr. Sweeney is an engineer with Frenchco, a California-based company that makes computers. Frenchco offers a range of medical care arrangements to its employees. The company pays the total cost of the cheapest plans in the area, which are two HMOs and something called a Preferred Provider Organization (PPO). It contributes a like amount toward Blue Cross–Blue Shield or coverage by a private insurance company. Since the cost of health insurance is higher than the HMOs or PPOs, employees must pay the difference. Because Mr. Sweeney and his family wanted to continue as patients of Dr. Ralph McLean, who had looked after them for several years and who happened to be part of the Blue Hills PPO, he chose membership in BHPPO.

BHPPO is an affiliation of primary-care doctors, specialists, hospitals, nursing homes, and pharmacies in the Blue Hills region, where Frenchco is located. Its doctors and institutions contract to offer comprehensive services to those who are signed up through Frenchco. Dr. McLean continues to practice independently, seeing PPO members like the Sweeneys without charge and his other patients on a fee-for-service basis. When Terry, the Sweeneys' eleven-year-old son, was knocked unconscious in an automobile accident, he was taken to a large hospital in the area, where he was cared for by a neurologist and a neurosurgeon associated with BHPPO. He recovered without surgery, and all the expenses were covered by the policy. However, when Mrs. Sweeney was found to have what turned out to be ulcerative colitis, the Sweeneys asked for a consultation with Dr. William MacMahon, a gastroenterologist who was not associated with BHPPO. Dr. McLean arranged for the visit, and the Sweeneys decided that they would like to continue to have Dr. MacMahon involved. They paid for his services out of their pocket, which presented no serious financial problem until an acute flare-up of Mrs. Sweeney's colitis made hospitalization necessary. Dr. MacMahon was not on the staff of Mercy Hospital, the acute care hospital associated with BHPPO. Rather than incur what could have proved very large personal expenses for care in the hospital where Dr. MacMahon practices, Mrs. Sweeney agreed to hospitalization in Mercy under Dr. McLean's overall care, with consultative advice from a gastroenterologist associated with the BHPPO.

Overuse of Emergency Units

In Britain 97 percent of people are registered with a general practitioner in their area. The GP serves as their gatekeeper. Millions of Americans have not developed such a relationship. As a result, if you visit the emergency unit of the hospital in your city, particularly at night or on weekends, you will find not only the accident victims and people with heart attacks brought in by ambulances. In addition, the unit is often full of people, rich and poor, with less serious conditions—sore throats, severe headaches, symptoms of a sexually transmitted disease or of anxiety, and other common medical problems for which they are seeking rapid diagnosis and treatment. Many well-to-do people without a primary-care physician who come to the unit pay more—sometimes much more—for the emergency unit visit than they would for a visit to a doctor's office. The price is high, because the emergency unit offers people with sore throats or headaches personnel and equipment that are much more specialized and expensive than their problems demand. They do so because the primary mission of their personnel and equipment must be to serve patients with head injuries or heart attacks. Further, the delay in treating the person with the sore throat is often considerable, for the heart attack victim must take precedence.

Medicine for Profit

Walk-In Clinics

The costs and the delays in hospital emergency units and the large number of Americans without primary-care doctors explain in part why large numbers of independent walk-in clinics—sometimes called "urgent care centers," surgical centers, emergency clinics, or "doc in the box"— are appearing in many cities. The clinics offer services to one group of patients found in the emergency units—those with the common and relatively uncomplicated medical problems that people want to have taken care of quickly. The clinics that are set up to make a profit—which means most of them—restrict their services to patients who can pay. Their rapid growth says that they are addressing a need that is not being met elsewhere at present. But they cannot be looked upon as doing more than filling a gap, and that in less than ideal fashion because they don't offer the comprehensive services that are important in a good primary-care arrangement. For example, most don't offer services around the clock. Therefore, the patient given penicillin for a strep throat who develops symptoms of an allergic reaction at 2 A.M. must look elsewhere for care. But many do not take responsibility for seeing that records are transmitted elsewhere to help ensure that penicillin is never given again. The diabetic patient who has abdominal pain may be correctly diagnosed by a walk-in clinic doctor as having appendicitis. But who will help the patient find a good surgeon and a good hospital? And who will help regulate the diabetes during and after the operation?

The growth of these clinics and some other for-profit medical facilities is contributing to important social and ethical problems. I will mention two. The first—often called "skimming"—is the sequestration of patients with illnesses that are readily cared for and for which compensation from third parties is relatively generous. An institution interested in its own financial well-being may set out to attract large numbers of patients with conditions like sore throats and appendicitis. The fees currently charged for the care of such conditions—and paid by third parties—may have been set in such a way as to reflect the *total* overhead costs of large medical institutions, which traditionally have cared for such problems as well as for patients, both paying and nonpaying, with complicated problems.

Some institutions that skim say they make money as a result of their efficiency.* But their profits come at least in part from avoiding the care of patients with expensive problems like burns and complicated heart or cancer surgery. Instead, they hospitalize people with "low overhead" conditions, like pneumonia and hernia operations. In addition, they take only patients who can pay.

Skimming has adverse financial effects on the nonprofit hospitals, particularly some teaching and all municipal hospitals, because they are left to care for patients with "high overhead" medical problems and for poor patients with medical problems of all kinds, but without any insurance coverage at all. This means a large increase in the overhead costs of such institutions. In the present climate of cost containment, they could have trouble maintaining their quality level, or even surviving. The weakening or disappearance of these hospitals would present all parts of society with a whole range of medical and social problems.

The second problem made worse by the growth of for-profit hospitals and clinics and the struggle for survival of many nonprofit hospitals is that of access to medical care for the poor. Many medical institutions now require payment or evidence that payment is available before a patient is admitted. And this is not only for nonessential care, say, cosmetic surgery. (In my view, this kind of medical care may properly be offered to those who wish to pay for it—and *not* at the taxpayers' expense.) But as the institutions demanding cash in advance replace others that don't require money as a condition of care, how will our society ensure essential medical services for people with needs but with little or no money? Consider as an example the poor child with a strep throat or with a heart valve that is deformed and in need of surgery (a condition that might have been prevented had an earlier strep throat—which caused it—not gone untreated for financial reasons!).

It should be of concern to all of us that for-profit health care institutions were—until very recently—among the most profitable investments in the equity markets at a time of strenuous efforts to control health costs. To the extent that profits result from greater efficiencies, the nation can take comfort. But those profits that result from shifting costs to government or to universities and from making care less accessible to the poor should be a source of great worry. I am not suggesting that for-profit enterprises have no place in the medical care system. Their increasing prominence speaks to needs *not* filled by the nonprofit sector. Nor do I propose that we leave

---

* Many studies thus far indicate that the for-profit institutions charge as much or more for services as the nonprofit.

to the for-profit sector the medical care of our disadvantaged. That is a responsibility that belongs to everyone in our society. But I believe that government involvement and coordination are required if we are to take advantage of the virtues of private enterprise and to see that vulnerable citizens are looked after. This problem will be discussed in more detail in Chapter 5, and one approach to its resolution will be described in Chapter 12.

The Gatekeeper: Access, Knowledge, Continuity, Commitment, and Rapport

Many of the people mentioned in this chapter have access to the advantages of American medical care. For some like the Carlyles, the Samuelses, and the Sweeneys, access is much easier than for others, because they have doctors who are in charge of their overall medical care. But gatekeeping is only one advantage provided by a personal doctor. Patients count on their doctor to remain abreast of rapidly developing medical technology so that new and useful concepts, tests, and treatments, such as those described in Chapter 4, will be available to them when they need them. Patients are equally dependent on their doctors for protection against developments that will *not* help them, particularly those that are widely publicized. This area, carefully assessing the benefits, risks, and costs of new and old interventions, which has received less attention from the academic community than it merits, will be discussed in Chapter 11. The doctor also ensures continuity of care, so that a problem resolved this year is not needlessly, and at some expense and some risk, raised again the next. People look to their doctor as a person who cares, who is available, and who has time for them. They can ask questions, no matter how personal or how seemingly trivial, and they can expect answers they understand. Many questions, such as "Is that test or operation desirable for *me?*" have no clear-cut answers. The doctor is the person who can lead the patient through the often complex facts that point to the best answer for today. Since the best answer will often differ from patient to patient, the patient must have the final word. We need more research to improve our capacity to deal with such questions, but we can do better with existing information for most Americans than we are doing today. Providing everybody with a gatekeeper could make it possible to do better for all Americans. Because in other countries, such as the United Kingdom and Canada, nearly everybody has that advantage, we know that it can be done.

4 Advances in Medical Technology

This chapter is a glance at—not an overview of—the cutting edge of some of today's medical technology. It would take volumes to describe all the recent developments in this large area. But in order to discuss the professional, financial, and social implications of the recent developments, it is necessary to suggest their quality and their magnitude. I shall also mention some health benefits we can anticipate from nonmedical factors. The distinction is important, so that whenever the nation decides where to spend money, it does so with realistic expectations.

Attacking the Major Killers

Diseases of the Heart and Blood Vessels

The most dramatic recent improvements in health have taken place in the field of cardiovascular disease. In the past two decades, heart attacks have gone down by more than 30 percent and strokes by more than 40 percent. But even with those changes, cardiovascular or circulatory diseases account for the deaths of more than 900,000 Americans each year, only slightly less than the total number caused by all other conditions combined. Over three fourths of cardiovascular deaths result from heart disease, more than 700,000 in 1981. Most of the rest are from stroke, a major complication of high blood pressure. Cardiovascular diseases are also at the top of most other lists that describe the effects of illness on our society. In 1983 they were responsible for more than 15 percent of all expenditures for health services, more than $50 billion. They accounted for more than 13 million years of potential life lost, a measurement determined by calculating how much longer individuals might have lived on the basis of average life expectancy for their age group. Thirteen million years of potential life lost is almost 40 percent of the total for all Americans. Cardiovascular diseases were the basis for more than 14 million physician visits, 19 percent of all days in acute-care hospitals, and 40 percent of those in nursing homes.

Were it not for modern technology, William Berry would have lost his life to cardiovascular disease several years ago: a life enjoyable to him and rewarding to society.

When Mr. Berry, a seventy-year-old businessman, philanthropist, and community leader, began to experience low back pain in the winter of 1970, he ascribed it to the snow shoveling he had done a few days earlier. But when the pain grew worse over the next two days despite aspirin, rest, and hot baths, he called his physician and arranged to meet at his office later that morning. By the time he was ready to leave his home, however, the pain was so severe that his wife decided to drive directly to the emergency room of a Boston teaching hospital five miles from their home. About half a mile from their destination, Mr. Berry screamed with pain and fainted. Fortunately, his wife maintained her composure and proceeded rapidly to the hospital. There an intern and a nurse helped pull the unconscious patient from the car while Mrs. Berry summarized the details of his illness. Recognizing that Mr. Berry was in shock, the intern and a resident who had joined them put needles into veins in both arms and started transfusions of salt solution, then plasma, then blood. Their initial examination persuaded them that he was bleeding into the abdomen. Their findings and Mrs. Berry's information suggested to them a tear in an abdominal aortic aneurysm, which is an outpouching of the wall of the main blood vessel carrying blood from the heart to the lower half of the body. Such outpouchings sometimes occur in the walls of blood vessels greatly weakened by atherosclerosis. In this disease fatty materials accumulate in the linings of the arteries, the blood vessels that carry blood away from the heart to the tissues of the body. (In contrast, the veins are the vessels that carry blood from the tissues back to the heart.) The accumulation of the fatty materials weaken the walls of the arteries and sometimes obstruct them, interfering with blood flow. When atherosclerosis occurs in the coronary arteries, the blood vessels that nourish the heart, it often blocks blood flow to the heart muscle and causes a heart attack. If the arteries that carry blood to the brain are affected, the result may be a stroke.

When atherosclerosis causes so much weakness in the wall of a large artery that it becomes distorted, the result can be excruciating pain. Had Mr. Berry's condition been recognized earlier, he would have been hospitalized at once and scheduled for surgery. However, when a previously unrecognized aneurysm of a main blood vessel ruptures, rarely is the patient within a few minutes of a hospital, as—by extraordinary good luck—was the case on this occasion. Equally fortunate was the presence of perceptive and skillful doctors, who almost immediately made the correct diagnosis.

Even while the doctors and nurses, now joined by a senior surgeon, were moving the patient to the operating room, they opened his abdomen, confirmed the diagnosis, and compressed the ruptured blood vessel with their hands to slow the bleeding. Meanwhile, blood to replace what he had lost from the torn artery was being transfused into both his arms. Once in the operating room, the diseased portion of his aorta was covered with a Dacron graft.

Within twenty-four hours Mr. Berry regained consciousness. During the next two weeks he was treated in the intensive care unit for the shock state that had resulted from the profound loss of blood and the consequent damage to his kidneys and other body organs. He convalesced during the next three weeks in the hospital and for three months at home. Four months later he resumed work.

Mr. Berry recently celebrated his eighty-sixth birthday. The intervening years have been marked by periodic mild illnesses, but his mind and body remain intact. He has spent much of his time and energy working for the civic causes that occupied him during his life "before the Dacron graft."

Many Americans know a William Berry whose life was saved by modern medical technology:

- By more rapid transport to the hospital, with better trained personnel and new technology making possible more prompt and more efficient emergency care.
- By intensive care units, not only in large medical centers but also in small community hospitals, so that patients can be monitored constantly when a few precious minutes can make the difference between survival and death.
- By electronic pacemakers that stimulate hearts to pump regularly when their own natural mechanisms fail.
- By a whole range of new drugs to control elevated blood pressure and to strengthen weakened hearts.
- By improved diagnostic techniques for localizing with exquisite precision diseased blood vessels.
- By extraordinary surgical methods, such as coronary bypass graft

surgery, for repairing or replacing those blood vessels.
- By improved anesthesia, which permits complicated diagnostic and therapeutic measures at greatly reduced risks.
- By new transfusion technology, which facilitates the rapid replacement of blood, blood products, other fluids, and nutrients.
- By newer antibiotics and other measures for fighting infections in patients whose resistance may be lowered as a result of chronic illness.

All of these developments and more have saved lives, lives that would have been lost a few years ago. And the progress continues. Eugene Grant is a recent beneficiary.

Mr. Grant, a fifty-five-year-old contractor in a large midwestern city, had been in generally good health, except for the fact that he was about fifteen pounds overweight. He smoked a pack of cigarettes a day. One night in the fall of 1985 he awoke with crushing pain that involved mainly the left side of his chest, but extended up into his jaw and down his left arm. He perspired profusely and felt sick to his stomach. His wife called Dr. William Sourwine, the internist who looked after the health of the family. Dr. Sourwine heard the story and immediately arranged for an ambulance to take Mr. Grant to a hospital, which was ten minutes away. The doctor was at the emergency entrance when the ambulance arrived and found a patient who looked desperately ill. The history, physical findings, and electrocardiogram were consistent with the doctor's impression at the time of Mrs. Grant's phone call: Mr. Grant was having a coronary attack. In this condition a block occurs in one or more of the coronary arteries, through which blood flows to the heart muscle. Blood carries to heart muscle—and all other parts of the body—the oxygen and chemicals that the muscle—and all other tissues—need to carry out their work and indeed to survive. When a tissue is deprived of blood, it undergoes progressive damage and then dies, unless the blood flow is resumed. Excruciating pain generally occurs when heart muscle is under such attack.

The common cause of obstruction to blood flow to the heart is a blood clot, which forms at a site of the fatty material that accumulates in coronary arteries affected by atherosclerosis; thus, the names "heart attack," "coronary attack," "coronary occlusion." All mean the same, as does "myocardial infarction," which is the medical expression for death of heart muscle (myocardium) as a result of inadequate blood supply (infarction). More than half the victims of fatal heart attacks die within a few minutes of onset, before they ever receive medical attention. What happens to the rest depends on whether any blood gets to the muscle that is fed by the obstructed artery. Normally, the muscle in any area of the heart is nourished by blood from a single main coronary artery. But some people have small tributaries that link their coronary arteries with each other. Then, if a block occurs in one artery, the tributaries may provide a detour route for blood to reach the muscle. In other victims of heart attacks, the clots appear to dissolve on their own. These are among the reasons that in many people with heart attacks, the damage to the muscle may be limited or even reversed. But in a substantial fraction—perhaps 20 percent of those who get to the hospital—the attack is fatal. And many survivors are left with permanent damage to their hearts, some so severe that they are completely disabled.

Until recently doctors could treat with varying success the *effects* of the heart attack—the pain, the disturbances in the beating of the heart, the shock sometimes caused, and other complications. But they were helpless to deal with the clots that caused the obstruction; they stood by as events played out to see who would die, who would be left disabled, and who would recover fully. Modern technology now makes it possible to interrupt the process in some patients.

Dr. Sourwine arranged for Mr. Grant to be seen by a specialist, who took him directly to a special procedures room. There, the specialist and her highly skilled team introduced a very thin catheter or tube into an artery in the patient's groin and threaded it up to the heart. Through the tube they introduced a dye, which made it possible to visualize the coronary arteries with X rays that were projected on a television screen. The X rays of the blood vessels, known as an angiogram, showed that dye passed normally through two of Mr. Grant's three major coronary arteries. But when it entered the third, the artery that supplies blood to the left ventricle, the largest chamber of the heart, it almost immediately met an obstruction. Here was the clot responsible for the heart attack.

The doctors then introduced into the obstructed artery a chemical that often dissolves newly formed clots. Unfortunately, Mr. Grant's clot was resistant to the chemical, forcing the team to take a more vigorous step. Attached to the end of the catheter was a small balloon. The team was able to slip the catheter into position so that the balloon was immediately adjacent to the clot. Then, by inflating the balloon, they disrupted the clot and stretched the inner walls of the artery, a procedure called an angioplasty. Two things happened simultaneously, heralding success. On the x-ray screen the team saw dye fill the remainder of the left coronary artery. At the same time, Mr. Grant, who had been only mildly sedated, was aware of wonderful relief from his pain.

The heart attack was over. His heart muscle had undergone some damage, but it would regain most of its function over the next few weeks. Mr. Grant remained in the hospital for another nine days while he recovered from the damage that had been done and so that he could be carefully monitored to ensure that another clot did not form. He began at once a weight reduction program, paying particular attention to lowering the amount of fat and cholesterol in his diet. He stopped smoking. He gradually began an exercise program and within three months was briskly walking three miles a day.

Eugene Grant was luckier than the vast majority of coronary attack victims, and not only because his problem was identified at once, and he was close to a place where it was appropriately dealt with. No more than 1 percent of Americans who suffer heart attacks now receive the kind of treatment Mr. Grant had. It was also Eugene Grant's good fortune that his atherosclerosis, which had led to the formation of the clot in a main coronary artery, was not nearly so severe as is usually seen. Most heart attack victims have clots and atherosclerotic narrowing in several sites in their coronary arteries. But the angioplasty is effective only against localized disease and even then only in some cases. An unsuccessful angioplasty or an angiogram showing *multiple* obstructions may be the basis for coronary bypass surgery, which involves bypassing areas of obstruction with normal blood vessel grafts. Indeed, because nobody could predict in advance the state of Mr. Grant's arteries, a surgical team had been ready to carry out bypass surgery on him, had the need arisen. He was lucky, too, because although the chemical treatment did not work, the balloon did open his blocked artery.

Like William Berry, Eugene Grant is both a victim of cardiovascular disease and a beneficiary of modern technology. Successes in many such patients have been brilliant. But as important as the technological advances have been, they explain only a part, and probably a small part, of the extraordinary fall in cardiovascular mortality of recent decades. A number of other factors—treatment of high blood pressure, less cigarette smoking, diets with less fat and cholesterol, more physical exercise, and others known and unknown—have played an even more important role.

Cancer

Cancer is the most dreaded of all diseases and, in this country, second only to cardiovascular diseases as a killer. It is now yielding to modern medicine lives that just a few years ago would have been lost. Michael Bell is one example.

Michael was two years old when he began to have nosebleeds and bruises on his skin. His mother noted that he was feverish and refused his feedings. His father, a young physician, suspected that the baby might have leukemia, a cancer of certain blood-forming cells in the bone marrow. The diagnosis was confirmed by their pediatrician and a specialist. The parents were aware that this disease, which had been almost uniformly fatal within twelve months a few years earlier, could be cured in more than 60 percent of children, with chemotherapy and, in some cases, radiation. The treatment, which lasted more than two years, was successful, and Michael, now an alert and vigorous eighteen-year-old without any apparent effects of either the disease or the treatment, has just entered college.

In Michael's case powerful chemicals and X rays were used to destroy the cancer cells that would otherwise have destroyed him. He and his family were lucky because his disease was recognized at once by his father. They were lucky, too, because they had available the specialists and the technology that led to cure of a disease that was almost invariably fatal before the era of modern medicine. Marian Cohen, another cancer victim, was also saved by today's medical technology.

Miss Cohen was a twenty-year-old college junior when she noticed afternoon and evening fevers of up to 102 degrees and a weight loss of 12 pounds. She consulted the doctor at her university's health service and was given a series of laboratory tests and X rays. These led to her hospitalization, a biopsy of an enlarged gland that the doctor had discovered in her neck, and a diagnosis of Hodgkin's disease, a form of cancer of the lymph glands. Extensive additional examinations indicated that the disease was confined to glands in her neck and under her left arm. During the next two months she underwent radiation treatment directed at the glands in her upper body, and her fever promptly disappeared. Following the treatment, she rapidly regained the weight she had lost before and during the radiation, and she returned to full activity. Now, eight years later, she is a practicing attorney, the mother of a healthy eighteen-month-old baby, and without any suggestion of the disease that, when it occurred twenty or more years earlier, was generally fatal.

Marian Cohen, like Michael Bell, almost surely owes her life and good health to medical advances. The development of so-called supervoltage radiation makes it possible to direct lethal amounts of X rays at areas of cancer without doing more than temporary damage to the surrounding normal tissues. New diagnostic methods permit identifying with great precision the areas where Hodgkin's disease has begun to grow. The combination of its relative sensitivity to killing by X rays and its tendency to remain confined to the body's lymph glands, on the one hand, and modern methods to localize and destroy it, on the other, means that what was formerly a usually fatal form of cancer is now curable in more than 60 percent of cases.

The cure of acute leukemia in children such as Michael Bell was originally viewed by many cancer specialists as a model for treatment of other cancers. Several other forms of cancer, particularly in children, have shown similar susceptibility and response to chemotherapy. In adults, too, certain cancers such as Hodgkin's disease, lymphoma, and acute leukemias (although a much smaller fraction of the latter than in children) can be cured with chemotherapy.* A few other cancers, while not curable, can be controlled for varying periods, often with considerable relief for their victims.

Unfortunately, however, these curable cancers are a small minority of the total. Fewer than 5 percent of cancers that would otherwise be lethal are cured by chemotherapy. The failures are not caused by the absence of sufficiently powerful drugs; many are available that can destroy every known form of cancer. The problem is, rather, that most of the body's normal cells, including many that are critical for our survival, are at least as sensitive to the deadly effects of the chemotherapy as most cancer cells. By delivering a dose large enough to destroy the cancer, so much harm would be done to normal cells as to kill the patient. Even the doses of drug needed to eradicate the most susceptible cancers temporarily damage many sensitive normal tissues, such as the blood-forming cells of the bone marrow, the hair follicles, and the lining cells of the stomach and intestine. As a result, the patient may suffer lowered blood counts with consequent bleeding and increased susceptibility to infection, loss of hair, and ulcers of the stomach and intestine, sometimes with bleeding and diarrhea.

Recent advances in tissue transplantation technology have made it pos-

---

* Early evidence suggests that chemotherapy following surgery also protects some younger women from recurrence of breast cancer.

sible to cure some patients with leukemia whose disease has not been cured by chemotherapy alone. This new approach is to treat with large doses of radiation and chemotherapy—enough to destroy both all the cancer cells *and* the normal bone marrow cells.* The destruction of the patient's bone marrow is then compensated for by transplanting bone marrow cells from a healthy matched donor. If the donor cells are not rejected, they will take over those marrow functions that are essential to life—making red blood cells, white blood cells (to protect against infection), and platelets (to permit normal blood clotting).

John Matson was referred to a Los Angeles teaching hospital for such treatment in January 1985.

Mr. Matson is a twenty-year-old artist, who had been diagnosed as having acute lymphocytic leukemia in 1977 and had been treated with chemotherapy and radiation. Four years later, when the leukemia appeared to have been cured, chemotherapy was stopped. However, in 1984, he again experienced symptoms that suggested leukemia, and leukemic cells reappeared in his blood. Six months later, he was referred to the Los Angeles hospital. Chemotherapy was resumed and appeared to control the disease. But the leukemia's recurrence after the prolonged period of apparent cure made it unlikely that it could be eradicated with drugs alone. Therefore, Mr. Matson was offered the new treatment of bone marrow transplantation. He accepted and was admitted to the hospital in January 1985.

He was prepared for the transplant with further chemotherapy and with sufficient x-ray treatments to destroy any remaining cancer cells; that combination also destroyed his normal bone marrow. After certain other preparatory steps, he received a marrow transplant from a brother whose tissue type closely matched his.

Because chemotherapy and x-ray treatments markedly reduce resistance to infection, Mr. Matson was protected from the ubiquitous germs that are readily dealt with by the body's normal defense mechanisms, but can be fatal to patients whose defenses have been compromised. Thus, for almost seven weeks, both before and after the transplant, Mr. Matson was kept in a special room fitted to purify the air.

The body's own immune mechanisms constitute another kind of obstacle to the transplantation of tissues. These normally help us reject "invaders" of all kinds, including not only germs, but also all tissues that the

---

* This approach can be used only against leukemia and a very few other cancers that are relatively sensitive to chemotherapy and radiation. To eradicate most cancers would require so much chemotherapy and/or radiation that many other organs essential for life would also be destroyed.

body regards as different from itself. Except for identical twins, each person differs from every other in many ways. When the body recognizes a tissue as foreign, or different, it calls into play a number of reactions that lead to the destruction of that tissue, or what we call rejection. New drugs are now available that lessen the rejection process and thereby greatly facilitate transplantation of many kinds of tissues. Mr. Matson was given some of these drugs in the weeks after his transplant. In addition, he required more than forty transfusions of blood and blood products to provide him with adequate red and white blood cells and blood platelets, until his new marrow cells were functioning properly.

After more than eight weeks in the hospital, by which time the bone marrow graft had been shown to be working and he appeared free of leukemia, he was discharged. More than a year later he continues to feel well, without evidence of leukemia.

It is too early to know whether John Matson has been cured. But it is possible to say without hesitation that without modern technology he would no longer be alive.

Meanwhile, even more profound changes have been taking place in the cancer field that are wholly independent of medical programs. For example, deaths from stomach cancer, which forty years ago was the leading cancer killer, have fallen steeply. If the disease were occurring at the same rate today as in 1930, it would claim over 60,000 more lives than it will take this year. Over the same period, deaths from lung cancer have increased by more than fivefold—to more than 120,000 per year. The two diseases are similar in their resistance to medical treatment—both are fatal in more than 90 percent of cases. But our understanding of their origins differs greatly. The cause of the fall in stomach cancer is one of today's medical mysteries; the role of the cigarette as the cause of the epidemic of lung cancer has been known for more than twenty years.

Advances in transplantation technology, which have kept John Matson alive, have also provided great benefit for people with conditions other than cancer. Americans who would have died of certain kinds of heart disease, liver failure, or severe forms of anemia are now alive, thanks to advances in the field of immunology and the applications of the new knowledge to the problem of transplanting human organs. The Stanford University Medical Center, which has had the most experience with heart transplants, reports that 80 percent of its patients are alive after one year, and more than 50 percent survive more than five years. These triumphs are extraordinary, but the total numbers are small: In 1984, in the United States about 400 people received hearts and 300 received livers. The largest experience is with kidneys. Each year, about 7,000 people who were kept alive by kidney dialysis three times a week are restored to far more pleasant lives by kidney transplants.

Trauma

Betsy Wiggins, whose potentially lethal trauma occurred in an automobile accident, is one beneficiary of a kidney transplant.

Betsy was seventeen years old and returning from her high school graduation dance when the car in which she was riding was struck by another. Her left kidney was irreparably damaged and had to be removed. Most people can survive such a loss and lead a normal life with their remaining kidney. But Betsy was born with only one kidney, and in years past, her accident would have been fatal. In this era of kidney dialysis and transplantation, however, she was extremely lucky. Dialysis kept her alive for several months until a donor kidney could be found and transplanted into her body. She now receives drugs that help prevent her body from rejecting the transplant.

Betsy's parents both have well-paid positions in the business world, and the family has comprehensive health insurance. But the more than $150,000 in medical bills since her accident has been almost fully paid by Social Security, which, following legislation passed by the Congress in 1972, covers the expenses of all Americans who are treated for kidney failure.

Three years following her accident, Betsy is about to enter her sophomore year in college. She requires continuing medical supervision, but her general health is remarkably good.

Most people with kidney failure have lost their kidneys to diseases caused by infections or by circulatory problems. In that sense Betsy Wiggins' case was unusual. But from another perspective her situation was typical. Injuries from accidents, poisoning, and violence are the third highest cause of death among all Americans, and first among those between the ages of five and thirty-five. The spread of trauma treatment services throughout the nation means that many people like Betsy now survive—people who, a short time ago, would have died in accidents involving cars, guns, poison, or fire.

Health Problems of Early Life

The early decades of this century saw brilliant progress in controlling the diseases of infancy and early childhood. Indeed, one sign of that progress is the fact that cardiovascular diseases, cancer, and trauma are now the leading causes of death in our nation. At the turn of the century the three major killers were influenza and pneumonia, tuberculosis, and infectious diseases of the stomach and intestine, which often caused death by dehydration from vomiting and diarrhea. Because they affected mainly infants and children, their control meant a marked decrease in death rates among the young. That, in turn, has meant that larger and larger numbers of people live to an age at which they are candidates for heart attacks, cancer, or accidents.

But health problems continue in early life, and modern technology brings great benefit for some of those problems. Among the most extraordinary feats are those that result from advances in the care of the newborn—advances that are taking place almost from day to day. Had Stephen Bradley been born fifteen or even ten years ago, he almost surely would not have survived the first day of life. He is now approaching his first birthday and appears in good health.

Marilyn Bradley went into labor in the twenty-seventh week of pregnancy and, at a community hospital near her home, delivered a baby weighing just over two pounds. Like all very premature babies, Stephen had difficulty in breathing. Therefore, he required mechanical ventilation and oxygen. "Premies" also need help with regulation of body temperature, heart rate, and blood pressure—other functions that are automatic in infants born after the normal forty weeks in the mother's uterus. All of these capabilities and more are available in neonatal intensive care units, which have been developed throughout the country. Because they are so expensive and require experts to manage them, a large medical foundation undertook a program in the 1970s to regionalize them. They helped link neonatal intensive care units in hospital centers in the nation's cities with smaller participating hospitals.

Fortunately for the Bradleys, their community hospital had such a linkage, and Stephen was taken directly by special ambulance to a teaching hospital ten miles away, where the regional neonatal intensive care unit was located. There, he was continued on mechanical ventilation. A radiant warming table was used to keep his temperature at a normal level, and his pulse and blood pressure were monitored. Like most very premature infants, he was incapable of taking fluids or nourishment by mouth. This meant intravenous feeding, but since the tiny infant is exquisitely sensitive to too much or too little fluid, a carefully regulated pump was required to deliver the total of 3 ounces of a special nutritious fluid that has to be given constantly over each twenty-four-hour period at the start. He received antibiotics to cope with the infections that are common complications. Premies often have brain hemorrhages. Stephen was lucky; periodic ultrasound studies of his head indicated that he had escaped that problem.

After fifty days of the most painstaking care by specially trained doctors, nurses, and technicians, he had almost doubled his birth weight and was ready for transfer to an intermediate care nursery. He remained there an additional three weeks. Then, when he was nearing what would have been his normal birth weight, he was discharged to the care of his parents.

The Bradleys were lucky because of the neonatal care that was available for their baby. Their good fortune was even greater, because he had escaped the complications often seen in such infants—brain hemorrhages, heart defects requiring surgery, chronic lung disease. Even many of those complications can now be managed, but they may require additional weeks or even months in the neonatal intensive care unit. Whether he will be entirely normal will not be known until he is older; as many as 25 percent of such babies are left with residual problems, but these are often mild—for example, a little clumsiness of movement or the need for glasses because of changes in the eyes.

The Bradleys were lucky too because their insurance covered their entire hospital bill of $54,000.

Between 1960 and 1982 the infant mortality rate fell by more than 50 percent in the United States, from 26 deaths for every 1,000 live babies born each year to 11. The fall is due, in part, to improved technology—medical care given in the first days and weeks of life. So-called low-birth-weight infants—babies weighing less than 5.5 pounds at birth—account for about 7 percent of all births in this country, but for over 60 percent of all deaths during the first year. Infants like Stephen Bradley, in what are called the very-low-birth-weight category, or less than 3.3 pounds at birth, are more than 200 times more likely to die in the first year of life than normal-weight babies. But the kind of care that Stephen received improves the odds greatly. Fifteen or even ten years ago an infant of his birth weight would have had less than a 20 percent chance of surviving; in the facility where he was treated, the odds of survival are now nearly 90 percent.

Despite the progress in infant survival, there is still much room for improvement in our country. Sixteen nations have better records than ours, including not only Finland, Japan, and Sweden, whose rates are the world's lowest, but Spain, Hong Kong, and Ireland. Within our own country profound differences exist. The babies born in some inner city areas are two or three times more likely to die in the first year of life than those whose mothers happen to live in prosperous suburbs. Infant mortality rates are twice as high for black babies as for white. Babies of mothers who are poor or adolescent or poorly educated, or who have had little or no prenatal care, or who, during pregnancy, have infections or are not well nourished or smoke cigarettes or use street drugs or misuse alcohol are all at greater risk of dying in the first year of life. And, not surprisingly, given the close relationship of low birth weight to infant mortality, the babies of such mothers are at greater risk of being very small at birth.

Not surprisingly, too, the countries with the lowest infant mortality rates have relatively fewer small babies than we do. The success in decreasing the infant mortality rate that has been achieved with medical technology suggests that one way to lower the rate still further would be to continue to improve the technology and to build more neonatal intensive care units around the country. But most experts in the field believe that we are reaching the limits of what can be achieved with high technology. To them the fact that low birth weight is so crucial a determinant of infant mortality suggests another approach: to decrease the incidence of low-birth-weight babies by means of preventive programs. From 1970 to 1980 more American women received early care (from 71 percent in 1970 to 80 percent in 1980 for white women, and from 45 percent to 63 percent for black women). But with the cutbacks in federal programs beginning in the early 1980s, fewer women received early prenatal care. In our inner cities, increases in infant mortality rates were apparent within two years.

Infectious Diseases

Tributes to newer technology are not intended to slight the importance of many medical interventions that have long been available. The doctor's own senses, often alone, sometimes accompanied by instruments as simple as the stethoscope, still lead to precise diagnoses. Many drugs and other medical and surgical approaches to treatment and rehabilitation that have been proved over decades or longer are still indispensable. Each year hundreds of thousands of people with heart disease, cancer, or trauma are cured of their problems or helped to live with them, often in comfort and for long periods, by technology that has been in use for decades.

In no area of medicine has success been greater than in the prevention and treatment of infectious diseases—particularly those caused by bacteria, like the streptococcus, which causes scarlet fever, and the tubercle bacillus, which causes tuberculosis, and some viruses. Control of the three leading causes of death early in the century—conditions that result from infections—are testimony to that success. The measures that had the greatest effects were in the category of public health technology—improved sewage disposal and other sanitary measures, purification of the water supply, better nutrition, and less crowded living conditions. But a crucial boost was provided by vaccines against the common childhood diseases and drugs that are effective against bacteria and some viruses. Sulfa drugs, fifty years after their discovery, penicillin, forty years on, and a range of younger drugs and vaccines continue to save lives and diminish suffering from the bacterial diseases and some viral diseases that were the most common causes of death and suffering in the early part of this century. The contributions of drugs and vaccines in medical history are apparent and relatively easy to measure.

If we needed evidence that we can never let our guard down with respect to threats to health, we have it now in the area of contagious diseases. The source of great alarm to health authorities and the public both within this country and around the world is a new disease, or group of diseases, the acquired immune deficiency syndrome (AIDS). It paralyzes the body's immune system, thereby inviting attack by a range of superimposed serious infections and some tumors. It is invariably fatal. It is caused by human immunodeficiency virus (HIV), or human T-cell lymphotropic virus III (HTLV III), which is transmitted by body fluids—particularly semen and blood. The major methods of transmission in the United States and Europe have been sexual (particularly anal) intercourse and exposure to blood, most often by contaminated needles, among drug users. In addition, a pregnant woman who is infected with the virus can pass it to her baby. As best we can tell, the HIV virus is entirely new to the human species, that is, never before has it infected people. This is in contrast to perhaps all other viruses and bacteria that have caused the major epidemics of past centuries. Because humans have experienced *those* germs over the millenia, we have developed some measure of resistance to them. Further, in part because of the AIDS virus's extraordinary capacity to change its character—that is, to mutate—nobody can predict what form it may eventually take, and how much havoc it will wreak. Thus, not surprisingly, no vaccine is as yet in sight.

But for AIDS, as for all other health problems that have dire effects and that are resistant to treatment, some steps *can* be taken, indeed are essential. First, we should institute the preventive measures that are known to be useful—in this case, avoidance of promiscuous sexual contacts, the use of condoms, and elimination of contaminated needles and of blood and blood products that come from unknown and untested sources. Second, we must encourage research on the problem. Third, we should avoid panic-inspired behavior, in which we hurt innocent people without any benefit to others—as, for example, in keeping out of school children who carry the virus (the evidence is strong that the virus is not spread except by the methods described). Finally, the victims of this terrible condition require all of the caring that doctors, nurses, and the public can muster.

Making Life More Livable

Most medical encounters are directed not at saving life, but at making it more livable—interventions sometimes called quality-improving. Modern technology can be very effective both in saving people's lives and in making their lives far more normal. John LeGrand bears particularly dramatic witness to both kinds of benefits.

John is a twenty-one-year-old farmhand who now has a functioning right arm despite the fact that it was completely severed while haymaking three years ago. Immediately following the catastrophe, a friend on the baler applied a rope as a tourniquet to the stump, thereby saving John from bleeding to death. He recovered the arm and rushed John and it to a hospital in a small Illinois town nearby. A surgeon cleaned the stump, put the arm in ice, and arranged for John's transfer by helicopter to a Chicago hospital. There, in an operation requiring eight hours, the blood vessels, nerves, and other tissues of the stump and arm were rejoined. Over the next two years, function returned to the point where John now has only moderate disability.

John's life was saved by his quick-witted friend who applied a tourniquet properly. The quality of his life thereafter was vastly improved by the reattachment of his arm by surgeons, followed by physiotherapy and retraining. Most interventions directed at improving life's quality are less dramatic, but they are no less important:

- Cataract extraction followed by artificial lens implants, which has restored vision to a vast number of people.
- Hip replacements, which make it possible for thousands of people

each year to return to what is often full mobility, with freedom from what had been constant pain.

- Lithium and other drugs, which have made it possible for many people with serious psychiatric disease to return to a normal or near-normal life from one of desperation.
- Contraceptive technology, which gives people, and particularly women of childbearing age, a degree of control over their lives never previously possible. It also permits the kind of planning that can lead to healthier babies.
- New drugs that heal previously intractable duodenal ulcers and allow patients to abandon the unpleasant diets that were previously thought to be essential parts of treatment and are now known to be useless.
- Hospices, which have made possible a release from pain and terror and the opportunity to die with dignity for many patients with terminal illness.

These are but a few more recent approaches that have improved the quality of life for millions of Americans with health problems and for their families. More are being developed. Since many are directed at problems of the elderly, the need for them is growing as our population ages. And as is true for life-saving technology, new quality-of-life-improving technology complements many measures that have long been on the scene and that continue to make life much more worthwhile. Aspirin, eyeglasses, and wheelchairs are simple examples.

The Price of Technological Progress

The Price in Money

Developing new measures, improving old ones, making both available to those in need—all of this requires resources, both money and people. Until recently, most Americans gave little thought to hospital bills; many never even bothered to look at them. When Mr. Berry was recently asked the cost of his hospitalization, he said he couldn't recall and thought he likely never knew. Most, he said, was covered by Medicare, and the balance by a supplemental insurance policy. Both at the time and in retrospect, however, Mr. Berry and his family say they would have regarded the price—whatever it was—as a bargain, given the outcome.

But the price of some modern technology is awe-inspiring, even if less so than the medical benefits it often brings. Eugene Grant's insurance company paid just over $20,000 for his ten days of hospitalization; had he required coronary bypass surgery in addition to his angioplasty, the bill would have been almost twice as high. The cost of the Bradley infant's hospitalization was $54,000. John Matson's 1985 hospital bill (which I will examine in detail in Chapter 5) was $133,000. It is not, of course, an average bill for an average hospitalization. But it does reflect the cost of some of our most extraordinary technology.

John Matson's bill of $133,000 covered a hospitalization of just over eight weeks. That was much more than the costs incurred by Michael Bell and Marian Cohen, who were cured of their cancer. It was higher, too, than the bills of most of the 600 children with cancers who were described in a recent article on the cost of cancer care in the *Journal of the American Medical Association*. But the mean cost of hospitalization for the children was over $15,000 per year, and the total annual cost of care was almost $30,000 per patient. Those whose cancers were most responsive had the lowest annual cost: over $26,000. For those who died, the mean cost of care in the last year of life was over $72,000. About 95 percent of all medical costs was paid by private or public insurance or by charities. But each family paid about 38 percent of their gross annual family income for the remaining medical expenses and nonmedical disease-related costs, like travel expenses, the costs of special diets, special education, and equipment. (Not included in these numbers is the loss of family income that resulted from illness.) The total cost of medical care alone—that is, not including the associated nonmedical but disease-related costs—over a five-year period for the children with cancer who responded well to treatment was $120,000.

The number of costly procedures that save lives and that make life more livable is increasing all the time. Heart, liver, and pancreatic transplants are limited by the number of organs that are available. But a variety of other procedures on the horizon have no such limits. For example, it is estimated that 35,000 to 50,000 Americans would be candidates for an artificial heart, and that an artificial heart program could add more than $5 billion a year to the nation's health bill. It is true, fortunately, that as procedures are done more frequently, the costs of some are reduced. But it is unlikely that the costs of most of those that involve high technology can ever be reduced to a level where they will not make major claims on our resources. For example, kidney dialysis and kidney transplantation— which together now prolong life for more than 70,000 Americans who would die without them—cost more than $2.5 billion a year. This is ten times the cost that some people predicted when the program began.

The Price in Time

The costs of new and old medical interventions must be examined in more than economic terms. Many demand enormous amounts of professional time. When patients are cured of pneumonia or of cancer, for example, they may no longer be patients. Then the need for the physician's time is generally much reduced or removed. But the need for continuing medical support is great for the person whose life has been saved but who is left seriously disabled—patients on dialysis, for example, or receiving chemotherapy for cancer, or with a heart transplant. I have described in some detail the significant time required—and deserved—by a patient like Jonathan Carlyle, for whose *disease* no specific treatment was available, but for whose person and whose family much was done. Similarly, the beneficiaries of interventions to improve the quality of life, such as people with chronic illness who are helped through crises, generally still require full measures of the doctor's caring function.

Lewis Thomas has written of "halfway technology," the kind that may save life but leaves behind a disabled patient. The polio victim of another era whose life was saved by an iron lung is one example. Today's patient on dialysis is another. The polio vaccine has almost eliminated the iron lung, but the patient on dialysis requires continuing medical care to survive. Thomas contrasts such halfway cures with people who will not be patients at all when scientific advances teach us how to prevent or cure kidney disease, as earlier advances led to the polio vaccine.

Here, too, the same considerations that apply to economic costs are relevant to physician time. Halfway technology leads to major needs for support from doctors and other medical personnel. The emotional requirements of the patient with the iron lung and the one on kidney dialysis present health professionals with great challenges. More such challenges clearly face us as medical capabilities increase and as our population grows older. And, just as the money expended for ineffective technology is unavailable for other interventions that do make a difference, so too a case can be made for being equally jealous of time expended on procedures that have questionable or no benefit. The minutes or hours of professional time consumed by an unnecessary test or treatment are minutes or hours not available to a growing population of the chronically ill and others in urgent need of doctors whose schedules give them adequate time to care.

The problem will not go away, nor would most people want it to. For the growing demand for medical care is in part the result of our successes, technical and socioeconomic. Technical success now makes it possible to do much that could not be done a few years ago. Socioeconomic success now means that a larger fraction of our society knows what medical technology can offer and is affluent enough to demand it. But millions of Americans today are denied access to that technology. In the absence of change in our system of providing the technology, their numbers will grow rapidly in the decades ahead. The next chapter will examine the system.

5 Money, Time, and Lives: Costs of "The System"

"System" is a misnomer. Health care for Americans is shaped by a jerry-built aggregate of institutions. Some overlap, some are redundant, some are separated by yawning gaps. Most are in a state of constant change but without any overall plan: schools of medicine, nursing, public health, pharmacy, social work, (recently) management, and others; tertiary care hospitals, which are designed for diagnosis and treatment of complex problems, like those requiring brain or heart surgery, but also deliver primary care to ambulatory patients through their emergency rooms and clinics; community or secondary hospitals, which were originally intended for simpler problems, like appendectomies, deliveries, and treatment of pneumonia, but are doing more and more tertiary work; chronic hospitals, usually for the mentally ill; special-purpose hospitals, like rehabilitation; nursing homes; clinics; community health centers; home care programs; for-profit corporations, including insurance carriers, hospital chains, ambulatory care centers, including many HMOs, and pharmaceutical and appliance manufacturers; non-health-related companies with large expenditures for employee health benefits; nonprofit organizations including Blue Cross and Blue Shield, some HMOs, like Kaiser and New York HIP, unions of health workers, non-health-related unions with health plans for their members, and various church groups; the research "establishment," including universities, institutes, nonprofit foundations, for-profit companies, and government agencies; a vast legislative and regulatory bureaucracy, both governmental and professional; federal, state, and local welfare programs; and a proliferation of lobbies and special interest groups, like the American Association of Retired Persons.

The continuing changes are partly a result of scientific developments or historical ones, like the control of some previously common diseases (e.g., tuberculosis) and the increase in others (e.g., cancer) or demographic shifts (e.g., an aging population needing more nursing homes). Some, like the revisions of the Social Security Act (and revisions of revisions), reflect legal tinkering resulting from a changing climate of public opinion. And some, like the new DRGs,* are bureaucratic efforts at cost containment.

Changes in one part of the system often have unexpected effects elsewhere. For example, the increase in medical students in the 1960s was intended to fill the need for primary-care doctors in underserved areas in the United States. It has done that to some extent, although many inner cities and rural areas still lack primary-care doctors, but it led to an unforeseen excess of specialists, and, as a result, unanticipated upward pressures on the costs of medical care.

The delivery "system" has progressed down the years by means of stalls, skids, and convulsive leaps. One index of its inefficiency: A *New England Journal of Medicine* article estimated that of the $355 billion spent in the American health sector in 1983, $78 billion, or 22 percent, went for administrative costs. The same article estimated that if a Canadian-style system were in effect here, the savings would have been $29 billion; a British system would have saved $38 billion. Another index of inefficiency is the widespread duplication of facilities.

The sociologist Paul Starr analyzes the system's historical development in terms of the medical profession's successful drive toward sovereignty. He reminds us that, even a century ago, hospitals were little better than charnel houses—places where the poor went to die or where "undesirables" such as the contagious and the mentally ill could be segregated—and that doctors were held in little esteem. By the middle of this century, however, hospitals had become "awesome citadels of science and bureaucratic order," and doctors were among the highest paid and most respected members of society, a self-regulating profession, Men in White, whose authority went unchallenged.

Doctors are being challenged now. Third-party payers (large corporations, insurance companies, and government agencies) want to be sure they're getting their money's worth.† Ever more sophisticated patients raise

---

* A fixed payment for hospitalization determined in advance largely according to the patient's diagnosis. See p. 86.

† Lee Iacocca found that Chrysler Corporation's health care program cost over $300 million in 1982. For example, it represented 10 percent of the price of each K car. He invited Joseph Califano, who had been Secretary of Health, Education, and Welfare in the Carter Administration, to reform the program. Investigating, Califano found "unnecessary care, inefficiency, even abuse and fraud." In 1984, reforms saved the company $58 million, yet in that year health costs still exceeded $500 per car and topped the total amount Chrysler paid its 65,000 pensioners.

questions concerning medical judgments. Growing numbers of malpractice litigants raise questions about both medical judgments and medical skills. Moreover, doctors are sharing or giving up responsibilities for which they need help, some because of conflict of interest, some because they haven't the training: "God committee" questions, matters administrative, legal, and scientific, and many issues of allocation and priority.

The three chapters immediately preceding this one include descriptions of what good health care can be, where to find it, and what it can do for us. But what does it cost to get it, in human and financial terms, and who gets it?

Rising Costs and Rising Expectations

It is not a new idea that all of us are entitled to health care. Americans are philanthropic, and our earlier hospitals were often supported solely by private charity. Well into the middle of this century many doctors gave as much as a third of their time to providing free services for the poor. An early legislative acknowledgment of the right to care was the Sheppard-Towner Act, which provided matching funds to the states for prenatal and child health centers. The act was passed in 1921, but discontinued in 1927. In those days, "care" meant only the most basic measures, since little else was possible. (See Chapter 2.)

In 1929, Americans spent just $29.49 per person on health. Expectations were low, and patients were fatalistic. Here is a contemporary account of a zero-cost treatment for cancer; the writer was British, but he had his American counterparts:

> Uncle Trevor has just died.—He was taken ill with "retention of urine" just before we left; and the current story is that he then took to his bed and refused to eat. The truth, confided to me under the seal of profoundest secrecy by Pippa [the author's sister] just now, is that a specialist who came in discovered that he had cancer. Whereupon Roland [the family doctor] with extraordinary good sense gave orders that he was to be given nothing to eat—so that in about a fortnight he died of starvation. There was absolutely no pain and practically no discomfort even. He died this morning at six.*

Here is a hospital bill, twenty-six years later, this time American, for another terminal case of a form of cancer:

* James Strachey to his wife, Alix, 1924, in *Bloomsbury/Freud: The Letters of James and Alix Strachey, 1924–1925,* eds. Perry Meisel and Walter Kendrick (New York: Basic Books, 1985).

Patient name: Williams, Nicholas

Diagnosis: Acute lymphocytic leukemia
Hospitalized: January 14–26, 1950

Room	$180.00
Medications and blood	65.00
Laboratory tests	45.50
Special procedures	30.00
Total	$320.50

Thirty-five years later, another young American with the same form of cancer, John Matson, whom we met in Chapter 4, received the following bill:

Hospitalized: January 2–March 3, 1985

Semiprivate room (12 days)	$ 3,720.00
Room with laminar air flow (47 days)	43,475.00
Medications, including chemotherapy	45,533.76
Radiation therapy	5,994.00
Blood bank	6,276.00
Microbiology laboratory services	5,465.00
Operating room	2,282.00
Additional charges described on 31 pages of computer printout	20,670.50
Total	$133,416.26
Physicians' fees	$ 7,200.00

The experiences of the two patients in their early twenties, suffering from the same disease thirty-five years apart, differed in three crucial respects. The first and most important difference was in the outcomes: The first patient died while in the hospital of a disease for which there was no specific treatment in 1950. The other left the hospital after fifty-nine days. Eight years earlier, when his leukemia was initially diagnosed, he was begun on chemotherapy, which at first appeared to control the disease. It returned, however, as it does in perhaps one third of children and young adults. Therefore, in early 1985 he was hospitalized for chemotherapy, radiation, and a newer form of treatment—a bone marrow transplant. He is now back at work without any evidence of leukemia. Although his doctors are hopeful on the basis of experience with a still limited number of others treated similarly, it is too early to know whether he has been cured.

The second difference was in the size of their medical bills. The third difference was in the method of payment for their treatment. Since the first patient was not able to afford private care, he had been hospitalized on the so-called ward service of the hospital, where no charge was made for physicians' services. His family was able to pay half the bill during the six months following his hospitalization; the rest was written off as "free care" by the hospital. The bills for hospital care and physicians' services for the second patient, whose earlier medical care had exhausted his savings and whose income was very limited, were covered almost completely by Medicaid.

In 1950, the United States health care bill was less than $13 billion, which was 4.4 percent of the gross national product or $82 per person. The bill for 1984 was $387 billion, about 10.6 percent of the GNP, or just under $1,600 per capita. If every American's health needs were in fact being met, the bill would be much higher than that. One thing is certain and cannot be changed: Future health needs will be ever greater, and meeting them could consume an ever-greater proportion of the GNP. That is partly because our capabilities are growing, and partly because more and more of us are surviving into extreme old age, when medical needs are greatest. In the last four decades, nongovernment and government health insurers, the so-called third parties in the financing of medical services, have spread the financial risks of illness to large populations, and thus have lifted a great burden from the ill and infirm. But the burden, which falls largely on the working population, will grow heavier as the number of aged people increases in proportion to the number of those who support them.

Direct Inflationary Pressures

Before examining "demographic" pressure on health costs, and making predictions about future needs, we will look at other inflationary factors, many of which could be controlled. And since the ultimate intent of this book is to propose that our national health policy be consonant with our nation's values, we will look at the failures and inequities in our present system. Later chapters will suggest means of redress.

What factors contribute to this extraordinary inflation (see Table 1)? The makeup of the population, of course. People of different age groups require different kinds and amounts of services. People from different income levels have different needs and demands. We'll come to that further on. There are what we may call historical factors: Had we shown figures for the 1940s, we would have seen the early effects of the private insurance programs, like Blue Cross and Blue Shield, which came into being in that

Table 1: Total U.S. Expenditure for Health, Absolute Amounts and Proportionate to GNP, 1950, 1960, 1970, 1980, and 1984*

Year	Billions of dollars		Percent of gross national product	Amount per capita	
	Contemporary	1984		Contemporary dollars	1984 dollars
1950	13	61	4.4	82	390
1960	27	97	5.3	146	528
1970	75	205	7.6	350	956
1980	248	312	9.4	1,049	1,321
1984		387	10.6		1,580

* Derived from Table 80, "Health Care Financing Review," by K. R. Levit, H. Lazenby, D. R. Waldo, and L. M. Davidoff. *National Health Expenditures 1984*, HCFA Pub. #03206, vol. 7, no. 1, U.S. Government Printing Office, Nov. 1985.

decade. The state of the nation's economy is a historical factor (the figures in Table 1 have been converted to 1984 dollars, to allow for inflation); the effects of boom and recession are slow—since it takes a long time to implement new programs or dismantle old ones. Questions of "value" are best reflected, perhaps, in per capita figures—out-of-pocket and private insurance expenditures, at least until 1966, tell us how much medical care "average" Americans were prepared to buy for themselves and their families.

Tax Policy

Tax policies have contributed. Tax exemptions for medical insurance programs in large organizations, for example, burden the general population, though indirectly. Health insurance premiums paid by employers are not taxable. Therefore, health insurance providing employees with a tax-free benefit is subsidized by those who do not have such benefits. The Congressional Budget Office estimated that in 1983, employer-paid health insurance cost the government $26 billion. This may be compared with the $19.2 billion the federal government and the $16.4 billion state and local governments spent on Medicaid that year. Moreover, there is an income-tax exemption for those who have very large medical expenses.

Social Policy: Medicaid and Medicare

Steep increases in health expenditures after 1965 reflect in large part the effects of the Great Society programs of the late 1960s. These acknowledged formally that our society has a duty to provide health care to all its citizens. That commitment was expressed in the 1965 amendments to the Social Security Act that established Medicaid, a welfare program for the poor, and Medicare, a public insurance program, primarily for the elderly.

Medicaid is intended to help the indigent of all ages, and mandates coverage of an earlier program called Aid to Families with Dependent Children. The federal government pays about 54 percent of its cost. The rest comes out of state funds. The states, of course, vary in population numbers, age of population, prevalence of certain diseases, per capita income, and level of taxation. So Medicaid consists of fifty-one separate programs that are administered by the states. Each state decides whether to participate (until recently, Arizona did not), who is "medically needy," what services to cover, and whether to require cost sharing. For instance, Medicaid in Georgia does not cover families in which both parents are in the home. In 1983, Medicaid recipients got, per capita, about $2,900 in New York, in Alaska about $2,560, in Connecticut $2,209, in Mississippi $1,030, and in California, where the cost of medical services is highest, $1,010.

Physicians are not required to treat people on Medicaid. About 32 percent of physicians in the medical specialties, 15 percent in the surgical specialties, and 40 percent of psychiatrists do not treat any Medicaid patients. Many avoid doing so because the reimbursements are so low, others because patients' Medicaid eligibility is determined on a month-to-month basis, and doctors may find that patients they treated last month with Medicaid reimbursement must now be treated at their own expense. As a consequence, Medicaid patients often rely on emergency-room care, which is very expensive. Many Medicaid plans are so structured that recipients have no incentive (indeed, may not be permitted) to seek comprehensive (and often, less expensive) coverage, such as is available in some capitation programs.

The Congress intended Medicaid to provide coverage for all citizens who could not afford medical services. Nevertheless, Medicaid covered only 40 percent of people living below the poverty line in 1981, *before* the major cuts of the 1980s were widely felt.

Most of the private insurance plans designed in the 1940s and 1950s, were intended to spread the risk of great expense for hospital treatment. The emphasis was on hospitals, because that's where people went for most costly problems, including emergencies, severe illnesses, surgery, and obstetrics. Visits to doctors' offices were much less expensive, since there was little technology there. Similarly, the home care then possible was generally simple, and a relatively small fraction of the population needed nursing home care. Unhappily, Medicare, the government's tax-supported insurance plan for the aged and the disabled (those covered by Social Security) of all income brackets, was designed like the earlier private insurance programs, though by 1965 age distribution, prevalence of medical conditions, medical and nursing capabilities, and family structure had all changed. There were a lot more old people, many of whom were chronically ill and needed care at home and in nursing homes, rather than in acute hospitals. Because Medicare does not cover most long-term care, that gap is filled, but only in part, by Medicaid. In 1981 almost 40 percent of Medicaid expenditures was spent for the care of 3.5 million elderly. An amendment to the Social Security legislation in 1972 also provides Medicare coverage for dialysis, kidney transplants, and other care for all patients with kidney failure.

Enactment of the original Medicare and Medicaid legislation was followed by major changes in health care and improvements in the nation's health, beginning in 1968. In the next fifteen years visits to physicians by poor people rose by 40 percent, from levels far below those of the nonpoor to levels that by 1973 were higher. This was not unexpected, since the incidence and seriousness of most diseases are much greater among the poor and considerable catch-up was necessary. Access to prenatal care rose dramatically for black women—in 1980, 63 percent of them received care during the first three months of pregnancy, as compared with 42 percent in 1969. The corresponding rise for white women was less, but gratifying— from 72 to 79 percent. A profound drop in such preventable diseases as rheumatic fever and measles also spoke to more comprehensive care. Infant mortality, which was 26.0 per 1,000 in 1960 and 24.7 in 1965, fell to 11.4 in 1982. The fall for black babies was even greater—from 44 in 1960 and 41.7 in 1965 to 21.8 in 1979. In the same period deaths of Americans from influenza and pneumonia dropped by 53 percent, from tuberculosis by 52 percent, from diabetes by 31 percent, and from meningococcal infections such as meningitis by over 40 percent.

Among the elderly, too, access to medical services was greatly improved. Health indices showed corresponding improvements. For example, between 1955 and 1967, the death rate for men sixty-five and over *rose* by an average annual rate of 0.2 percent, but in the decade after 1968 there was an annual average *drop* of 1.5 percent. Almost surely, the services to which Medicare provided access accounted for a portion of this dramatic difference. In addition, both medical progress and Medicare made available to many older people a variety of measures, such as hip replacement and cataract extraction, that while not life-saving, can make life much more rewarding. Between 1970 and 1980, there was an almost twofold increase in cataract operations in people over sixty-five. That operation has been greatly improved as a result of the insertion of an artificial lens within the eye at the time of the removal of the cataract. In the last few years the number of such improved operations has tripled.

At the fifteen-year mark, the evidence available to the President's Commission for the Study of Ethical Problems in Medicine and Biomedical and Behavioral Research spoke of extraordinary health benefits following the Medicare-Medicaid legislation. But the evidence uncovered by the commission conveyed additional messages. It said that the job was only partly done and done inequitably. For example, although infant mortality for the nonwhite population fell relatively much faster than for the white, it is still two or three times higher in many inner cities than in prosperous suburbs. These differences account, at least in large part, for the fact that the United States is seventeenth on the list of world nations ranked according to infant mortality. Additional testimony to greater health needs of the poor continue to accumulate—more heart disease, hypertension, asthma, emphysema, diabetes, and arthritis are found among poor than nonpoor Americans.

Not surprisingly, the achievements of Medicare and Medicaid cost a good deal of money—in 1982, $83 billion to cover 20 percent of our population. Thus, the program was a factor, although only one, in the recent escalation in health costs. But it was set up to address a major need and not to save money. It did address that need very well, even if not completely. And contrary to widespread belief, increases in the cost of the programs in recent years—once they were under way—have been no larger than the increases in the costs of other medical care programs supported by nongovernment sources. Overall, Medicare and Medicaid accounted for 29 percent of all health spending in 1982. The two programs covered 35 percent of all hospital expenditures, 23 percent of physicians' services, and 50 percent of nursing home care.

How Inflationary Factors Interconnect

A range of other factors, many of which have little to do with unmet medical needs, contributes to the inflation of health care costs. These include historic and demographic factors, which we can't do much about. Others are often interconnected:

1. The structure of our payment system, which has helped shape
2. the structure of our delivery system, both of which contribute to

3. the kinds and amount of services we deliver.
4. An oversupply of doctors, which is affected by 1 and 2 and affects 2 and 3.
5. Malpractice suits, which are encouraged by 1 and contribute to 3 (see Chapter 2).
6. Our tax policies, which are affected by 1 and contribute to 2 and 3 (see p. 74).

The Payment System

In 1950, when Nicholas Williams, the young man with leukemia (p. 72), was hospitalized, Americans paid directly out of pocket for more than 65 percent of all the health services they received, including over 80 percent of their doctors' bills. At that time private insurance for hospital care, which had been spreading through the country for more than a decade, covered about half the American population. In the years since, the spread of private insurance has continued, so that now more than three quarters of the population is insured for at least part of their hospital expenses. Further, coverage has been extended, although in much more limited fashion, to other medical services, including physicians' bills, expensive outpatient procedures (such as ambulatory surgery and complicated diagnostic measures like CT scans), nursing homes, home care, and drugs. But coverage as comprehensive as this is now restricted mainly to so-called capitation plans, where for an annual premium per individual, most health services—preventive, therapeutic, and many rehabilitative—are covered. Many of these plans cover prescription drugs and appliances, long-term care, and some psychiatric service.

Most insurance payments until very recently were cost-based and retrospective; that is, the bill was submitted for a test or hospitalization or a visit to the doctor after the fact, and payment followed. As a result, the individual seeking the service and the individual or institution providing it had little reason to seek economies. Because neither doctor nor patient had reason even to ask the cost of "one more" (or the first) test or one more treatment, the prevailing philosophy was, why not order it if there is even the remotest chance that it may be useful? ("Let's order a [or another] CT scan. It's extremely unlikely to tell us anything we don't already know, but it won't cost you anything.") Until very recently, doctors had little reason even to know the costs of what they ordered.

Since existing health insurance plans do not cover all Americans, their inflationary pressures have penalized the poor and near-poor who *don't* have insurance. For them the costs of individual items of medical care mount as steadily as for those who are insured, and who have not had immediate reason to be cost-conscious.

Paradoxically, most private and public programs are structured so that they provide incentives for more, rather than less, costly approaches to medical care. For example, an insurance policy that covers, as most do, expensive tests for patients in, but not outside, the hospital encourages doctor and patient to opt for hospitalization to save the patient from paying for the tests, even though the overall cost to the system will be much greater.

The most extensive coverage by far is for hospital care. In 1950, hospital care accounted for 31 percent of all health expenditures; in 1982 it was 42 percent. In 1982 federal government covered 40 percent of this, state and local government 13 percent, and private health insurance 33 percent. The remaining 12 percent was paid by individuals out of pocket.* For all other health services much larger fractions came directly from patients.

An increasing fraction of hospital money goes into the most expensive ones, the acute care institutions. Thus, in 1982, 84 percent of total hospital funds went to hospitals that provide primarily acute care, 8 percent to federal hospitals (mainly those operated by the Veterans Administration and Department of Defense), and 4.5 percent to state and local psychiatric hospitals.

As has been mentioned, Medicare pays for doctor and acute hospital services, but not for preventive services, mental health services, or for long-term care, neither at home nor in nursing homes or other facilities. Thus, Medicare covers most hospital expenses of the sixty-five-year-old person who suffers a heart attack or who requires bowel surgery for cancer. On the other hand, it does not cover instruction in diet and other elements of life-style that could help prevent or delay heart attacks and most other preventive measures, or custodial care at home for the victim of crippling arthritis or of Alzheimer's disease. In addition, it provides only limited coverage of nursing home care and none of drugs. For example, in 1978 the Medicare population spent $12.6 billion on nursing home care, and $3.2 billion for drugs, but Medicare paid for only 3 percent of the first and none of the second. The only way in which Medicare recipients can receive public support for such medical needs is by pauperizing themselves, thereby making themselves eligible for Medicaid. That happened to Mrs. Sophie

* Totals less than 100% result from rounding the percentages.

Booker. In the process her daughter was forced to give up most of her savings.

Mrs. Booker is a ninety-one-year-old widow with long-standing diabetes and high blood pressure. Four years ago she developed gangrene of both legs and underwent amputation of one. A few weeks later it became apparent that the other leg could not be saved, and it too was removed. In both cases the surgery was uncomplicated, her diabetes was well managed, and she rapidly recovered. Her hospital bills were covered by Medicare.

Before the operation, she lived with her only close relative, a sixty-two-year-old single daughter who worked as a secretary. Because she could not manage at home following her second operation, she was transferred from the hospital to a nursing home. Her Medicare did not provide for her care there, and as a result, she paid her bills by withdrawing $450 weekly from a savings account that she and her daughter held jointly. Her daughter was told that in their home state, Massachusetts, Mrs. Booker would be eligible for Medicaid only after her savings were less than $2,000. The $60,000 the two women had accumulated was exhausted in less than three years, and the nursing home costs are now met by Medicaid. However, the savings account that her daughter had expected to be available to supplement *her* Social Security benefits after her retirement now contains just under $2,000.

Mrs. Booker was provided ready access to some of the medical technology she needed—the surgical and medical treatment of the gangrene that was a complication of her diabetes. However, despite the fact that she was not indigent, at least at the outset, the other technology that she needed—nursing home care—was not available to her except at the price of her becoming impoverished. With tragic irony, the banking arrangement that she and her daughter had made in order to protect each other in the event of the death of one led to the impoverishment of her daughter as well.

The net cost to society of the overuse of expensive short-stay hospitals is sometimes higher than if more appropriate and often less costly facilities were used. For example, a pilot study in New York was recently reported as having shown savings of $2.5 million in hospital and nursing home expenditures following an investment of $500,000 in home care services.

Too Many Doctors

The number of doctors in practice is steadily increasing, not only in absolute terms, but relative to the population. In an effort to increase the number of primary-care doctors practicing in underserved areas, between 1965 and 1980 the federal government subsidized new medical schools and increases in the size of existing ones. As a result, the number of medical school graduates more than doubled, from about 7,500 to more than 16,000 per year. The number of physicians in practice, which was 335,000 in 1975, increased to 410,000 in 1980 and 464,000 in 1983, and is expected to reach almost 600,000 in 1990. This meant that the number of practicing doctors per 100,000 population increased from 141 in 1950 and 140 in 1960 to 174 in 1975, and 197 in 1980, and is expected to reach 240 in 1990. That ratio will be among the highest in the world. The larger number of doctors will exert pressure on costs in part because of their own earnings: In 1985 average physician net annual income, according to the American Medical Association, was over $108,000. The total accounts for just under 20 percent of the nation's health bill. But more significant will be the fact that more people will be directing expenditures in the health sector. By deciding the frequency of return visits, what tests are done, who is hospitalized and for how long, who is operated on, and what drugs are prescribed, physicians are responsible for about 80 percent of spending for personal health services.*

Too Many Tests and Treatments

The progressive increase in the cost of physician services is due not so much to a greater number of doctor visits as to a rapid increase in what is called intensity of care—that is, the number and type of services, such as electrocardiograms and endoscopic examinations and sophisticated blood tests, carried out during each visit. Often these procedures cost more than the visit itself. Over the last several years, the number of surgical cases has increased by 2.4 percent annually, and the volume of tests on patients outside the hospital by 15 percent per year. An undetermined, but likely sizable, fraction of these tests are ordered by doctors to protect against malpractice suits. (See Chapter 2.)

* A 1974 study showed that the incomes of physicians in the New England and the East South Central regions of the United States were comparable, though the average New England physician saw fewer than 60 percent as many patients as did the East South Central doctor.

Difficulties in access to medical care "save" money for the millions of Americans, almost exclusively the poor and the near-poor in our society, who fail to receive the care they need. But for millions more from all income groups who lack a primary-care doctor, difficulties in access often lead to too many medical procedures of the wrong kind. This produces waste as well as poor medical care. John Nichols (Chapter 3) was one example. Barbara Wallace is another.

Mrs. Wallace is a vigorous widow of seventy-eight, who had a series of headaches over a two-month period. Because a few years earlier she had had headaches during an episode of sinusitis and since the headaches started shortly after a severe cold, she wondered whether the sinus trouble might have recurred. She consulted the ear, nose, and throat specialist who had looked after her earlier episode of sinusitis. His examination revealed no evidence of sinusitis, but to be absolutely certain, he had sinus X rays taken. When she returned to see him a week later, he reassured her that her sinuses were not the cause of her headaches. However, in the course of their discussion he learned that she was also having mild discomfort in her neck, presumably related to long-standing arthritis in the upper part of her spine. Arthritis in that area can cause headaches, and she might want to see the neurologist who had seen her when her arthritis had flared up a year earlier and caused severe pain radiating down her arm.

After his examination, the neurologist told her that her neck was not the source of the problem. Even more important to her peace of mind, he mentioned in passing that he saw no reason to suspect a brain tumor, a possibility that had occurred to her. When she told him that the vision in her right eye was poorer than last year, he suggested she see an eye doctor; a change in her glasses might control the headaches. The ophthalmologist never got around to refracting her eyes, for he saw a suspicious area in the retina of her right eye. For several years the vision in her left eye had been markedly impaired as a result of a clot in a blood vessel in that eye. Therefore, he and she were particularly concerned to think that her good eye might be in trouble. He sent her to a retina specialist, who thought it might be a tumor and made an appointment for her to have an angiogram.

At this point a physician friend suggested she get a second opinion concerning the angiogram. He arranged for her to see another ophthalmologist, Dr. James Roberts. Dr. Roberts found a pigmented area in the retina, which he thought was probably of no clinical significance. But he said it was important to watch it to be certain. Further, he learned from her the name of the specialist she had seen twelve years earlier when she had had the blood clot in the other eye and wrote to him for a copy of his record. He also asked her to return in two weeks so he could determine whether the suspicious area in her good eye was changing.

She kept the return appointment—now about six weeks following the visit to the first eye doctor, who had told her that she might have a tumor. Dr. Roberts had not yet received the report from the doctor she had seen twelve years before, but he did reassure her again, stating that the lesion had not changed and that he was now virtually certain it had no clinical significance. His secretary called the office of the doctor she had seen years earlier and learned that the original request for information had apparently gone astray. She arranged for the immediate dispatch of the record in question. After it arrived, Dr. Roberts called her to report that the original description made clear that, whatever the nature of the pigmented area in the eye, twelve years earlier it had apparently looked exactly as it did now. Thus, it was surely no threat. Mrs. Wallace, who expressed enormous relief, said that she had been even more anxious than she had confessed. After all, at seventy-eight she was not eager to have her one good eye removed for cancer.

What about the headaches? They had disappeared some weeks earlier, shortly after her daughter had completed several weeks of radiation treatment for cancer. In retrospect, she now thinks, the headaches may have been related to her concern for her daughter's health. In any event, they were insignificant as compared to the worry she had been carrying around about the possibility of losing her good eye to cancer.

Mrs. Wallace didn't know the cost of the medical events that were part of a search for the cause of her headaches. But surely many hundred dollars is a conservative guess for doctors' fees, X rays, and laboratory tests. Her time was perhaps worth less to her than it would have been had this happened at an earlier time in her life when she was working, and her family was dependent on her not missing time on the job. As for the emotional trauma, the relief she has experienced in knowing that she does not have cancer in her eye and that there is no present threat to her vision outweighs by far, she says, the anxiety of what for most people would have been a nightmarish experience.

Mrs. Wallace's story is not unique. She found her own way into the system of medical care and was exposed to some of its technology. But it was technology she didn't need. It was costly, and her original problem disappeared before it was really addressed.

An arrangement that would provide a primary-care doctor for all citizens not only would help ensure that people get into the system properly, but also could save a good deal of the money now spent for tests and treatments that are unnecessary.

Faulty Incentives

Some incentives built into much of our health insurance give signals that distort medical practice and inflate costs. Further, some have helped create gaps in the system. For example, because there has been little financial incentive, facilities for the care of patients with chronic and terminal illnesses have not been developed in most communities to the extent that they are needed. Independent of income, many people have learned of this gap only when they fell into it. The family of Philip McCormick is an example.

Mr. McCormick was a sixty-year-old New York stockbroker who consulted his physician when his morning "cigarette cough" of many years' duration became more pronounced and continued through the day and much of the night. On occasion his sputum included some flecks of blood. He had smoked a pack a day for forty years, despite at least three serious attempts to break himself of the habit. A chest X ray confirmed his and his doctor's fear that lung cancer might be the cause. His situation, however, seemed more favorable than that of about 75 percent of the 150,000 Americans who will be found to have lung cancer this year, because extensive examinations following hospitalization showed no evidence that the cancer had extended beyond the lung. After the operation to remove the lower lobe of his right lung, the surgeon told him of his good fortune: There was no apparent spread at the time of surgery. He recovered slowly, and despite residual shortness of breath, he was able to return to work two months after his operation.

Six months later, however, he complained of severe pain in his back and weakness in his left arm and leg. He was hospitalized again, and X rays demonstrated that the cancer now involved his bones and his brain. Any spread of lung cancer to other organs means that cure is not possible. However, temporary relief of symptoms can usually be achieved, and for that purpose he was subjected to radiation treatment. The pain disappeared, and he recovered full function of his arm and leg within two weeks. A month later, however, pain recurred in his limbs, his chest, and his neck. Dizzy spells and headaches added to his discomfort, and he returned to the hospital for precise localization of the cancer and for further radiation. In addition, he was begun on the first of what proved to be a series of drugs to control his pain.

When discharge from the hospital was discussed with him and his wife, they sought a nursing home where he could be kept comfortable. None of the facilities then available appealed to either of them, and they decided that he would return home and be transported by ambulance to the hospital for radiation each day. He again experienced pain relief from the radiation, but within three weeks pains in new areas of his body were occurring almost daily. In addition, the spread of cancer within his brain caused increasingly severe headaches and weakness of his left arm and leg. His appetite, which had been waning, now disappeared, and nausea and vomiting added to his misery. His wife had great difficulty in finding attendants who had the compassion and the skills that she insisted on and who were willing to come to their home. On one additional occasion his physician in desperation did have him readmitted to the hospital for supportive treatment, but this was carried out against considerable resistance of the hospital admitting office, which stressed that its beds had to be kept for situations for which the hospital's technology was required. The patient and his wife understood this need, but were unsuccessful in finding a place in their community where *their* needs could be met. Mr. McCormick was finally admitted to a nursing home, where he was kept relatively comfortable with heavy doses of morphine administered by needle every four hours. There, eight months after his operation, he died.

Some months later, Mrs. McCormick reflected about the problems in finding satisfactory care that confronted her husband and herself—people for whom expense was not an issue—and wondered what happens to the poor faced with similar needs. It was, of course, a rhetorical question.

Efforts at Cost Containment

In certain important areas, measures that contain costs can make for more efficient and effective health care. Prevention (see Chapter 9) is always better than cure and sometimes cheaper. By evaluating medical practices of all kinds (Chapter 11), much expense and waste (and bad medical practice) can be eliminated. By eliminating duplication of facilities and generally establishing more rational systems for paying for and delivering medical services (Chapter 12), we can provide better access to care at less expense.

From the beginning, Medicare provided for home care, but only the skilled kind. In 1980 and 1981, this was slightly modified, to encourage more people to use this cheaper form of care. In 1982, coverage of (also cheaper) hospice care was begun.

In the Social Security amendments of 1983, the Congress changed cost-based reimbursement to payment of a predetermined amount by enacting a prospective payment system for certain acute care hospitals treating Medicare beneficiaries. Patients are classified into categories determined by their diagnoses (diagnosis-related groups, or DRGs) and a set amount is given for each DRG. For example, a hospital receives a fixed sum for every patient hospitalized for an uncomplicated heart attack, and another for each patient hospitalized for an appendectomy. Hospitals whose average costs are lower than the prospective rates are permitted to keep all of the difference, while hospitals whose costs are above the DRG rates must absorb the loss. Thus, the system encourages hospitals to watch expenditures carefully, and early evidence suggests that it is helping reduce hospital stays that were previously often too long.

But it is too soon to be certain that its overall effects will be to save money. For example, it has swollen the bureaucracy. Its costs have included the hiring of 6,000 new fiscal personnel and the purchase of hundreds of millions of dollars of computers and other equipment. Further, its across-the-board regulations are leading to the premature discharge of many seriously ill people, particularly the elderly. In some places this has led to readmission to hospitals of such patients, thereby creating unanticipated increases in *total* hospitalization. (The new system has no incentive to limit the *number* of admissions.)

Thus, it is not too early to say that the DRG system is having some adverse effects on the quality of patient care. Patients have a legal right to request a written note of discharge, which they may then appeal. But few patients know that or do that. Hospitals may not discharge patients on the explicit grounds that their DRG time is up, since DRGs technically set limits on amount of payment, not length of stay. But hospitals naturally reckon their charges by combining costs per day with the number of days.

Here, as in many experiments in health services—since the DRG program must still be regarded as unproved, and therefore experimental—it would have been better to have tried the program in a few places to see how it worked before applying it throughout the country. (The tryouts that did take place involved programs that differed greatly from what has been instituted nationally and in haste, as a result of a bill signed by President Reagan only four months after its first presentation to the Congress.)

Starting in 1983, Medicare has required that beneficiaries pay a deductible for inpatient hospital care with a copayment for lengthy stays. In 1987 the deductible was raised to $524, and the copayment to $130. This has accelerated the impoverishment of many elderly, who cannot qualify for Medicaid until their funds are extremely low. It also provides some insight into the fact that almost 40 percent of Medicaid funds are used for the care of the elderly.

Other Government Programs

Besides Medicare and Medicaid, health expenditures from the federal government included $7 billion for veterans' medical needs in 1982. Of that amount 82 percent was spent for care in veterans' medical centers and other hospitals around the country. This money covered 24.5 million days of hospital and almost 9 million days of nursing home care. Another $5.5 billion was used for health care of Department of Defense personnel and their dependents. Federal funds are also used to provide personal health care through the Indian Health Service; in 1982 this activity consumed just under $500 million. Public health programs, primarily those at the Centers for Disease Control and the Food and Drug Administration, received $1.3 billion. The federal government has traditionally provided funding for the health needs of poor mothers and children through what are called maternal and child health programs.* This activity received $896 million of federal funds in 1982. Federal support of just under $700 million was used for programs concerned with problems of alcohol, drug abuse, and mental health. Support for these activities has been shared by federal and state government. In 1982 overall federal contributions for them were reduced by 18 percent from the level of spending in 1981.

Of the total of $5.9 billion spent in 1982 for medical research, $5 billion came from the federal government, mainly via the National Institutes of Health (NIH). The NIH is placed administratively in the Department of Health and Human Services. Much of the department's budget is in entitlement programs, which are relatively protected. Therefore, reductions in the budget of the department can fall disproportionately on research. The dangers of cuts in research support to the nation's health and perhaps to our economic well-being are discussed in Chapter 10.

State and local governments operate 1,750 community hospitals that provide general medical care and more than 200 hospitals for patients with

---

* Cutbacks in maternal and child health funds in the 1980s were intended to save money. They have deprived expectant mothers of necessary prenatal care, however, and in many places where that has occurred, infant mortality rates have risen. This is partly the result of an increase in low-birth-weight babies. The care of such babies has meant greater demands on expensive neonatal intensive care units. Some of the survivors will need costly special education and other programs in later life, thereby diminishing further the "savings" achieved.

mental illness. The total cost of these facilities, not offset by Medicare or Medicaid funds and therefore borne by state and local government, exceeded $5 billion in 1982. State spending for health care for the poor who were not covered by Medicaid was just over $2 billion. State and local government provided more than $7 billion for public health activities, $500 million for maternal and child health programs, and $500 million for biomedical research.

An area of neglect in health services today that perhaps dwarfs all others is the care of patients with mental illness. The present situation can be traced in part to a well-intentioned program that began in the early 1960s. The development a few years earlier of drugs to treat mental diseases and the deplorable state of most hospitals for mental illness prompted authorities to begin to discharge patients to the community—the so-called deinstitutionalization movement. The plan was to build community mental health centers, where patients could be looked after outside hospitals. More than three quarters of almost 600,000 hospitalized patients were discharged, but fewer than half the needed centers were built. As a result, large numbers of people in desperate need of attention have been neglected. Hundreds of thousands live alone in rooming houses or in dingy hotels and have little or no medical supervision. Much worse, similar numbers are homeless. One expert estimated that more than half of a vagrant population of 2.5 million in the winter of 1983 suffered from mental illness.

The neglect is not limited to the mentally ill who are homeless. As many as twenty percent of Americans, according to some estimates, at some time in their lives are moderately to severely impaired in mental (and often, as a result, in educational, social, and job-related) functioning. Their difficulties, in turn, place great burdens on families and caretakers as well as on clergy, law-enforcement agencies, teachers, and others. The debilitating effects on individuals and society of such illness are the more tragic as more effective preventive and therapeutic measures come to be recognized. Social measures could likely prevent some of this illness. Psychotropic drugs could effectively alleviate more. A blanket system of primary care linked to social services would help identify some potential problems early and treat existing problems before too much damage was done. This could reduce the suffering of large numbers of Americans and buffer their impact on our society.

Many states, pinched by federal cutbacks and rising costs, have also been reducing expenditures. They can lower appropriations across the board, like California under Proposition 13 or Massachusetts under Proposition 2½, or alter eligibility requirements. In 1982 California eliminated its Medicaid program for indigent adults under sixty-five. A disruption in care followed and then a worsening of health status of, for example, people with high blood pressure. The victims include even people in need of emergency, life-saving care. The fate of two such people was described recently in a medical journal.

One patient, a thirty-six-year-old uninsured man, was taken to a private hospital emergency room in California after being beaten. After two neurosurgeons refused to respond to the emergency physician's calls for assistance, the patient was transferred to a public hospital. There he was found to have a skull fracture and bleeding into the brain, and he never regained consciousness.

The other, a twenty-one-year-old woman, was hit by a truck and taken to the nearest emergency facility, which was a private institution. Since she was uninsured, she was transferred to a municipal hospital thirty miles away, despite the fact that she had multiple fractures of her ribs, pelvis, leg, and ankle, and severe internal bleeding. At the municipal hospital the bleeding was found to be coming from a tear in her aorta, the main artery that carries blood from the heart. Because the public hospital lacked facilities for chest surgery, she then had to be transferred to yet another hospital for repair of the artery.

Both patients were in a group of 458 individuals who were transferred from private hospitals to a municipal hospital in Oakland, California, in the first six months of 1981. More than half of the patients were without health insurance. Only one of the 103 patients whose records were reviewed in detail was transferred because the private hospital lacked appropriate facilities necessary for care. In the rest it was for economic reasons. In thirty-three instances the transfers were judged by the doctors who studied the records to have placed the patients in jeopardy.

Privatization

For-profit hospitals have grown rapidly in the 1970s and 1980s. Whereas early in the century, proprietary hospitals were very common (in 1928 there were more than 2,400), by 1968 the number had fallen to 769. As of 1984, there were more than 1,000, or 15 percent of the acute care hospitals in the nation. About half belonged to large corporations specializing in medical care. Simultaneously, the for-profit sector is also delivering a growing share of the nation's services in nursing homes, home care programs, and diagnostic laboratories.

The growth of the for-profit sector in health care has been ascribed by some to the need in the health area for the more efficient management practices and the competitive spirit of American industry. Inefficiencies surely exist in health institutions, and the absence of competition has likely had adverse effects in some areas. It remains to be seen, however, whether the for-profit hospitals will prove more economical. Some reports in medical journals indicate that their charges are similar to those of nonprofits. Indeed, one component of their "efficiency" is a form of economic triage: They often exclude indigent patients and any insured patients whose treatment would cost more than they would be reimbursed by insurance carriers—people with severe burns, for instance, and elderly patients with complicated and prolonged illnesses. Such policies contribute to a practice that is more and more frequent and that involves many nonprofit hospitals as well. This practice is rather inelegantly called dumping. Patients who are regarded as economic risks are refused admission and sent instead to public and some nonprofit teaching and nonteaching hospitals. The 458 patients who were transferred to the public hospital in Oakland were victims of this practice. So were most of the 467 patients moved to Chicago's public Cook County Hospital from other area hospitals in the last six weeks of 1983 and described in the *New England Journal of Medicine* in 1986. The Cook County Hospital doctors who wrote the article reported that many of the patients were in no condition to be moved because of bleeding, serious infections, very high blood pressure, or other grave medical problems. As one might have predicted, the death rate among this group of patients was much higher than among patients with comparable medical problems who had not been transferred. Thus, dumping can mean inexcusable threats to life and health of uninsured Americans. The burden on the resources of the receiving institutions can readily be pictured.

Not surprisingly, the issue of responsibility for injuries to patients who are refused essential care has been placed before the courts. For example, the Arizona Supreme Court recently considered the case of a young boy who was brought to the emergency room of a private hospital after he was seriously injured in an accident. Because he was from an uninsured family, he was transferred out of the private hospital at a time when his condition was critical. At the receiving hospital he underwent emergency surgery. However, he was left with a permanent injury to his leg that might not have occurred had he been promptly treated at the private hospital. The court found the private hospital liable for refusing emergency care. It found that the physicians at that hospital had wanted to keep the patient there and were therefore not liable.

Arnold Relman, the editor of the *New England Journal of Medicine,* predicts that as economic pressures on hospitals grow, more and more patients will be refused necessary care for financial reasons. The transfer of more hospitals from the nonprofit, and even the public, sector to the private will make the problem worse. Long before the Medicare-Medicaid legislation, most large communities had a public hospital where poor people could go for emergency and often nonemergency care. The nonprofit hospitals had facilities, usually called wards, for the care of patients who, like Nicholas Williams, the young man who was hospitalized for leukemia, could pay little or nothing. In many institutions the quality of ward care was high, but even there, a sense of two classes of medical care existed. Memorial Hospital, the institution often mentioned in Chapter 2, was such an institution. But many of its staff, including Daniel Beck, took pride in the fact that the Medicare and Medicaid legislation was followed by the closing of the wards and the conversion of the entire hospital to a single class of medical care, in appearance as well as operationally. In some hospitals, however, "ward" medicine in pre-Medicare and Medicaid days was inferior to "private" medicine. The legislation did go a long way toward eliminating two standards of medical care—one for the poor and one for the nonpoor. Some communities closed public hospitals and arranged for the nonprofits to look after patients whose health insurance was covered by government and those who were not covered by insurance.

The recent sharp reductions in government support have led to a return to two classes of medical care, particularly in communities where public hospitals have been taken over by private investors. In some such places, understandings have been reached by them with public officials guaranteeing emergency (and sometimes more) care for the poor.*

But in others, a single standard of care has been achieved, although not in the way that the architects of Medicaid had in mind. In some of those communities *no* care, not even for emergency purposes, is available to poor Americans. Janice Brown and her husband can attest to that.

Ms. Brown is a twenty-three-year-old married woman who in 1981 lost

---

* In early 1986, the Texas Board of Health ruled that hospitals must treat all emergency cases, may transfer patients only for medical reasons, and must forward complete medical records with transferred patients. National legislation on this issue was passed in March 1986, but its provisions are much less rigorous.

her job as a retail store clerk in a small city in the southeastern United States. One year later, she awoke one night with severe abdominal pain, nausea, and vomiting. The pain worsened over the next hour, and she found that her temperature was slightly elevated. Her husband, who had lost his job as a laborer shortly after she lost hers, took her to the emergency room of a hospital within a mile of their apartment. Before they could even describe fully her excruciating pain, they were asked for evidence of medical insurance or a cash deposit for the services she might need. They had neither, and she was refused care. Her husband took her to another hospital, six miles distant, where they were also turned away. They were told, however, that she could be treated in the municipal hospital of a city twenty miles farther on. There she was admitted and diagnosed as having an ectopic pregnancy—that is, a pregnancy abnormally implanted in one of her tubes. If not promptly corrected surgically, this condition can lead to death from hemorrhage or infection. She was operated on, and she recovered uneventfully. She and her husband have a bill of $2,800, which they understand must be paid sometime in the future.

In 1983 the President's Commission for the Study of Ethical Problems in Medicine and Biomedical and Behavioral Research said that in our nation, "Society has an ethical obligation to ensure equitable access to health care for all." But the commission found that in the late 1970s as many as 25 million Americans were without health insurance and 27 percent of the poor were uninsured. The uninsured are now believed to exceed 37 million. A recent study indicated that 28 million Americans, including 7 million children, have difficulty in obtaining care.

Among the least fortunate and least visible Americans are the families bereaved by the major cutbacks in federal support programs of the 1980s. While it is too early to assess fully the results, early data show increased infant mortality rates in Boston, Detroit, North Carolina, Alabama, and other cities and states throughout the nation.

I do not suggest that the private or the nonprofit hospitals should be asked to assume financial responsibility for the care of uninsured Americans. That responsibility belongs to society. But for the privilege of serving a community, every hospital, whatever its financing arrangements, may be expected to accept every patient for whom transfer would be a risk, and every patient with a medical problem requiring hospitalization for which the community has agreed to pay.

If Americans seriously faced the fact that our jumbled policies and blinkered initiatives are literally killing many of us and damaging many more, they might well act in concert to mend the situation. If they faced the certainty that the burden is growing, they might do so very rapidly. And if they could be persuaded that this human damage could be avoided by spending *today's* health budget more wisely, then surely they would demand immediate action.

Upward Pressures in the Future

Discussions concerning the upward surge of medical costs in the future relate not to whether they will continue, but rather in what categories and how great the increases will be. This is because of the growth and aging of the population, the continued development of medical technology, and the increasing number of physicians, dentists, and other health professionals directing the use of the technology. With a conservative estimate of an increase of 1.8 percent per year in health care spending, rather than the 3.3 percent of the previous fifteen years, government analysts project that expenditures for health care in 1990 will be $755 billion, which will be about $3,000 per person, or 12 percent of the gross national product.

In the year 1990, assuming that the system doesn't change, $684 billion will be spent for personal health care (as compared to the 1984 figure of $387 billion and $10.9 billion in 1950). Hospital care will claim $340 billion, physicians' services $142 billion, and nursing home care $67 billion. These expenses are particularly influenced by an aging population, since people over sixty-five years of age require, on average, three and one-half times as much care as those under sixty-five. In 1980 the almost 11 percent of the population over sixty-five used 29 percent of health dollars. If the relative spending of this group continues, the 14 percent in this category in the year 2000 will consume 33 percent of health money.

It is estimated that in the absence of major change, in 1990 31 percent of all health care bills will be paid out of pocket, 26 percent from private insurance, and just under 42 percent by government. The federal share is projected to increase to 31.5 percent from its present level of just over 29 percent in part because of aging of the population. The projections assume no major new government programs. However, given the increase in costs and the consequent progressive increase in risks to the uninsured or partly insured members of society, the demand for new programs will likely rise.

The future health needs of our larger and older population are, of course, conjectural. Some experts like James Fries of Stanford University suggest that the elderly will be healthier. They do not, of course, visualize a pop-

Table 2: The Absolute and Relative Size of Various Population Groups, 1945–2050

	Under 20	Population (millions) 20–64	65+*	Working age as a percentage of total population†	Aged as a percentage of total population	Aged as a percentage of working-age population‡	Aged 80+ as a percentage of total aged
1945	46.2	83.2	10.5	59.5	7.5	12.6	13.3
1950	51.6	87.9	12.4	57.9	8.2	14.1	13.7
1955	59.8	90.8	14.5	55.0	8.8	16.0	14.5
1960	73.1	98.7	17.1	55.2	9.1	17.4	14.3
1965	80.0	104.1	19.0	51.3	9.3	18.2	16.5
1970	80.7	112.6	20.7	52.6	9.7	18.4	18.9
1975	78.9	122.6	23.3	54.5	10.4	19.0	20.0
1980	75.4	134.6	26.4	56.9	11.2	19.6	20.1
1985	73.5	144.8	29.3	58.4	11.8	20.2	21.7
1990	74.7	151.5	32.6	58.5	12.6	21.5	23.4
1995	76.4	157.4	35.0	58.6	13.0	22.2	25.8
2000	77.2	164.1	36.2	59.1	13.0	22.1	28.5
2005	76.4	171.7	37.5	60.1	13.1	21.9	31.2
2010	76.2	177.1	40.6	60.3	13.8	22.9	30.9
2015	77.1	178.2	46.4	59.1	15.4	26.1	27.4
2020	78.4	176.8	53.3	57.3	17.3	30.1	24.8
2025	79.2	174.2	60.8	55.4	19.4	34.9	24.4
2030	79.4	173.1	66.3	54.3	20.8	38.3	27.0
2035	79.5	174.4	68.6	54.1	21.3	39.4	30.9
2040	80.1	176.7	68.8	54.3	21.1	39.0	35.6
2045	80.9	178.6	68.6	54.4	20.9	38.4	38.8
2050	81.6	178.9	69.7	54.2	21.1	38.9	38.3

Source: The 1984 Annual Report of the Board of Trustees of the Federal Old-Age and Survivors Insurance and Disability Insurance Trust Funds; U.S. Bureau of the Census, Current Population Report, Series P-25, nos. 98, 310, and 952. Data for 1945–1980 are actuals; for 1985–2050 they are projections based on the mid-range series of Census and the Social Security actuaries. From ''The Economic Consequences of an Agrarian Society,'' by John L. Palmer and Stephanie G. Gould. *Daedalus,* vol. 115, no. 1, 1986. Reprinted by permission of *Daedalus,* Journal of the American Academy of Arts & Sciences, Cambridge, Mass.

* The aged counts for years 1945, 1950, and 1955 are from Census data, whereas all subsequent years are from the Social Security actuaries. These latter include the total population eligible for Social Security and Medicare benefits who are 65 years or older. Historically this number has been several hundred thousand higher than the Census count of the United States aged population (65 and over) because it includes people who live overseas.

† Population 20–64 as a percentage of total population.

‡ Population aged 65 and over as a percentage of population 20–64.

ulation living indefinitely. Rather, they see a society in which most people survive in good health into their eighties and then quietly and relatively painlessly die. The analogy has been drawn to Oliver Wendell Holmes's "one-hoss shay," which runs well for many years until the day on which it collapses because all parts crumble together. Indeed, the ideal goal of medicine has been described as keeping people well until they die. When that day arrives for our society, all projections will, of course, have to be changed radically.

But most health experts foresee a great increase in the incidence of chronic diseases and senility and a corresponding increase in demand for facilities and personnel appropriate to the needs of a society with such problems. In fact, the marked reduction in death rates of recent decades and the consequent increase, both relative and absolute, in the numbers of older citizens has not been accompanied by much change in the health needs of the elderly. Thus, it seems prudent to assume that their future health needs will reflect their current patterns of utilization of health resources and their projected numbers.

As part of the process of making the *Queen Elizabeth II* conform with government regulations, the Cunard Line has to insure that lifeboat space is provided for more than the total number of passengers and crew. Thus, for a recent world cruise with a crew of 911 and 1,300 passengers, the *QE 2* carried twenty lifeboats with a total capacity of 2,326 places. Compare our medical resources with a lifeboat; with the productive age group dwindling, in the future we won't have so many to pull the oars (see Table 2).

By 2020 we will have to enlarge the lifeboat's capacity by 40 percent. It will have to be differently equipped as well. The nation will need not only more, but also different kinds of help from the health professions. This applies to research and teaching, as well as to service. For example, more research is required into such problems as senility and incontinence, and for better ways to deal with impairments in hearing, vision, and mobility. Social scientists can contribute much to efforts to improve methods of providing good and compassionate care alternative to institutionalization—foster care homes, retirement communities, home care, homemaker services, and adult day care centers. Changes are required in health insurance programs, which up to now have encouraged the use of acute care hospitals. They are not only expensive, but often inappropriate to the needs of the elderly. Education programs for doctors, nurses, and other health professionals must put greater emphasis on training in skills that address the needs of the elderly.

It can be done. We are beginning to do so. Great Britain has a figurative, as well as a literal, *QE 2*. The proportion of elderly people there is higher than here, the standard of medical technology is as high as ours, and resources are far more constrained. Yet basic health care is guaranteed—and delivered—to every citizen. And the cost to the nation is less than one third per person of what we spend. There are gaps—long waiting lists for important procedures like hip replacements and cataract removal. Some life-saving measures, like kidney dialysis, are withheld from older people. It's far from ideal, it's true. But there are no Sophie Bookers, for whom and for whose families chronic illness is catastrophic in economic as well as in medical terms. And no Janice Browns, who are refused emergency measures at times when refusal can be a death sentence.

II

LESSONS

FROM ABROAD

6   Lessons from Britain

In Britain, in August 1984 *The Guardian* ran an editorial entitled "Hollie: the Heroic and the Humdrum," about the unsuccessful struggle for life of an infant who had undergone a heart transplant. It concerned even more a subsequent event—the appeal for supplemental government funds by the London hospital where the surgery had been carried out. The hospital's heart transplant team had exhausted a whole year's budget in four months. Unless it received additional funds from the Department of Health and Social Security, the hospital warned, twenty patients who might otherwise have been saved would die during the remainder of the year. The editoral sympathized with the dilemma that the hospital had placed before the government, but suggested that giving the hospital more money could make the problem worse.

The editorial quoted Sir George Godber, who was for many years chief medical officer of the Department of Health and Social Security and believed by many informed people to have been key to the early development and success of the National Health Service (NHS). Two years earlier Sir George had stated that no nation can afford to provide open-ended health care to all. Rather, he urged a policy of providing "the most for the most, and not everything for a few."

The newspaper pointed out that "surgical success does not lessen medical demand but increases it. When the National Health Service was set up, it was assumed that better medical care would improve the nation's health and so eventually diminish the demand for treatment. But the unforeseen developments in medical technology meant that a bottomless pit of demand was opened up." It continued, "Since more people can benefit from less . . . sensational procedures, and since more still can avoid much disease in the first place if money is spent on disease prevention programmes, the ethical case for spending more on such measures and less on transplants is very strong. . . . Transplants do not cheat death, but postpone it, possibly, for a few. But everyone, surely, should be given most opportunity to make the most of the lives they have."

Because the NHS has a record of making medical care available to all residents of Great Britain and Northern Ireland (and to visitors from many other countries who get sick in the United Kingdom) with little or no financial charge at the time and at less than one third the per capita cost of medical services in the United States, it is important to understand how it works.

Centralized Funding, Regional Budgeting

About 95 percent of health expenditures in Britain are from the government, and these funds are principally derived from general taxes. Most of the remaining 5 percent comes from private health insurance. Eighty percent of the health budget is spent for hospital and community services, which comprehend all hospital inpatient and outpatient treatment for acute and chronic illnesses, including mental disease and mental handicap, community nursing, and preventive services. All specialist consultations and care come under this heading. The remaining 20 percent of the health budget covers general medical and dental practitioner care, drugs, and eyeglasses and other medical appliances.

The budget for hospital and community services is administered on a regional basis. The country is divided into regions of 2 to 5 million people, each large enough to have the most specialized health services that a population requires, such as heart surgery or high voltage radiation treatment for cancer. The health budget is allocated to each region by the Department of Health and Social Security and is administered by a Regional Health Authority appointed by the minister. The authority, in turn, assigns its resources in part to highly specialized regional programs for such procedures as heart surgery and radiation treatment, but primarily to its constituent districts, each with an average population of 250,000 people. (There are about 200 districts in the country.) The governing board for each district, which is appointed by the regional authority, decides how to divide its budget among its facilities. District facilities include at least one hospital that cares for patients with the most common and relatively less complicated problems, such as most heart attacks, appendectomies, and the pneumonias that require hospitalization. They also include community hospitals, which are primarily for the care of the elderly, home nursing, and facilities for the care of the mentally ill and the mentally handicapped. Because Britain is densely populated, few patients live as much as twenty-five miles from a general hospital. The administrative arrangement permits overall budgetary control at a national level and a great deal of local flexibility with respect to the way in which the budget is used.

Universal Primary Care

More than 97 percent of the population is registered with, or "on the list" of, a general practitioner, their gatekeeper, who is responsible for the overall care of the people on his or her list. People can choose their GP from those in their general area. GPs, in turn, can decide for how many and which patients they will accept responsibility, within a maximum of 3,500 that the government now permits each GP to have. About 80 percent of GPs work in groups of three or more (but seldom more than six). They see their patients in their offices (called the surgery) or in health centers. If the patient's condition dictates, GPs often make house calls, especially on older people. Because their patients are generally from circumscribed areas near their offices, GPs' home visits can be made without extensive travel time. For example, on a visit to London, I made three house calls in a three-block area in a period of about one hour with a GP I know. We then proceeded to the GP's health center in five minutes by car from the last patient's home.

A special strength of British medicine is the close link between general practice and social services within the community. That link permits the GP to arrange for domestic help for the sick or handicapped as well as for sophisticated professional skills in the home.*

Specialists, who are called consultants and who mostly have their offices in hospitals, normally see patients only on the recommendation of their

---

* Dr. DeWitt Stetten, Jr., a distinguished physician-scientist who was for many years deputy director of the U.S. National Institutes of Health, would have appreciated such a link, had he found it in the United States. In an article published in the *New England Journal of Medicine,* he described his difficulty in finding the kind of technology he needed during the years when he was losing his sight. He reported that during that period he consulted several leading American specialists, all of whom gave him the same technical information. They agreed on the diagnosis. They also agreed that the condition was incurable. Dr. Stetten accepted all of this. What he found unacceptable, however, and the reason he wrote his article, was that not one of the specialists offered suggestions concerning how he might adjust to his handicap. He subsequently found major resources that instruct blind people how to get around, how to find books, magazines, and newspapers, how to meet each other—in short, how to begin to re-create meaningful lives for themselves. But for all of this he had to provide his own access. In a touching and effective way, he alerted his medical colleagues to their responsibility to link their (expert) medical care to the social services that are essential to improving the quality of their patients' lives.

GP. The specialist, often after consulting the GP, decides whether hospitalization is necessary. In this way, one doctor—the patient's GP—is in a position to keep a comprehensive record of each patient's medical problems. Further, the doctor and the patient, rather than the patient alone, makes the judgment as to which kind of, or whether, a specialist is needed.

Consultants in hospitals receive an annual salary that is independent of the number of patients they see and the number of procedures they do. Most consultants are on full-time or nearly full-time contracts; full-time doctors are required to attend to their medical responsibilities ten half-days ("sessions") each week and for any emergency needs of their patients. They may see private patients at other times and thereby supplement their income. However, at least until recently, relatively few (mainly surgeons) have done so to any substantial extent, and many do no private practice.

GPs are also paid an annual income, which is determined in part by the number of people on their list, rather than on the number of times they see their patients. The average list size is about 2,100. The present goal is to have lists no larger than 2,200 patients per GP. Except for a few procedures carried out by GPs, such as immunizations, contraceptive advice, and cervical smear tests for cancer, a fee-for-service arrangement is unusual in the NHS.

Doctors' salaries are set by an independent pay review body set up by the government, which considers evidence from the medical profession and other sources. Their incomes are, on average, considerably less than half those of doctors in the United States, but they compare favorably with those of British business executives and lawyers. The GPs are paid nearly as well as hospital doctors, and among the latter, discrepancies in salaries are not nearly so wide as they are among American specialists. For example, most British pediatricians, internal medicine specialists, heart surgeons, and GPs all have about the same incomes. In contrast, the incomes of some American specialists like heart and orthopedic surgeons may be five times or more larger than those of pediatricians or family doctors. A merit award system permits about 4 percent of British specialists who are judged A$^+$ to receive as much as twice the salary of less eminent colleagues and GPs and another 30 percent to have one of three intermediate level awards. More than half of new medical graduates now opt to go into general practice. This is, many believe, at least in part the result of a deliberate policy of recent years that has led to an equalization of income among doctors.

Doctors: Number, Distribution, and Specialization

Government policy ensures geographical distribution of doctors and does not permit oversupply. Consultant positions are determined by the needs of the districts and are filled by selection after advertisement. GPs too can practice only in areas where numbers are not already sufficient. The GPs' list sizes are monitored by an oversight committee, which can offer incentives to GPs to locate in areas where lists are large and restrict their entry into places where lists are small. (With rare exceptions, the amount of private practice available does not permit doctors without an NHS post to earn a livelihood.) This means that no more general practitioners, pediatricians, or heart surgeons are able to practice in, say, London or Bristol than the number considered appropriate by the expert committees that advise the government on such matters.

This policy offers interesting contrasts with the situation that prevails in the United States. For example, the United States has ten times as many neurologists on a per capita basis as Britain. Indeed, only 159 neurologist positions exist in all of the United Kingdom, whereas each year more than 350 *new* neurologists graduate from training programs and seek clinical positions in the United States. One result, according to Dr. T. J. Murray, a prominent Canadian neurologist who has studied training programs in each country, is that English neurologists may see such important but relatively infrequent problems in their field as myasthenia gravis or Guillain-Barré syndrome three or four times a year, while many of their American colleagues confront them once in three or four years. As a result, the Canadian specialist says, most British neurologists are better able to keep their neurological skills sharpened than most of their American counterparts.

Many observers also ascribe the control of costs of British medicine in part to the policy of restricting the number of doctors. The large number of American specialists often means that they see more patients who don't really require their services. This may also explain the fact that the British do half as much of some forms of surgery, such as gallbladder operations, as their American and Canadian counterparts.

How Good Is the British System?

What do the British get in return for an investment in health that is much smaller than that of the United States and most western European countries? It is difficult to answer that question because the yardsticks to measure health are so imprecise, a problem that has been mentioned frequently in this book (and wherever one attempts comparisons in the health field). They do, of course, have comprehensive personal medical care for the whole population. British life expectancy is slightly longer and their infant mortality lower than ours, although neither compares favorably with those of most other western European nations. Surveys over the years show a continuing high level of satisfaction with the National Health Service on the part of the British public, and this attitude appears to be independent of political party.

But the NHS is not without important problems. Although the health of the poor has improved considerably since the NHS came into existence, major differences in death and sickness rates continue. A government committee of experts appointed to examine this problem a few years ago confirmed and documented the differences with extensive figures. Although they were unable to pinpoint precise causes, they reached two major conclusions. First, they agreed that social change would be required to make major impact on the overall problem. Second, recognizing that resource limitations made it impossible to do all that needed doing at once, they proposed that the major focus of early action should be the health and welfare of children.

Against this background, they made several recommendations. In the realm of child welfare, these included better access to prenatal and child health clinics, better day care facilities, free milk, adequate school meals, and measures to reduce accidents to children in the home and outside. The steps proposed for the population independent of age included greater emphasis on, and additional resources for, health education, preventive measures, and care of the disabled. Other recommendations included a range of social measures, such as better housing, larger allowances for the disabled, and improved conditions in the workplace. Recognizing Britain's severe financial straits, the committee proposed that some of its recommendations be financed by redistribution of resources.

Their view was that no additional vaccines, medical screening programs, or prophylactic medication could have as profound health benefits as such social measures as improving housing, reducing unemployment, and providing financial help to the unemployed, particularly those who have responsibility for children, to those who are pregnant, and to the elderly. Such prescriptions are now also in urgent need of filling in the United States.

One criticism frequently leveled against the NHS is that there now are long waiting lists for important procedures, such as hip replacement. This operation is now universally agreed to be extremely important in terms of its capacity to improve the quality of life, often dramatically. And yet the waiting list for the operation is over a year in many regions of the country. (These waits apply only to what are called elective operations; emergency or urgent procedures for the patient who has fractured a hip, for example, are done at once.) The increasing delay for the elective operation is ascribed in part to the competition for the same orthopedic services for emergency problems such as those resulting from highway accidents. People also blame shrinking hospital budgets in some parts of the country, particularly London. But waiting lists exist as well for many other important procedures, such as cataract removal, hernia repair, and gynecologic surgery.

The delays in medical care have led many in and out of government to suggest that more reliance on private insurance, private hospitals, and fee-for-service arrangements, or what is often called privatization, will help solve British health problems. In fact, 25 percent of elective hip replacements are now done in the private sector. Some kidney dialysis is also done by teams working outside the NHS. These teams, however, work under contract with the NHS, treat patients referred by the NHS, and are paid by the NHS and not by the individual. In contrast, those people who have hip operations and most other procedures privately pay from their private insurance or from their own pockets. These private arrangements permit people to avoid the delays of the NHS, a practice called queue-hopping. It is a source of great concern to many Britons, for by making important medical procedures available on the basis of ability to pay, it violates the equity principle on which the NHS was founded.

The NHS has also been criticized, particularly by American observers, for its failure to treat with dialysis or transplants all people with kidney failure. The British have about as much kidney disease as the United States and other European countries. Yet, on a per capita basis, about three times as many Americans and twice as many French as British are treated with dialysis. These differences are very much age-related; that is, dialysis is begun on about as many British under the age of fifty as in any other country. But many fewer Britons with kidney failure between fifty and sixty-five years of age, and almost none over that age, are begun on dialysis. A leading British kidney expert estimates that if an additional £50 million annually were committed to the kidney program, 2,000 lives could be prolonged. Almost no chronic dialysis is performed independent of the NHS because of its expense.

Much high technology medicine—for example, radiation therapy for cancer, treatment of hemophilia with blood products, and bone marrow transplantation—is practiced as frequently in Britain as in the United States.

Other high technology measures—including cancer chemotherapy, intensive care, CT scanning, coronary bypass surgery, as well as kidney dialysis—are used less often. Some critics consider the differences to reflect the rationing that inadequate resources force on the British system; others have, without much evidence, blamed the system itself. Most British experts acknowledge that their system could effectively use more money, and some say that new technology does not reach the public as rapidly in Britain as in the United States. They argue, however, that many differences in the use of high technology medicine reflect American overuse rather than British underuse. The available evidence suggests that the truth lies somewhat between: Survival and quality of life are not always benefited by the much higher levels of technology used for many medical problems in the United States; on the other hand, more resources in the health system, for treatment of kidney failure and to reduce the long delays for hip replacement, for example, would surely save some lives and more rapidly improve the quality of many others in Britain.

Administrative arrangements in the United Kingdom permit the government to shift resources geographically and from one program to another, in response to what it perceives are relative needs. For example, in the mid-1970s, a government-appointed group of experts concluded, after comparing death rates and the structure of the population in the several regions of the country, that more health money should be put into areas other than the southeast, that is, away from the Greater London region. Further, the government proposed that services be increased for the elderly, for the mentally ill, and for the mentally handicapped. This proposal was linked to widely supported efforts to shift care into the community, even if it meant taking resources from large institutions. In general, the goal was to put more emphasis on the relief of pain and suffering and the maintenance of independence, rather than on high technology within acute care hospitals. The decision to take these steps was made in part to address the health needs of groups that have traditionally been neglected in British society (and most other societies). In addition, as is the case in the United States, demographic factors suggested such priorities; for example, the over-seventy-five age group, which in Britain requires more than seven times as much health spending as younger adults, increased by 500,000 from 1976 to 1982. Also as in the United States, the over-eighty-fives, whose health needs are even greater, are rapidly increasing in relative and absolute numbers. The over-sixty-fives are now more than 15 percent of the British population, as compared with 11 percent in the United States.

Since the proposed increases in spending for the geographic and programmatic areas of special need were to take place with very little increase in the overall health budget, health funds would have to be diverted from elsewhere, in this instance, primarily from the London regions and from high technology institutions. Such shifts could not, of course, be made without major disruption. As a result, a long-term plan to effect just such shifts was developed and discussed and for the past five years has been gradually implemented.

The results thus far do not support those who predicted that the public would not stand for cuts in some budgets to support others. For example, from 1976 to 1982, overall increases of 18–20 percent in health spending occurred in some areas of the country, whereas the corresponding increase in large parts of the London region was about 4 percent. Further, medical schools and large teaching hospitals in London are combining their resources, while more money has been committed to community programs for the elderly in the same areas and elsewhere.

The involvement of local groups in allocation decisions permits overall policy to be modified to allow for regional preferences. When a government body recommends greater emphasis on, for example, care for the elderly, programs differ from one district to another. Indeed, there are three regions of the country where that priority is in general respected, but where a hospital is carrying out heart transplantation, although in very limited numbers, and with the approval of the central government.

In general, consensus concerning health policy somehow appears to exist from one area to another. For example, a national policy regarding who is a candidate for kidney dialysis cannot be found in writing. However, the local boards responsible for allocating funds in all regions appear to allocate to the hospital in their area with dialysis and kidney transplant capabilities only enough money to treat about half the patients found each year to be dying of kidney failure. Doctors throughout the country generally have adjusted to this limit by referring for treatment only patients under the age of sixty years. Such locally set priorities can, at least in principle, be superseded by the central government. For example, the government could in theory direct enough additional money to the regions to assure treatment of all patients with kidney failure not now being treated. However, given the growing health needs and demands of the population and the nation's overall economic problems, few people expect major additions to the health budget. Thus, if the government were to intervene on behalf of the kidney program, it would be expected to indicate where corresponding cuts in other health activities should be made.

One crucial difference between the British health system and our own is that 95 percent of resources spent on health comes from a single source—the national budget. As a result, the British have the means not only to decide on health policy, but also to implement it. For example, when they decide to give more emphasis to general care for the elderly, at the expense of heart transplant programs, they can readily do so. The single source of funding would, of course, make it equally easy for them to set a reverse policy, that is, one that would favor transplants over care for the elderly.

Contrast this with the American experience with a related technology. More hearts are transplanted in California than anywhere else in the world. Achievements in that field at Stanford University are considered the model for programs elsewhere. Yet in the same state, medically uninsured people have died for lack of access to emergency services. (See Chapter 5.) The sources of funds for the heart transplant program are diverse but do not include the state Medicaid agency. However, that is the agency which is unable to pay for basic medical services for all of California's poor. Thus, even if the citizens should wish to do so, no way exists to give priority to the provision of emergency services for all citizens over heart transplants for a few, for the funds now used for the two programs come from different pockets.

Our diversity of sources of funds is seen by most Americans and some Britons as an advantage—and it does provide mechanisms for overriding government policy with which some in the private sector might disagree. But by the same token, such diversity makes it difficult or even impossible to translate priorities into practice.

The private sector in Britain uses its resources for purposes it judges important and often with government cooperation. For example, a lithotripter was recently purchased and installed in a London teaching hospital by a private insurance company. This machine, costing £1 million, crushes kidney stones by high frequency sound waves and thereby avoids surgery for many patients, The Department of Health and Social Security is sponsoring a controlled trial of its usefulness, and the cooperating doctors and patients are from the National Health Service.

What are some of the lessons that Americans can learn from the British experience? First, few of us would dispute the view that one feature of the NHS worthy of emulation is universal coverage, independent of the geographic location or economic status of patients. This coverage throughout the nation applies not only to primary care by GPs, but also to hospital and specialist care. The system is so arranged that nobody in need is turned away. The incentives encourage doctor and patient to decide on the best place for management of a problem—doctor's office, acute care hospital, home, or chronic illness facility—on the basis of the problem and the wishes of patient and family, rather than on financial grounds.

Another advantage of British as compared with American medicine relates to the gatekeeper function of GPs. If Barbara Wallace, the American widow with headaches mentioned in Chapter 5, had lived in the United Kingdom, whether in Liverpool, in a small rural community in the north of England, or in London, she would have telephoned her GP when her headaches led her to seek medical advice. The GP, in turn, would have decided whether she needed a consultant. Had she ultimately been referred to an eye specialist, the GP's records might have revealed the presence ten years earlier of the same swelling in her retina that caused her so much worry and led to so much expense.

The regionalization of services that the NHS is developing is important for three reasons. First, it does provide access to even the most specialized forms of medical care at centers throughout the nation. A person from a rural community in northwest England in need of heart surgery does not have to travel all the way to Birmingham or London for it. (The availability of such specialized services as heart surgery is, however, still not as great in many regions of the country as in London. Correction of this disparity is one of the goals of the present program of redistributing resources.) Second, because highly specialized problems are dealt with in relatively few places, the teams dealing with those problems have good opportunities to maintain their skills. Finally, as a result of regional planning, costly duplications are generally minimized. Thus, competing programs in heart surgery in the same region are not supported.

The fact that overall decisions concerning areas of need are made by the central government, but that resources are ultimately distributed locally, permits decision making at appropriate levels. Thus, a central government body decides on more funds for the northeast and less for London, and recommends more for care of the elderly and less for heart transplantation. The overall health budget is then divided accordingly and assigned to regions. The regions, in turn, and then their constituent districts decide how the monies that each receives are ultimately distributed and used.

Perhaps the NHS, by allowing greater financial incentives for specialists, might increase their productivity. It is possible, for example, that some orthopedic surgeons and other personnel would be pleased to have the opportunity to work an additional session or two a week, if they were compensated for so doing. (Some have been doing this without compensation since the NHS was begun.) Under such circumstances, assuming that operating rooms and other facilities are available, one could reduce the waiting list of patients in need of hip replacements without increasing physical plant or even the number of specialists.

More money for the NHS and for social services might not eliminate completely such existing problems as the inability to treat some patients with kidney failure or the very long waiting periods for cataract surgery. But it would make a big difference. The British government, however, beset with many other severe financial problems, is seeking to deal with this and other difficulties in the NHS not with increases in budget, but rather by emphasizing better management, greater efficiency, and competition. The government is also encouraging the private sector to become more involved in the delivery of health services. It will be of interest to see whether privatization improves the nation's health. It will be crucial to the future of the NHS to see whether in the process the commitment to equity is retained.

In this respect the British record will be of great interest to Americans. Important cultural differences, of course, distinguish the two nations and therefore how each goes about its business. It is difficult to visualize Americans accepting without extensive public debate—and perhaps not even then—an implicit policy that denies life-saving treatment to people over sixty years of age, the unspoken policy with respect to kidney dialysis in Britain. But one challenge for us is to find ways to incorporate into our system those aspects of British medicine that appeal to us, while retaining those of our current approaches that will help us reach our goals.

7 Lessons from Canada

If Sophie Booker, the elderly Massachusetts widow described in Chapter 5, whose illness bankrupted both herself and her daughter, had been a resident of Canada, she would be in a nursing home that provides care such as she now receives in a small city near Boston. But she and her aging daughter would still have their modest joint bank account, which they had to exhaust almost completely before she was eligible for support for nursing home care from the commonwealth of Massachusetts. Had she lived in Quebec or some other Canadian province, she would be paying the nursing home a nominal amount, determined by her income and assets. The government would be paying the rest, and she and her daughter would have kept most of their savings.

Canada and the United States have, of course, much in common. The two countries share a continent and have populations with strong similarities in history, ethnic origins, language, social goals, age distribution, and patterns of illness. Until recently their medical care systems, too, were much alike, in terms of both structure and financing. In both countries medical services were traditionally provided on a fee-for-service basis by private practitioners inside and outside acute care hospitals, most of which are owned by nonprofit organizations and run by individual boards of trustees. Nursing homes are both proprietary and nonprofit.

Until the late 1960s medical care was paid for in both countries by a combination of insurance from government, nonprofit, and for-profit sources, and by individuals out of pocket, while government insurance covered primarily acute care hospitalization. Similar fractions of the health care dollar—between 55 percent and 60 percent—were consumed by hospital and physician bills. Both nations experienced health care cost inflation in the same period. Between 1950 and 1971 Canadian health expenditures rose steadily, from 2.95 to 7.5 percent of the gross national product, while those in the United States were rising from 4.4 percent to 7.8 percent.

The 1970s, however, saw the development of profound differences in the health care picture in the two nations. First, a universal entitlement program in Canada made ambulatory, acute and chronic hospital, and long-term home care available to the entire population without direct charge. Nursing home care at a modest cost was subsequently added. In other words, a one-class system of medical care that covers everybody and that is financed by the government was implemented throughout the nation. Second, medical cost inflation in Canada was slowed to the rate prevailing in other sectors of society, so that the fraction of the gross national product consumed by medical services remained under 7.6 percent throughout the decade.* All of this took place while costs were rising to 9.5 percent (in 1980) in the United States, and efforts to meet the health care needs of the entire American population were not succeeding.

The two achievements in Canada, universal access to medical services and cost control, are among the most eagerly sought and, thus far, most elusive social goals of the United States. Indeed, many Americans (and others) assume that universal access and cost control are in conflict, that is, that achieving either would almost inevitably put the other further out of reach. How did Canada do it?

Universal, Comprehensive Health Insurance

Canada's central government collects both personal and corporate taxes. The nation's 25 million people live in ten provinces and two territories. The provincial governments are responsible for shaping and implementing much domestic policy, including health and social programs. The provinces differ—in some instances, markedly—from each other in income, population size, and approaches to social problems. In 1946 the province of Saskatchewan enacted a hospital insurance program. Variations were adopted by other provinces, and in 1958 the federal government proposed a program of universal hospital insurance. By 1961 all of the provincial governments agreed to participate, although with considerable variation from one to another.

In the early 1960s Saskatchewan extended its insurance program to cover doctors' bills. Similar programs were adopted in other provinces. In

---

* One should note that the legislation did not cover most dental care and a few medical services such as cosmetic surgery. It is of interest that costs for these continued to escalate.

its 1966 Medical Care Act, the federal government offered strong incentives for all provincial governments to develop broader health insurance programs. Fifty percent of the costs would be paid from federal tax revenues, if the provincial governments paid the rest and set up programs that were comprehensive, including ambulatory as well as acute hospital and long-term care, provided universal access, were portable—that is, valid in all provinces and, to some extent, outside the country—and publicly administered. Between 1968 and 1971 that challenge was accepted and implemented by all the provincial governments, again with important differences from one province to another.

Regional Administration

The history of health insurance in Canada may have lessons for the United States. Despite the fact that their population is only slightly greater than one tenth of ours, the Canadians' universal health insurance program was not begun at the federal level. Rather, it began locally, evolved as a result of local initiatives, and spread so as to permit variations that recognized the marked differences that distinguish one part of the country from another. The federal carrot—the use of federal funds—was used to assure for all parts of the country programs that are comprehensive, provide universal access, and have other attributes agreed by the central government to be important for all citizens. It is of interest that the program continues to have the strong support of the major political parties.

The general arrangement in each province provides that budgets for hospitals and nursing homes are set at regular intervals by its ministry of health. The hospital budget covers only operating costs. Separate negotiations are required for capital expansion, for example, for new beds or expensive new equipment. This is in contrast to the situation in the United States, where hospitals may pay for expansion from their own funds or by borrowing on the capital market. The constraint on capital expansion permits each Canadian province to develop and carry out programs designed to better integrate its hospital system. Thus, if its ministry decides that the province would do better in a given year by assigning more of its resources to long-term beds in some areas and to heart surgery beds in another, and less to other acute care beds throughout, there is a mechanism for translating such policy into action. Policy development and implementation have not been without problems, but many observers say that the new arrangement is a great improvement over the previous situation, which was similar to that in the United States then and now.

Cost-Control Measures

The ministry also negotiates fee schedules with associations of physicians. Typically, the ministry agrees to a specific total annual allocation for a federation of groups of doctors and leaves to the federation how that sum is to be divided among its members. It is now a matter of federal policy that doctors not charge in excess of the negotiated fee scale—that is, they may not extra-bill. Certain other billing practices are also believed to have helped control costs. For example, in some areas the original legislation permitted doctors to charge different sums according to the amount of work done during a patient visit. When it became apparent that a seemingly excessive number of visits to doctors' offices fell into the "major complete" category, for which higher bills could be charged, in some provinces a single fee was set for all visits. Second, fees may be charged only for the services of practitioners, not for their employees. This restriction is controversial, for it may encourage doctors themselves to carry out procedures that could be done equally well by less trained personnel. Finally, most diagnostic services are performed in hospitals or in some provinces in centralized laboratories. Since many of those services, such as endoscopic examinations of the stomach and intestine, can be extremely lucrative sources of income for physicians, this arrangement is believed by some to have discouraged unnecessary examinations and thus to have kept costs down. It does help ensure that complex procedures are carried out only by those with considerable experience.

Such measures are intended to restrict costs incurred by doctors already in practice. However, as is true in the United States, Canadian health policy analysts worry about the escalation of costs that generally occurs when more doctors go into practice. In one effort to control that problem, Canada has taken steps that severely limit the number of foreign-trained doctors entering the country. But, as in the United States, Canadian medical schools were greatly expanded in the 1960s. The resultant continuing increase in numbers of their own medical graduates also presents a problem that must be dealt with. Some Canadian provinces are addressing this issue. For example, British Columbia will not reimburse physicians who set up practice in areas that the province considers overdoctored. Since it is virtually impossible to make a living unless one receives government fees for services, this effectively restricts new doctors from going into practice in areas where they are not needed. (The constitutionality of this policy is being challenged in the courts.) Some provinces use financial incentives to encourage the entry of doctors with backgrounds that are in short supply and to discourage specialists in areas that are considered overrepresented. In Quebec the proportion of family physicians and general practitioners has increased from 50 percent to 65 percent in the past decade, while funding has been cut in half for training programs for specialists.

Access to Long-Term Care

Long-term care, which is now the right of all citizens and the responsibility of the provincial government, may be delivered at home or in nursing homes. In the province of Ontario, for example, a medically oriented home care program for all residents is among the goals of the health insurance program and is now available to some. It includes medical and nursing services and up to eighty hours of homemaking in the first month and forty hours in each subsequent month. Had Mr. McCormick, the man who was dying of lung cancer described in Chapter 5, lived in Ontario rather than in New York, his wife would likely have been referred to the home care program. Although he was able to pay, home care would have been free for him, as it is for all provincial residents. The amount of care he needed would have been determined by a so-called case manager, who is generally a nurse or another health professional, and who is located in the district in which a patient lives, in consultation with his doctor and his wife. The nursing and homemaking services he received would have been provided by nonprofit or proprietary agencies at rates that are negotiated periodically with the provincial government ministry.

All provincial residents are eligible for nursing home care, which, like home care, is based exclusively on medical and social needs, and not at all on income or assets. Patients pay a modest to a moderate fixed room charge, which is determined by income and assets. This arrangement permits a continuing small income for even those whose sole support is a government pension. Thus, Mrs. Booker would have paid a small amount from her government pension and perhaps her savings each month, and the provincial government would have paid the rest. Most of the savings account held jointly by Mrs. Booker and her daughter would have remained in their possession.

Most nursing homes are privately owned, and they are paid on a per diem basis, at a rate negotiated annually for the whole province. Nonprofit nursing homes are paid in a fashion similar to nonprofit hospitals—on the basis of prospectively negotiated global budgets. Additional charges for private rooms and other amenities are permitted, but strictly controlled.

Some who have studied long-term care in Canada have commented favorably on the benefits that result from the competition between the for-profit and nonprofit agencies that are involved.

How Good Is Canada's System?

What have been the effects on the Canadian health picture in the fifteen years since Canada and the United States went separate ways in health policy? First and foremost, all agree that our northern neighbor has removed financial barriers to medical care; that is, Canada has moved closer to equity and universal access to health services for all of its citizens. Contrary to the concerns of some, this has *not* led to discernible overuse of medical resources and obviously not to uncontrolled expenditures. Community care—medical, nursing, and social services (such as the home care program that Mr. McCormick might have used had he been a Canadian), and nursing homes and other facilities for the chronically ill and the elderly—has been increased. But some resources for which the demand is great are in short supply. In several provinces the waiting lists are long for nursing home beds.

The stability of overall costs of health care has already been emphasized. The cost per elderly resident of long-term care facilities, which are more comprehensive and widely available in Canada, seems no greater than in the United States. The 1982 public expenditure per nursing home bed averaged about $10,000 in the United States and slightly less in Canada. The number of beds per 1,000 elderly residents varies widely from province to province, with the United States ratio about in the middle range.

The administrative costs of running the payments system are now about 3 percent of health expenditures, an even lower fraction than in Great Britain. Prior to the public plan they ranged from 10 percent to as much as 50 percent of private premiums. In the United States 11.1 percent of private insurance premiums went for administrative expenses in 1984, while 3.2 percent of the revenues of public programs are so spent.

Since in Canada many services have been increased at a time of overall budgetary restraints, particularly in the early 1980s, priorities have had to be set, and difficult trade-offs have been required. These have differed from one province to another, but the general pattern has been to shift resources away from acute care hospitals and from doctors' incomes. The number of acute care hospital beds has been reduced as a matter of policy—over the past decade by about 30 percent per practicing physician. The amount of new medical technology has been severely limited. For example, in late

1984 Quebec had a total of thirteen CT scanners for a population of 6.5 million, or about 15 percent as many on a population basis as in the United States. Ceilings have been placed on government reimbursement to certain groups of physicians.

The effects of these changes on the overall health of the population are difficult to assess accurately for, as has been frequently noted, the available indices are limited and measures of quality are difficult to come by. However, by the usual yardsticks—increase in life expectancy, fall in infant mortality, decrease in deaths from heart disease, increase in deaths from cancer, particularly of the lung, etc.—the overall health picture in Canada continues to look like that in the United States. The much worse health indices among the poor as compared with the nonpoor seen in the United States continue in Canada—poorer Canadians have life expectancies as much as seven years less than those of their fellow-citizens—as they have in Great Britain under the National Health Service. This provides further evidence that even unlimited medical care cannot compensate fully for the health penalties of poverty.

The factors primarily responsible for the dramatic leveling off of medical costs cannot be defined with certainty. However, the legislation of the late 1960s did not change the delivery system. For example, fee-for-service payments for doctors were left intact. It did, however, radically alter insurance arrangements. Therefore, cost control is widely ascribed to two attributes of the new system. First, funding for almost all health care now comes from a single source. And, second, that source is an appropriate one—the provincial ministry of health. Unlike what went on previously in Canada and what still prevails in the United States, neither hospitals nor doctors can charge individuals, private insurance companies, or competing government agencies for services that the primary insurer—the provincial government—refuses to pay. This can keep costs controlled, but it requires a knowledgeable primary insurer fully aware of the needs and problems of both public and providers of care, both in general and in the context of local conditions. R. G. Evans, a Canadian health economist, believes that provincial governments are appropriate agents for this purpose, because they "have the political legitimacy, technical expertise, and financial leverage and incentives to offset the influence of providers of care."

The Canadian arrangement has been criticized by some because it does not allow for capitation programs. Therefore, it has not exploited the efficiencies that those critics believe can be achieved by that approach. In addition, it has been faulted by those who believe that cost sharing would save money. With increasing needs for health services and the growing capabilities of medicine, the pressure for cost sharing will almost surely increase, as it is increasing in Great Britain. It is true that some experiments in the United States have shown that when the patient must pay a portion of the cost of medical services, utilization is reduced by as much as 30 percent. However, if Canada's extraordinary recent record of cost control is in large part attributable to having all health funds flow through a single funnel, then cost sharing itself could be inflationary.

With the recession of the early 1980s, pressures have increased on every medical care system, including Canada's. That makes the more remarkable Canada's continued efforts to give special attention to neglected health areas, such as community care programs for the chronically ill and the elderly. In fact, Canada's progress in addressing such needs has continued during recent years when the United States, which has made a much larger investment in health, has been cutting back on its health commitments, particularly to the elderly and the poor.

Whenever priorities are set, some people are inevitably less favored. When they are set in times of overall budgetary constraints, hardships will be the greater. Thus, it is no surprise that some groups have experienced difficulties. For example, some physician organizations in Canada have expressed concern that doctors' incomes have not kept pace with inflation within the country. It is true that marked discrepancies exist in the fees paid for some common procedures there, as compared with the United States. For example, the prevailing charge in California under Medicare in 1984 for an appendectomy was $734 (median throughout the United States $600) and in Ontario $259, for a hysterectomy $1,393 (median United States $901) as compared with $503 in Ontario, and for a lens extraction in California $1,341, in Ontario $368.

An expert who has served as an impartial arbitrator on physician compensation issues in Canada feels that the rigidity of the system is probably its most serious defect. He points out that medical school tuition is very low as compared with the United States—as low as $1,000 per year, which is 5 percent that in some U.S. schools. Doctors in training are well paid—perhaps twice what their United States counterparts receive. As a result, doctors enter practice not saddled by the enormous debts they might have incurred had they had their education and training south of their border. In addition, their starting incomes are generally high as compared with United States doctors, and their incomes compare favorably with those of other professional groups. But their upward financial potential is more limited than in the United States, and few opportunities exist to provide financial recognition of variations in the quality of performance from one doctor to another.

The upward pressure on costs of new medical technology and of increased medical demands have continued in Canada, as they will continue in all countries, independent of the system of medical care. Indeed, in the early 1980s the costs of medical care in Canada rose to 8.5 percent of the gross national product. It is not clear whether this reflects the downturn in Canada's overall economy during the recession of those years, with continuing stability of medical costs, or an absolute and relative increase in the latter.

What is clear, however, is that important lessons for the United States are to be found in Canada's medical experiences. Three are worth our most serious attention. The first is that conditions can be created that permit universal access to comprehensive health services without runaway costs in a nation very similar to our own. The second is that health resources can be allocated according to agreed-upon priorities if those resources are controlled by a single authority. In Canada that authority is at the level of the provincial governments, thereby permitting variations that reflect the tastes of the diverse population groups that make up the nation. Finally, initiatives in the delivery of health services can, and perhaps should, begin at the local level. The unit must be large enough to require the presence of all components of comprehensive health services. In Canada, the level has been the provincial government, recognizing local variations in needs and desires and permitting local diversity. The role of the federal government has been to encourage, to facilitate, and to ensure that the medical needs of all citizens are met.

8 Third World Health Problems: Lessons and Opportunities

The Example of China

Americans in need of hospitalization for appendicitis or pneumonia would not choose the Seven Treasures Commune Hospital in a rural section of Shanghai county, China. But such problems are often confronted there, and despite the concrete floors and operating room equipment like that seen in the United States fifty years ago, they are managed successfully.

What is remarkable about the Seven Treasures Hospital is not its technology, but its existence, and even more, the achievements of the system of which it is a part. Since 1949, life expectancy in China has increased from thirty-five to sixty-eight years, and the annual death rate has fallen from 25 to 6.2 per 1,000 of the population. In 1949, the infant mortality rate was over 200 per 1,000 live births. Today it is 12 in large cities and 50 in rural areas.

Although China remains very much a developing country in terms of its economy, its health picture is much more like that of industrialized countries. And it has made the transition in a fraction of the time required by most countries. For example, babies born a century ago in the United States, Great Britain, or France had about the same prospects for survival as babies born in China, El Salvador, or Ghana in 1948. Now the chances that a baby will survive the first year of life are ten to twenty times greater in industrialized countries *and* in China than in many developing nations. Thus, in twenty-five years the outlook for a Shanghai baby improved as much as it did for New York, London, and Paris babies over a century.

In striking contrast, a devastating health picture still prevails in most Third World countries. Eleven million babies die before their first birthday.

Half the world's population does not have safe drinking water, and three fourths of the Third World has no sanitary facilities, while most sickness and deaths in the Third World are attributable to contaminated water. Almost half a billion people suffer from hunger and malnutrition. An estimated two thirds of all couples in the Third World lack ready access to family planning services.

In 1984 fewer than 40 percent of Third World children were immunized against the six major diseases of childhood—measles, tetanus, whooping cough, diphtheria, polio, and tuberculosis—and 4 million die of those diseases each year. More than 2 billion people live in malarious regions, and 1 million children die of malaria each year in Africa. Schistosomiasis, a parasitic infection that is transmitted by snails in contaminated water, kills directly relatively few of the estimated 200 million people who have the disease, but like several other tropical infections, it commonly leads to so much weakness and suffering as to make its victims unable to support themselves. An estimated 30 million people suffer from river blindness, which has led to the abandonment of large tracts of fertile African farmland and, in some villages, to blindness in half the adult males. Sleeping sickness, which threatens 35 million Africans, Chagas' disease, which causes sickness and often death from heart disease in more than 10 million Latin Americans, and an infection that prevents livestock production in much of Africa are all forms of trypanosomiasis. Eleven million people around the world have leprosy. These diseases not only cause untold misery and much death, but also help prevent large numbers of people from being able to work and to sustain themselves and their families. The horror story is the more tragic because much could be done to modify it considerably, as the Chinese experience has shown.

Prevention at Low Cost

The Chinese have emphasized preventive as well as curative programs and have built an integrated health system that attempts to reach every part of the country and every group within it. High on their priority list has been improved nutrition, for malnourished people are more susceptible to, and are much more likely to die of, many diseases which in industrialized countries are generally quite innocent. Measles, for example, is the leading cause of childhood death in many Third World countries. But China does not rely on improved nutrition alone to deal with the common childhood diseases. Immunization is now almost universal against infections like measles for which vaccines exist. Polluted water transmits intestinal infections, which account for as much as 30 percent of all deaths in some Third World countries. In China, a nationwide campaign to upgrade sanitation and to reduce exposure to contaminated water and food has also been crucial to improved health.

An extensive curative system has also been developed in China. It begins with a primary-care network involving "barefoot doctors" and reaches up through commune hospitals, like the Seven Treasures, and county hospitals to the teaching hospitals in the major cities. The system permits simpler and more common problems to be managed close to home and the more complex to be referred upward. In the teaching hospitals of Shanghai, Peking, Harbin, and other centers patients undergo heart valve replacement and kidney dialysis. But it is the emphasis on prevention and on primary care that helps keep the curative system from being overwhelmed.

China's health advances are also noteworthy for their limited cost. In Shanghai the annual per capita health expenditure in 1981 was about $25. Nationwide, the average was $7 and in remote areas less than $4. The difference from the corresponding American per capita expenditure of $1,200 that year was attributable to a range of factors. For example, hospital services are far less comprehensive and comfortable than ours. Salaries are, of course, vastly different. Chinese doctors receive from $40 to $120 monthly, rarely somewhat more.

Cuba, Sri Lanka, Costa Rica, and the province of Kerala in India are other places where remarkable advances in health have occurred in relatively short periods and without the very large expenditures for health made by industrialized countries. The precise explanations for progress differ from country to country, but in all of them priority seems to have been given to preventive measures, nutrition, health education, and some form of primary care.

Many Third World countries, in contrast, spend a large fraction of their health money on high technology medicine designed for diagnosis and treatment, and little on primary care and prevention. In the capitals of some African, Asian, and Latin American countries with widespread infectious disease and malnutrition, much or most of the health budget may be used in Western-style tertiary care hospitals. I recall visiting health stations in rural areas of one African nation on the second day of the month and finding the month's supply of antibiotics already exhausted. Milling around the stations were large numbers of people, mainly pregnant women with infants and children with infections, most of which would have responded to antibiotics. The following day I made rounds in the teaching hospital in the nation's capital. After I was shown the relatively well equipped facilities for cardiac surgery, it came as no surprise to be told that the hospital consumes 70 percent of the national health budget. (I was also not surprised to learn that when one of the leaders of the country needed heart surgery, he went to London for treatment.)

China's lesson is also relevant to the United States, despite profound cultural and political differences. It demonstrates the importance to health of improved social conditions. It underlines the economic, as well as the human, benefits of some preventive measures. It suggests that important savings could be achieved by regionalizing expensive diagnostic and therapeutic facilities.

Finally, the lesson of the recent past bears on health policy issues now confronting China. Recent changes in the political economy of rural areas have led large numbers of barefoot doctors and others to give up health roles in favor of better-paying agricultural jobs. This provides the government with the problem of deciding how health services will be organized for the 800 million Chinese who live outside the cities. Simultaneously, pressures have grown to build more high technology hospitals in the cities. Thus, the competition for scarce funds is keen within (as well as outside) the health area. It will be of interest to see how the Chinese remember and interpret their own health experience in the next phase of their development.

Population Control

Not all of the Chinese health program is universally applicable. Democratic nations would find unacceptable the totalitarian approaches that the Chinese have taken to some health programs. It is surely true that population control is easier to achieve in a nation where severe economic sanctions are applied if people depart from regulations for family size. In this and other such areas, the Chinese lesson, however impressive, is of limited value.

Some people have expressed reservations about large-scale efforts to reduce the burden of disease in Third World countries on the grounds that, in the absence of population control, they would only lead to increased deaths from starvation. In fact, there is much historical evidence that limitation of population generally takes place only *after* important control of disease begins. People everywhere and at all times seem to need reassurance that their offspring will survive *before* they begin to limit their numbers. That was true, for example, in Great Britain, where very high birth rates began to fall in the late nineteenth century, well after public health and other measures had caused very high death rates to decline. Interestingly, this began in Britain and in many other countries long before the availability of modern contraceptive technology.

Prevention and Social Change

Although better social conditions are crucial for improving and maintaining the health of communities, the prevention and treatment of disease with present-day medical measures can bring rich benefits even in the absence of social change. For example, both the spread of tuberculosis within a community and the seriousness of the disease in those who contract it are greatly reduced when living conditions are improved. But tuberculosis in American Indians, in poorer people in New York City, and in citizens of India, among other groups, has been shown to be very responsive to antibiotics even when the standard of living has not changed. Similarly, immunization against measles, whooping cough, tetanus, and other childhood diseases will protect malnourished as well as healthy children. Indeed, because infections cause their victims to burn more calories, they can make malnutrition even more severe. This is not, of course, a reason to opt for immunization instead of improving the diet. Rather, it tells us that both measles vaccination *and* dietary supplements are important.

As is true for tuberculosis, measles, and many other infections, the impact of tropical diseases can be greatly reduced by better nutrition, sanitation, and improvements in other social conditions. But in recent years, modern biomedical science has also led to extraordinary progress toward their control and at a cost that is relatively modest. For example, the Special Programme for Research and Training in Tropical Diseases sponsored by the World Health Organization, the United Nations Development Program, and the World Bank has had remarkable benefits in the development and testing of drugs and vaccines against the diseases themselves. (River blindness is among those with particularly promising results.) It has led to better methods for controlling mosquitoes, flies, and other vectors that transmit the diseases. It has trained growing numbers of scientists, particularly from Third World countries, who are now working on these problems. The total cost from 1974 to 1982 was less than $118 million, of which the United States contribution was $15.4 million. This effort as well as programs to deal with the problems of overpopulation, contaminated water, and hunger could be advanced in a major way by the commitment of additional resources. Additional sums that are almost trivial as compared to the costs of the arms we send to many Third World countries could save lives and greatly benefit the quality of life.

Enlightened self-interest, as well as humanitarian arguments, can be marshaled for our giving more support to programs designed to address Third World health problems. The lessons Third World countries can teach us about how to get the most out of scarce health resources have been mentioned. Another kind of lesson emerges from the crippling effects that disease and malnutrition have on the economy of most developing countries. Many experts in the field of economic development say that it is crucial to tie development activities to programs in health and in education. For example, vaccines exist that would control the six major diseases of childhood. The 100 million children born in the developing world each year could be immunized at a cost of $5 per child. Immunization could protect against diseases that kill 4 million children and leave disabled another 4 million each year. That, in turn, would not only reduce the burden on already strained health care systems, but leave healthier populations to build sounder nations. The United Nations Children's Fund has undertaken a campaign to immunize all of the world's children by 1990 and is making impressive progress toward that goal.

International Cooperation

Finally, a lesson that is constantly asserting itself: Disease recognizes no national borders. The large numbers of American servicemen who returned from Viet Nam with malaria and other devastating tropical diseases are among the witnesses. So are American travelers abroad who come home with debilitating intestinal infections. The epidemics of influenza that begin in Asia and sweep eastward, as well as those that begin in the west and travel to Asia, pay little attention to local health regulations. Perhaps the most serious expression of this lesson is the rapid spread of today's most feared scourge, AIDS. The best evidence is that the disease began in Africa. The reluctance of some African governments to cooperate in studies of AIDS in their own countries may impede greatly not only our understanding of the disease, but also our capacity to contain it. For example, some evidence says that a relatively benign variant of the potentially lethal AIDS virus that affects Americans, Europeans, and many Africans may exist in Africa. At least one African AIDS virus infects people, but seems not to produce serious disease. Some scientists suggest that if that should prove to be the case, the African variant might provide the basis for a vaccine that would protect against the malignant virus that is so devastating. This would be similar to the use of cowpox virus for the vaccine that protected people against smallpox. These two viruses are similar, but cowpox produces only a small and temporary sore at the vaccination site and sometimes a few hours of fever. In contrast, smallpox killed and disfigured millions of people over the centuries. Two hundred years ago over 90 percent of Europeans contracted the disease, and one seventh of them died of it. But cowpox virus was so close in its nature to smallpox virus that it provided vaccinated people with immunity against smallpox for years.

The use of that vaccine to conquer smallpox represents one of the extraordinary achievements of all time. It tells us what international cooperation can mean in the health field and also provides an insight into what relatively small sums of money can do when directed at constructive and well-considered goals. In 1967 the World Health Organization launched a campaign to eradicate smallpox. Ten years later, the campaign was successfully concluded; the world had seen the last case of naturally occurring smallpox that should ever occur. (The three cases that have been recorded since were in laboratory technicians working with the virus and in a person who had applied compresses to the arm of a soldier who had just been vaccinated.) The total cost of the eradication campaign, which was estimated to have been $300 million, was borne by contributions to the WHO by nations throughout the world. The United States' share averaged $3 million annually—an amount that may be compared with the $130 million that we now save each year by our having been able to discontinue surveillance and quarantine programs and vaccination of the population at large.

As the competition grows for resources, it will be more and more difficult to protect even the relatively small amount of money the United States now commits to international health. But the smallpox story should remind us of what we can do. And the state of the Third World's children and the staggering implications of AIDS should remind us of what needs doing. Both are crucial as we think about how to spend our money.

III

PROPOSALS

An Introduction: Proposals in Perspective

In an article in a medical journal in 1975, I likened the resources used for medical care to the grazing area on a common pasture, and the medical practices drawing on those resources to the grazing animals. The analogy was taken from Garrett Hardin's "The Tragedy of the Commons," which concerned a class of human problems that Hardin believed had no solution. As the number of cattle approached the capacity of the area, Hardin indicated, each additional animal contributed to overgrazing. Each herdsman, attempting to maximize his own gain, could reasonably assume that the addition of one or a few cattle to his holdings would have minimal effect on the general welfare. But all herdsmen reasoning and acting individually in this fashion would destroy the commons. "Freedom in a commons," Hardin concluded, "brings ruin to all."

In that 1975 article, I stated: "Nobody would quarrel with the proposition that there is a limit to the resources any society can devote to medical care, and few would question the suggestion that we are approaching such a limit. . . ." I cited a recommendation that had recently been made by a doctor who felt that coronary bypass graft operations should be carried out much more widely than was then (or is even now) the case. He was quoted in the lay press as having proposed that the United States should be equipped to do each day 80,000 coronary angiograms, the x-ray study of coronary arteries that was crucial to the diagnosis and treatment of Eugene Grant, whose heart attack is described in Chapter 4. That advocate for more bypass surgery was urging that angiograms be done on people without, as well as with, symptoms of heart disease. His idea was that "preventive" surgery would then be recommended for all people with any narrowing of the coronary arteries. Since atherosclerosis occurs in virtually all adults, this could mean surgery for a very sizable number of apparently well people. The recommended x-ray assessment alone would then have cost in excess of $10 billion a year. The annual cost of the resultant surgery would have exceeded $100 billion, which was almost equal to the total spent on all health care that year.

Since that time the number of angiograms and the number of coronary bypass operations have continued to increase; in 1985 an estimated 200,000 Americans had bypass surgery at a total cost of more than $4 billion. (Most of those who had the operation were greatly benefited, but careful studies indicated that as many as 30 percent would have done as well or better with medical treatment instead of surgical. More will be said about the effectiveness of bypass surgery and of other technology in Chapter 11.) Although the procedures have not been disseminated as widely as proposed by some advocates, Eugene Grant's Dr. Sourwine (of Chapter 4) would suggest that we have only begun to address the problem. He points out that only 1 percent of coronary attack victims are now treated as Grant was. Suppose that today's research were to confirm his impression that most people with coronary attacks should be managed in the "Grant" way, that is, with an angiogram and then, depending on the results, with treatment by chemicals to dissolve the clot, an angioplasty in some, and coronary bypass surgery in others. If the approximately 800,000 Americans who survive a heart attack each year were so treated, that could mean an additional annual investment of more than $20 billion for coronary care.

The financial and personnel implications of such a possibility are even more sobering when one considers the geographic issue, for the $20 billion estimate assumes the use of existing facilities. But present facilities would not do the job, given the importance of the time factor. Recall that Mr. Grant was ten minutes away from a hospital and had his blocked coronary artery open within ninety minutes of the onset of his pain. Had a lot more time elapsed, his heart muscle would likely have been irreparably damaged, and he could have died or been invalided. To be useful for all citizens in need, the capability to perform angiogram, angioplasty, and bypass surgery would have to be within perhaps two hours' reach of every place in the United States where people have coronary attacks. That, in turn, means virtually every corner of the nation. The demands on the medical commons would be staggering.

The prospect of greater demands is not restricted to treatment programs and not, of course, to the management of heart disease. The importance of preventive measures in lowering deaths and disability from cardiovascular disease has been mentioned and will be discussed in more detail in Chapter 9. Among the programs of great benefit are those designed to control high blood pressure. About 30 million Americans have moderate to severe high blood pressure. Perhaps an equal number have less marked elevations of their pressure, but high enough to warrant treatment. Most are not now effectively treated. A treatment program for all those in need would cost more than $15 billion. As will be emphasized in Chapter 9, and in contrast to popular belief, preventing the complications of high blood pressure, like most other preventive programs, saves lives, illness, and suffering but not money. And, as is true for treatment programs, the dividends in health benefits that preventive programs yield may be more than adequate justification for calls on the medical commons, even when those calls are formidable.

My prediction of 1975—that we were then approaching the limit that the nation was prepared to spend on health services—has not been borne out. Each year since, the amount of resources taken from the medical commons has increased—from $132 billion then to more than $400 billion in 1985. This represents an annual growth of 3–4 percent above the combined rate of increase in price levels and population, and an increase from 8.2 percent to 10.6 percent of the gross national product.

Although my crystal ball was cloudy in 1975, I am bold enough to use it again, this time to predict that soon health spending relative to the nation's total expenditures will level off, and in a more rational and equitable way than we have recently seen. For instance, had Americans and their representatives understood the demand medical care for low-birth-weight babies would make on the medical commons, they might have made a different decision concerning the reduction of maternal and child health care program funds. We need professionals to bring together, to analyze, and to put before us that kind of information.

What We Can Do

The four chapters that follow will suggest ways in which, from within the resources we now commit to health, we could increase health benefits. One important policy change would be to commit a larger fraction to prevention. As Chapter 9 will point out, success in one prevention program alone, the abolition of cigarettes, would avert more than 300,000 deaths a year, enormous suffering, and in the short term a heavy economic drain on the medical care system.

Our limited capabilities in dealing with many patients with cancer, atherosclerosis, mental disease, and aging, and our helplessness in dealing with some others, point to the challenges before us. Our primitive understanding of the underlying basis of those conditions and many others is testimony to how much we need to learn. There is no way to predict where to look for many of the crucial bits of information that will ultimately lead to ways to prevent or treat Alzheimer's disease, many forms of cancer and arthritis, and many other diseases that are now resistant to medical intervention. Therefore, we should give high priority to the support of first-rate basic research. The importance of research in the natural sciences will be emphasized in Chapter 10.

A second kind of research and development—in health services—is also crucial. It involves medicine and the social sciences and is in a much younger stage of development than is research in the natural sciences. Health services research includes technology assessment, the subject of Chapter 11, which helps us know when a CT scan or coronary bypass surgery is likely to help the patient, and when it represents an unnecessary risk and an unnecessary cost. By telling us of the costs, risks, and benefits of worthwhile programs, it also may guide us to choices as we more and more often find that we can't afford to do all that we want to do.

Much health services research is directed at streamlining the delivery of health care. Health 2000, the plan presented in Chapter 12, is an example of the kind of experiment that addresses some of the cost and access problems of today's delivery system. One routine practice in research in the laboratory sciences should guide the approach to health services research. Every natural scientist carries out trials on a small scale before undertaking any major experiments that consume large resources in time, money, equipment, other materials, and hope. Thus, before trying to make large quantities of a product like interferon, a biologist would exhaustively carry out small pilot studies looking for optimal conditions for its production, indeed, to see whether the underlying theories are valid.

Experiments designed to improve the system of health care deserve no less, but frequently the crucial preliminary phase is skipped. The results can be expensive in human terms, as well as in money. For example, had the program to "deinstitutionalize" psychiatric patients begun in the 1960s been subjected to small trials in one or two parts of the country before it was applied nationally, we likely would have had advance warning of the troubles that it unexpectedly caused. Then, knowing that one result would be large numbers of homeless and helpless people, many worse off than before, we could have modified or stopped the program until the unexpected consequences had been dealt with. This points to another need for social experiments that is often overlooked: Built into every such undertaking should be provision for evaluation. If conditions are to be modified on the basis of consequences as the experiment progresses, as well as after its completion, we need careful observations of all outcomes, expected and unexpected.

Even when the theoretical basis for a change is established, local conditions may speak for considerable variation in application from one part of the nation to another. The size and complexity of our country are another reason for undertaking pilot studies: What works well in New Jersey or Florida may be much less useful in New Mexico or Idaho.

Providing more efficient (which often means better) health care will require the participation of government, the general population, and a range of professionals not traditionally involved in health, as well as those who have been central in the past. Until recently the physician was *the* key figure in the health arena. Perhaps that was natural. The perception was widespread that medical measures were—with few exceptions—all that mattered in restoring or maintaining health. Further, the middle years of this century saw a great expansion of effective medical treatments, particularly the antibiotics like penicillin and streptomycin that controlled scarlet fever, tuberculosis, and other infectious diseases. Indeed, the extraordinary effectiveness of such drugs encouraged the familiar "magic bullet" mentality. In the minds of many, the principal objective of medicine became the discovery and application of cures for cancer, heart disease, arthritis, and the other diseases that afflict us.

Simultaneously, and perhaps partly as a consequence, the emphasis in medical education, medical research, the distribution of medical care, and payment arrangements for medical services has been oriented toward diagnosis and treatment of the individual. This has often turned out to be expensive and sometimes heroic. Much less attention has been focused on the promotion of the health of society as a whole. One reason is that medicine and health have been widely regarded as synonymous. But there is growing appreciation that medical care, however crucial, is only one determinant of the health of individuals and of population groups.

We need now to involve all sectors of our society in decision making. That could help lead to a more efficient and more healthful utilization of our health resources, one that reflected the wishes of the American people. As Chapter 5 shows, "grazing" takes place on a variety of medical "pastures"—some that are "cultivated" by federal, state, and local government, others by a variety of insurance and other kinds of private sector companies, and still others by individual Americans paying out of pocket. Many of those pastures are unconnected. How some are used may or may not conform with the wishes and interests of society as a whole. As a result, the nation is limited in its capacity to make choices and then to implement them. For example, suppose that the American people decided to limit access to the commons for the artificial heart until more care had been provided for the elderly, or to divert resources away from additional neonatal intensive care units and toward community programs that would provide more care for pregnant women, or that some funds now used for treating lung cancer would be directed at smoking control programs, or the other way around. We could not now do so; the diversity of individuals controlling access to the commons impedes our capacity to carry out decisions that reflect the interests of society as a whole.

To use medical resources in ways that reflect our values and that are more efficient requires one more very basic decision: We must decide whether we are prepared to take control of our "commons."

9   Prevention: Its Value and Its Cost

A Problem: Moderation Has No Sex Appeal

Consider how well Jack Washington takes care of himself. At the age of fifteen he smoked a few cigarettes, but decided he didn't like them and never took up the habit. He enjoys wine and most evenings has a glass or two with dinner. He has a varied diet, prefers chicken and fish to steak, and eats large quantities of whole grain cereals and green, leafy vegetables, few eggs and relatively small amounts of dairy products other than low-fat milk. On occasion, he has dinner in his favorite French restaurant and orders whatever takes his fancy. He swims or plays a set of tennis three or four times a week. He always wears a seat belt and generally follows posted speed limits. He is happily married and has never been sexually promiscuous.

Aged fifty-three, he visits his doctor's office once a year and has his blood pressure measured and leaves specimens of his stool to be examined for blood. His wife does the same. At the same time, she has a Pap smear and, on alternate years, a mammogram, an X ray to detect early breast cancer. No result of these tests has ever been abnormal. Because both the Washingtons work in the garden, they are careful to have tetanus booster shots every ten years.

At the age of forty-three he did not have a few weeks of coughing, spitting up blood, and weight loss of fifteen pounds and was not found to have lung cancer. Therefore, he did not then have an operation on his chest, followed by radiation. At forty-nine he did not experience crushing chest pain and collapse, was not found to have obstructions involving all three main coronary arteries (nobody has—as yet—looked into those arteries), and did not undergo triple bypass coronary surgery. He does not have cirrhosis of the liver. Two years ago, while driving home from a cocktail party where he did not drink, he did not have a head-on collision with another car and was not taken to the emergency unit of a large metropolitan hospital for emergency surgery to remove a large blood clot on his brain. In short, he can boast an impressive list of negative accomplishments with respect to his health.

And all of this was added to the endowment for his longevity and good health with which he began life. His father died of cancer at the age of eighty-four years, and his mother is still in remarkably good health at the age of eighty-seven. Neither of the Washingtons nor their parents had high blood pressure, diabetes, or heart disease.

In recent years he and his wife have read extensively about medicine and health issues. As a result, they believe they call their doctor less often than many of their friends, who seem more easily intimidated by symptoms than they are. In addition, they feel that their reading has increased their (already deep) commitment to disease prevention and health promotion.

Several case histories presented in this book include fictional names. "Dr. Daniel Beck" is so disguised. Anything I could say about him must imply my respect, and I don't want to embarrass the unpretentious person whom I consider a model physician. But Mr. and Mrs. Washington, uniquely in this book, are pure fiction. Paragons like them surely exist, but since I have not yet (knowingly) met one, I had to make them up. In fact their medical history is pretty boring. But that's the problem that confronts those who promote the general topic of disease prevention. Have you ever heard of a philanthropist endowing a professorship in a medical school in honor of the fact that her father was *not* treated in the university hospital by world experts for a dread disease because he didn't have it? How many politicians demand that the budget be doubled for research on the relationship of poverty to disease? Do very many of us enthusiastically give up today's pleasures for the promise that a condition we think is unlikely in any event will therefore be less likely, or for the possibility of five more years of life thirty years on?

His exemplary behavior notwithstanding, Mr. Washington owes much of his gift of good health to factors over which he had no control—the genes he inherited from his ancestors. When he married a woman with a family history like his own, he did for his children's health what had been done for his. The Washingtons follow with admiration and sometimes wonder the remarkable advances in medical technology. But they are aware that the major steps forward in the control of heart disease and some kinds of cancer in recent years have resulted much less from modern diagnosis and treatment than from changes in environmental factors. Because they are prosperous and well-educated, the Washingtons have been in a good position to control many environmental factors that influence their health.

Inheritance and Environment

The mention of environmental factors warrants a few words of amplification. A stir was created a few years ago when it was pointed out—quite correctly—that most cancer is related to environmental factors. This led many to think that large numbers of contaminating chemicals in air, water, and foods were responsible for most cancers (and a variety of other diseases as well). But pollution of air and water account for no more than 2 percent, and food additives for much less than 1 percent, of all cancers in this country.

The confusion stems from a misunderstanding concerning the term. In fact, "environmental factors" means all *outside* influences on our bodies, as distinguished from the genes that each of us has inherited from previous generations. Environmental factors are diverse, ranging from the foods that we eat—the wheat itself, as well as any additives that may be in a slice of bread—on the one hand, to whether women become pregnant and, if so, their age when they do, on the other. They include not only physical, chemical, and biological, but also the social factors to which we are exposed in life.

Genetic factors determine the color of our hair, skin, and eyes, the shape of our ears, our fingerprints, and other characteristics handed on to us from our parents. Some diseases—phenylketonuria (PKU) and sickle cell anemia are examples—are traced mainly to our genes, but even they are influenced by environmental factors. For example, the brain damage caused by phenylketonuria can be greatly reduced by dietary measures; people with sickle cell disease can die when exposed to the reduced oxygen concentrations of high altitudes. All other diseases—lung cancer is a striking example—are related primarily to environmental factors, although many, like diabetes and coronary heart disease, are strongly influenced by genetic factors. But most, and perhaps all, are affected to some degree by genes. For example, many people who smoke moderately get lung cancer, while some very heavy smokers do not. This may be the result of inherited differences in the capacity to dispose of the cancer-causing chemicals in tobacco.

The principal environmental factors that have been implicated with respect to cancer, then, are—in the United States—*not* toxic chemicals in air and water, but cigarettes, which are responsible for about 30 percent of all cancer deaths; diet, about 35 percent; infection, 10 percent;* reproductive and sexual practices, 7 percent;† alcohol, 3 percent; and asbestos, 2 percent.

The figures differ in other parts of the world. In China and many African countries, for example, infection with hepatitis B virus is a crucial factor in the development of primary cancer of the liver, which is a common cancer in those areas, but relatively infrequent in the United States.

Environmental Change and Health

Most Americans take for granted control of many environmental factors that were so hazardous to the lives and health of their forebears. Many would be surprised to learn that before the middle of the eighteenth century a quarter of all people born did not survive to their fifth birthday. Most deaths at that time and most in their grandparents' generation were the result of infectious diseases, which are caused mainly by bacteria and viruses. These were controlled to a considerable degree by clean water, pasteurized milk, sewage disposal, uncrowded living conditions, personal hygiene, and later by vaccinations.

It is likely that the dramatic cures by antibiotics, and the prevention by vaccines, of the infectious diseases that were the nation's major killers until the early twentieth century have had two effects on many people's thinking. First, there is a sense that similar "magic bullets" can be expected for the conditions, like heart disease, cancer, and stroke, which have replaced the infectious diseases as the nation's principal health hazards. Second, the importance of environmental changes in the control of even the infectious diseases is not widely appreciated.

The Washingtons take a more than casual interest in the history of medicine and public health. Their reading has in no way diminished their

---

* It must be emphasized that the percentages offered for diet and infection are less precise than that for cigarettes, in the sense that the nature of the dietary factors and the infecting agents remain to be better defined. As a result the opportunity for cancer control in these areas is at this time much more limited.

† Much information concerning environmental influences in this sphere is even more difficult to exploit than that relating cigarettes to cancer, because of its implications. For example, the evidence is strong that women who have their first pregnancy in their teens are 50 percent less likely to get breast cancer than those who become pregnant for the first time in their thirties. But how is that translated into health policy in a democracy? And would we want such a policy, even if we could democratically arrange it? Consider just a few of the problems—school dropouts, low-birth-weight babies, child neglect—associated with teenage pregnancy. Here, as in so many other health issues, there are trade-offs. The lessened likelihood of breast cancer seems hardly a reason to take on the burdens of teenage pregnancy.

appreciation of the power of modern medicine. But it has helped them understand that the major diseases of today are far more complex in their origins than the infectious diseases, each of which is caused by a single kind of microbe. Therefore, they are much less optimistic that atherosclerosis, the mental diseases, cancer, arthritis, and other problems seen mainly in later life will be cured by single drugs like penicillin or streptomycin. Further, they know that environmental changes had great benefits on the infectious diseases long before effective medical treatments were found. For example, deaths from scarlet fever among English children fell from 25,000 per million children per year early in the nineteenth century to 25 *before* the first antibiotic was discovered. This in no way demeans the importance of penicillin; with the availability of this and similar drugs, *nobody* should die of streptococcal infections, and almost nobody does. Unless the patient is allergic to it, penicillin is mandatory for everybody with strep (and many other) infections. Its benefits in terms of diseases cured and complications prevented are matched by few other medical measures. But well before the antibiotic era, improvements in many environmental factors, such as nutrition and hygiene, contributed to the remarkable decrease in deaths.

Similar stories can be told about other potentially fatal infections. For example, in the United States tuberculosis was among the leading causes of death from the middle of the nineteenth century, when health statistics first began to be collected. In the late nineteenth century more than 300 people per 100,000 population died of tuberculosis each year. At that time, many environmental factors, including malnutrition and overcrowding, were contributing to the devastating spread and ravages of the disease.

In the mid-1940s, streptomycin, the first antibiotic effective against the disease, was introduced. But by then, deaths had already fallen tenfold, to just over 30 per 100,000 per year. What had happened? Improved nutrition and better housing conditions, as well, many experts believe, as changes in other still unidentified environmental factors, were responsible.

The diagnosis of tuberculosis is now, of course, an automatic signal for the institution of appropriate drug treatment. Such treatment leads to control of all but the most advanced cases. But even in the present antibiotic era our knowledge of the conditions that facilitate the spread and the grave consequences of tuberculosis and the use of that knowledge are important in preventing, as well as curing, what was once considered an uncontrollable problem.

The Washingtons' reading about health matters has informed them of the many facets of atherosclerosis, the condition that causes most heart disease. It has important genetic components; the chances of Jack Washington's dying of a heart attack at an early age are very small because both his parents lived to their eighties. But susceptibility is also heavily influenced by environmental factors. Despite his genetic background, a heart attack would have been more likely had he been a chain smoker, thirty pounds overweight, inactive, and under constant severe emotional stress.

To sort out all the factors responsible for the nation's recent marked decrease in heart disease deaths may never be possible. But the effort is important, particularly because most of today's treatment programs, however effective, do not—in contrast to penicillin for strep infections—cure. Medical technology can sometimes repair, open, or bypass arteries damaged by atherosclerosis—often with life-saving results, as William Berry and Eugene Grant can testify. But you don't "get over" atherosclerosis; you prevent it. Thus, identifying and controlling the causes of atherosclerosis should be high on the list of today's medical agenda. The same can be said for all the other chronic diseases that take heavy tolls in our society.

Cancer is another good example. Cures as a result of modern chemotherapy treatment programs represent major milestones in medical progress. The cures are the more notable because the principal beneficiaries are the young; perhaps 3,000 cancer victims under the age of thirty years, like Michael Bell and Marian Cohen, are saved every year. Perhaps twice that number of older people with cancer are also cured with drugs. Experts in the cancer field debate what chemotherapy *could* do. But a realistic assessment suggests that until we know a lot more about cancer, it is unlikely that the total number of patients cured by chemotherapy will exceed 30,000 per year. That would be a remarkable achievement, but more than 460,000 Americans died of cancer in 1985. Thus, the number of potential cures is low in terms of the size of the overall cancer problem. It is also small relative to the more than 150,000 persons who die each year of smoking-related, and therefore preventable, cancers, particularly lung cancer.

If lung cancer deaths were occurring at the same rate now as in 1930, annual deaths from that cause would be less than 10,000. The difference—that is, an increase of more than 116,000 deaths per year from lung cancer—does not indicate *less* effective medical treatment. Rather, it reflects what is really an epidemic of the disease as a result of cigarette smoking. Cancer of the lung now strikes more than twelve times as many Americans as it did fifty-five years ago. Treatment programs cure fewer than 10 percent of people with lung cancer. As a result, in the past half century lung cancer has risen from a position of sixth on the list of fatal cancers to first by a wide margin—it now takes more lives than the next three most common causes of cancer deaths combined.

In sharp contrast, stomach cancer, which was first on the list of fatal cancers fifty-five years ago, has been steadily decreasing over the years, to seventh position at the present time. It is still an important problem; it claimed more than 14,000 lives in 1985. But if it were occurring at the same rate as in 1930, it would now be causing more than 77,000 deaths a year. In other words, more than 60,000 people are "saved" annually from stomach cancer deaths. As is true of lung cancer, the change is unrelated to medical programs. Indeed, like lung cancer, cancer of the stomach continues to be among the most resistant to treatment. Fifty years ago, of those who got stomach or lung cancer, fewer than 10 percent could be cured. Treatment results today are only slightly better; about 15 percent of stomach cancer and 10 percent of lung cancer victims are cured. Thus, it can only have been changes in environmental factors that led to a marked drop in stomach cancer deaths. In other words, we can credit environmental changes with the saving of more than 60,000 lives per year from that disease.

We know what is responsible for the increase in lung cancer. We have only guesses as to what has caused the decrease in stomach cancer. (One guess is that refrigeration and preservatives have decreased the presence in foods of cancer-causing toxins, which, the theory goes, are made by contaminating organisms.) We can say with confidence that medical treatment can neither be credited for the marked decrease in deaths from one, nor faulted for the even more marked increase in deaths from the other. However, we can also say that whatever the factors responsible for the decline in stomach cancer, they have decreased the immediate need for medical services, just as cigarettes have been increasing the need.

Meanwhile, a few other fatal cancers have increased and a few have decreased, independent of treatment. Cancer of the pancreas, for example, which is incurable in all but a very few patients, kills about 24,000 people a year, almost three times the number that would die if the disease were occurring at the same rate as in 1930. More than 25,000 men die of cancer of the prostate annually, a figure about 35 percent higher than the number that would die if deaths were at the same rate as half a century ago. On the other hand, liver cancer, which is also incurable, is decreasing; about 10,000 deaths are expected in 1985, as compared with the 28,000 people who would die of the disease if its rate of occurrence were unchanged from 1930. We don't know why. The changes are the results of changes in environmental factors, mostly unidentified.

The steps that can be taken to prevent disease can conveniently be thought of in three categories. Some require action by society, such as purification and fluoridation of the water supply. Some are the responsibility of the primary-care doctor or other health professional, such as immunization against measles, flu, and other infectious diseases. The most important are under the control of the individual and are often referred to as actions affecting life-style, such as weight control and the use of seat belts and of contraceptives, both those aimed at birth control alone *and* those aimed at preventing sexually transmitted diseases.

Preventing Noxious Habits

One program in disease prevention would do more for the health of the American people (and the people of every other industrialized country and a growing number of people in Third World countries) than any treatment or other prevention program, or combination of programs known to affect health. The abolition of cigarettes would avert more than 300,000 deaths a year in the United States alone, and much suffering associated with cigarette-related diseases, particularly several cancers, coronary heart disease, and certain chronic and life-threatening lung diseases. This would include a reduction of one third in total deaths from cancer (primarily of the lung, but of a variety of other organs as well, including mouth, throat, larynx, bladder, kidney, and pancreas). It would eliminate chronic obstructive lung disease, a condition which often leads to death from suffocation, and which has been among the most common causes of death in Britain and is increasing in the United States. It would reduce heart attack deaths by one quarter. It would reduce appreciably deaths from strokes and a variety of other vascular diseases.

The message is getting across, but thus far mainly among the more educated and more affluent citizens of the United States, Britain, and most other industrialized countries. (Cigarette smoking is rapidly *rising* in Third World countries. As a result, they can soon expect epidemics of the tobacco-related diseases prevalent in our country.)

The lung cancer epidemic is slowing in the United States. The number of new cases in men in 1983 was 4 percent less than in the previous year, the first drop in at least fifty years. This was due in part to a more than 50 percent reduction in tar content of cigarettes between the 1950s and the 1970s. But it was also due to the reduction in smoking that began in men about twenty years ago.* Lung cancer among women is still increasing and will continue to do so, for there has been little overall drop in smoking among women.

* For reasons that are not clear, there is a latent period of fifteen to thirty years between the first exposure to cigarettes (and most other carcinogens) and the appearance of cancer. Thus, today's incidence of lung cancer reflects patterns of smoking of twenty years ago.

The fall in heart disease deaths that has occurred in the United States is also partly attributable to a reduction in smoking (although not to the decreased tar content of cigarettes; the cardiac effects of cigarettes may be due to nicotine or carbon monoxide or something else, but not to tar). Since the cancer-producing effects of cigarettes take about twenty years, the benefits in terms of reduced cancers require that long to show up. In contrast, the harmful effects of cigarettes on the heart occur at once. Similarly, the benefits of the reduction in smoking are also quickly apparent.

No single measure will deal successfully with the problem. It's all very well to tell people that cigarettes are harmful, but how does the person who is physically addicted use that advice? Research, both biological and behavioral, on the nature of addiction and how to deal with it is urgently needed. Surprisingly little is yet pinned down concerning the chemical substances in cigarettes responsible for the various devastating health effects. Tars are believed to cause cancer, but precisely which substance or substances are cancer-causing is still unknown; the other harmful agents are even less well understood.

Among the steps that the government might take are to ban advertising and to raise the tax on tobacco. With respect to the first, the Norwegians found that cigarette sales leveled off after their total ban on cigarette advertising went into effect in 1975. Objections to such a ban have been raised in this country on constitutional grounds. The issue is troubling to every American committed to the First Amendment, but I consider this objection outweighed by the vulnerability of children becoming addicted to cigarettes before they are old enough to be able to evaluate the often misleading and seductive advertising. A larger tax might be particularly effective in discouraging young people from starting to smoke, and it is this group that one wants particularly to influence. Clearly, the number of questions that are still unanswered is large, and a broad program of research is important for permanent control of the problem.

To turn to other programs in prevention, many could be mentioned. Some depend on evidence more fragile than that linking cigarettes to several diseases. None would have the sweeping health benefits of cigarette control. However, those that I will mention can be defended on sufficient grounds to warrant changes in policy. Further, preventive strategies can complement each other. Indeed, evidence suggests that some combinations have even more than additive effects. For example, it has been proposed that cigarettes don't do as much harm to the hearts of Japanese as to American or British smokers, because of the protection offered by the Japanese diet, which is low in fat and cholesterol.

Next to cigarettes, diet is likely the area in the lives of Americans where change could have the greatest health benefits. It is true that no single dietary factor can be linked specifically to today's common diseases with the certainty that, let's say, influenza viruses have been shown to cause flu. But a growing body of information points to an important role for diet in the development of coronary heart disease and some kinds of cancer. The uncertainties are compounded by the fact that today's most serious diseases are almost surely caused, or at least influenced by, a range of factors. As a result, those who insist on unequivocal evidence may never find enough basis for action.

Epidemiologic research often provides the basis for health whodunits described in fascinating fashion by writers like Berton Roueché. It has also provided the underpinning for much of contemporary thinking about the relation of environmental factors to disease. Consider, for example, that stomach cancer is seven times more frequent, and cancer of the breast about one fifth as common, in Japan as in the United States, but that Americans of Japanese extraction have the same patterns of stomach and breast cancer as other Americans. This says at once that the cancer differences are not genetic but rather are related to environmental factors that distinguish the Japanese and the American cultures. Nobody can as yet say which are the key differences, but it is likely related at least in large part to diet.

Epidemiologic studies tell us that, in contrast to what was once believed, diseases like atherosclerosis and cancer are not inevitable consequences of living or aging, since they differ from one country to another, and within the same country from one time to another. Thus, when their causes are known, it ought, at least in principle, to be possible to eliminate them, or at least to reduce them sharply: in principle, because the identification of the biggest offender of all, the cigarette, has not led to the control that might be expected. The decline of stomach cancer and of atherosclerosis proves that, strictly speaking, identification of cause is not essential for control. However, it would obviously make no sense to leave to chance the environmental changes that can prevent or greatly decrease the occurrence of cancer, atherosclerosis, and the myriad of other chronic and often fatal health problems that beset Americans. After all, the possibility of changes like those that are leading to more pancreatic cancer seems no less likely than those that have led to less cancer of the stomach.

The results of such epidemiologic studies will be more and more relevant as society finds it necessary to choose among various possible investments in health programs in a climate of limited resources. Then, it will be particularly important to know accurately the achievements of the various approaches that have been taken in the past. For example, the budget of the National Cancer Institute rose from $230 million in 1971 to more than $1 billion today (or an increase of more than 65 percent in constant dollars). Those funds have been used for a range of programs, including some extremely important basic research. A larger fraction has been devoted to chemotherapy programs. Much less has been spent in the prevention field. It would be foolish to neglect any of these. But when we are forced to make choices, it would be shortsighted to concentrate funds largely on chemotherapy programs *at the expense of* basic research and prevention programs.

Immunization

The preventive measures that require a doctor, nurse, or other trained person include those directed at the infectious diseases of childhood for which effective vaccines exist, such as measles. Most Americans regard this as a mild disease, causing a typical skin rash, fever, and few symptoms, and disappearing in a few days. That was an accurate description for the vast majority of the 4 million Americans who contracted the disease each year before the development of a measles vaccine. But measles also has serious complications—ear infections that may be followed by deafness, severe pneumonia, and inflammation of the brain, or encephalitis, which can lead to permanent mental deficiency or even death. Indeed, in the United States in prevaccine days, 400 children died of the disease and 4,000 contracted encephalitis each year.

Although both Mr. and Mrs. Washington had measles as children, their good general health, particularly their state of nutrition, meant that they had virtually no risk of dying of it, and they didn't get very sick. Their children, having been immunized, never even got it. In contrast, measles may be fatal in 10 percent of children in many African and Latin American countries. This is because malnutrition leads to greater susceptibility to infections of all kinds, including measles, and far less resistance in those infected. Thus, in some Third World countries measles rivals malaria and severe intestinal infections as threats to life and health among children. But immunization does work in such populations, despite the malnutrition.

Soon most Americans should have little frame of reference for thinking about measles at all. The isolation of the virus in 1954 made possible the development of a vaccine, which was first used on a large-scale basis in American children in 1963. Within five years the annual incidence of the disease had fallen from more than 4 million cases to 22,000, and now only a few hundred cases occur each year throughout the nation.

Most immunization programs, like many others in the prevention area, require continuing participation by government. This lesson was brought home in the late 1960s and early 1970s. Then, following the elimination of federal funds for measles immunization, the number of measles cases began to rise, and in 1971, 75,000 cases were reported. Renewed attention to the disease followed, and by the late 1970s measles eradication, a far more ambitious goal than measles control, became a national priority of the surgeon-general of the Public Health Service.

Vaccines can also prevent other childhood diseases, including rubella (German measles), whooping cough, diphtheria, and polio. Newer vaccines are now available to control other infections that may cause serious disease in adults. Examples include influenza and a form of pneumonia that is caused by the bacterium pneumococcus and is often fatal in older people. A vaccine now exists to prevent infections by hepatitis B virus, the cause of a chronic and sometimes fatal form of hepatitis in the United States, as well as of liver cancer.

Vaccine development is an important area of research worldwide. A vaccine may soon be available against malaria, which is perhaps the single greatest killer among the infections in Third World countries. In recent years malaria has been occurring with greater frequency in the United States, particularly among our military forces, as intercontinental travel increases. Now that the virus that causes AIDS has been isolated, the search is on for a vaccine. But the AIDS virus mutates or changes its genetic structure rapidly, more than 100 times as fast as flu viruses. And flu virus itself mutates frequently. It is this frequency that reduces the protective value against next year's flu epidemic of a vaccine made with this year's virus. Thus, most virologists hold little hope for an effective vaccine in the near future. Vaccines will likely one day be available against some of the infections that contribute to certain forms of cancer, such as that of the uterine cervix, which appears to be closely related to infections with human papilloma virus.

Several research programs are now directed at searches for agents that might protect against today's most frequent killers. For example, a large-scale study among doctors is now under way to determine whether a small daily dose of aspirin will lessen the chances of heart attacks in people over fifty years of age. The suggestion that vitamin C would help prevent cancer has been disproved, but a test is now being carried out to see whether beta-carotene offers protection. Many people seem more willing to add to, rather than to subtract from, their diet as a means of disease prevention.

Screening Tests

Several years ago Dr. Daniel Beck stopped doing annual comprehensive "checkups," because most components of the examination are expensive and yield little or no *useful* medical information. For example, while a chest X ray every six or twelve months may detect an unsuspected cancer of the lung, treatment of cancers detected in such surveys is no more successful than when patients seek medical attention because of symptoms. Therefore, he decided that it made no sense to put his patients to the trouble, risk, and expense of periodic chest X rays in a search for early lung cancer. On the other hand, he is persuaded from recent reports in medical journals that mammograms every one to three years in women over the age of fifty might save as many as 25 percent of the 35,000 women who die of breast cancer each year. Here, then, is a place where early diagnosis makes a difference. He has long been convinced that treatment of people with high blood pressure, at least those with severe and moderate elevations, can reduce markedly the incidence of strokes and heart attacks, which are serious and often fatal complications.

Beck also recommends a few other tests at intervals, including hearing tests and examination of the mouth for cancer. Counseling in contraceptive practice is clearly important for women of childbearing age. Stool examination for traces of blood, as a means of detecting unsuspected cancers or precancerous polyps of the bowel, and Pap tests for uterine cancer are also useful. Dr. Beck has another reason for periodic contact with all or most of his patients—to encourage their coming forward with problems, physical and psychological, when they occur. This is especially true for his elderly patients, lest serious problems go unrecognized.

He has always urged the use of condoms for his patients who are active sexually with more than one partner. He adds even greater emphasis to that advice now that the AIDS epidemic is so devastating. He alerts expectant mothers early in pregnancy to the need for many kinds of healthy behavior, including a good diet, the treatment of infections, and the avoidance of cigarettes, alcohol, and drugs of all kinds. He helps them establish a relationship with an obstetrician early in pregnancy. Early and continuing prenatal visits have probably been an important factor in the marked fall in infant mortality that has occurred in the United States in recent years. He suggests amniocentesis or other means of sampling fetal tissue for his patients in high risk situations who would consider interruption of pregnancy if certain disorders like Down's syndrome or sickle cell disease were found.

Social Measures

Societal involvement was essential to maintain clean drinking water and sewage disposal in order to control the many water- and food-borne diseases that were major causes of death in the early part of this century. Residents of communities with fluoridated drinking water have much less tooth decay. Unfortunately, only 50 percent of Americans have access to this benefit, many because they live in areas remote from public water supply. They should take dietary supplements of fluoride. Regrettably, a large number of people are deprived of fluoride in public water because of the misconception of some that the small levels of fluorine involved are dangerous.

Many concerned citizens are aware of the benefits of monitoring exposure to unhealthy substances in the workplace and in the community. Some have led efforts to test for and remove lead paint in urban neighborhoods where lead poisoning was prevalent. Such campaigns not only saved many children from terrible and sometimes permanent damage, including mental retardation, but saved their communities considerable money in averted hospitalization and medical bills.

Americans who are privileged with respect to income and education have the advantage of being able to control many environmental factors that could be threats to their health. In contrast, citizens who live in poverty have burdens of illness that are often quite resistant to medical intervention. For example, infant mortality rates among the disadvantaged are twice the national average. Death rates among the poor are higher from heart disease, lung cancer, and cirrhosis. Days of hospitalization and days lost from work are also more numerous. Whether poverty begets illness, or the reverse, cannot be said with certainty. In all likelihood, both are true. But it is clear that no medical measures protect fully against the illnesses that owe to poverty a large part of their origin and/or severity. In Britain inequities in health among the poor have received special attention. In the late 1940s, many Britons (and others) thought that the ready availability of medical services to all citizens made possible by the National Health Service would eliminate those inequities. That has proved not to be the case. (See Chapter 6.)

Another group in great distress in the United States is our mentally ill. While no vaccines exist to prevent their underlying sicknesses, this large group of Americans now lacks many medical and social measures that could have profound benefits.

The burden that poverty and perhaps the apathy bred by poverty put on the health care system was reflected in a report a few years ago of the conditions that brought most people to the emergency units of two inner city hospitals in Chicago. The problems were not heart attacks, stroke, and cancer. Rather, they were (in order) automobile accidents, interpersonal attacks, accidents other than those involving cars, bronchial ailments, alcoholism, drug-related problems, and dog bites.

The hospital staffs dealt with these problems medically, of course. But they did more. They looked for ways to reduce the number of victims that would need help. When they traced many automobile accidents that involved children to a hazardous crossing near a busy parking lot, they had the police change traffic flow. They also learned that a pack of wild dogs was free in the neighborhood and arranged for their destruction by the authorities. Immediately, the number of accident and dog bite victims decreased. But for most of the problems they could do little.

The steps they did take and the many more that were outside their power to take are not, of course, generally looked at as health measures, but that in no way lessens their health benefits. However, they are not included in my discussions of cost, because they normally appear in a part of the national budget different from that concerned directly with health. But whether or not such measures are pursued, and particularly when they are not, the poor urgently need programs in both therapeutic and preventive medicine. They need vaccines, prenatal care, health programs for the elderly, control of cigarettes, attention to diet, and the rest. Their need is greater, because many poor people have had little access to health education, and most have even less access to medical programs like those that Dr. Wendy Bates (in Chapter 2) initiated at Rosehill. As Dr. Bates discovered, some measures, like antibiotic treatment of tuberculosis, are helpful even for populations whose unhealthful living conditions are not otherwise changed. But, as she also learned firsthand, many medical programs make little difference in the absence of social change. In fact, she was already well acquainted with that conclusion from the observations of other doctors described in many medical articles. For example, one from the Southwest which is widely quoted showed that ready availability of doctors, nurses, and modern medical measures had little effect on the health of impoverished Indians when their living conditions were unchanged.

What would be the effects on the health of the nation of applying all that we know about disease prevention? Our society would have much less cancer, particularly of the lung, heart disease, stroke, and emphysema and other forms of lung disease. We would have many fewer deaths and injuries from automobile accidents and fewer suicides and homicides caused by handguns. Infant mortality rates would be reduced, as would the number of low-birth-weight babies. We would have less sexually transmitted disease, like gonorrhea, genital herpes, and AIDS.

We would have an even larger number of the elderly than is presently anticipated. Present projections are that the over-seventy-five-year-olds will quadruple—from 10 million in 1980 to 38 million in 2040. A larger fraction of this group would have less of the chronic illness of old age than at present.

But this world is far off, and not only because preventive measures receive less emphasis than they merit. Once again, a major stumbling block is the state of the art. Here, as with many other health issues, our knowledge of cause is still relatively primitive (as, for example, the reasons for the decline of stomach cancer). Further, we don't know how to apply effectively much of the information we do have about cause (as with teenage pregnancy, cancer, and heart attacks caused by cigarettes, or the trauma inflicted by handguns). The need is great for research, biological, social, and behavioral. That will be discussed further in the chapter that follows.

Where Prevention Saves Money ... And Doesn't

There is a widespread perception that preventive programs will save money. And many will. For example, a group from the Centers for Disease Control, the federal agency responsible for overseeing the measles immunization program, calculated that the first five years of the program led to the avoidance of almost 10 million cases of measles, averted more than 3,200 cases of mental retardation, and saved almost 1,000 lives. The cost of the program was just over $100 million. The net direct economic savings from averted doctor visits, hospitalization, and long-term care of those who would have been permanently disabled exceeded $275 million. Almost as great were what economists call indirect savings, which include earnings that would have been lost from work during the illness by victims of the disease or their guardians, and lifetime earnings of those killed or permanently severely disabled. As a result, one can calculate that in addition to the enormous benefit in human terms, there was a greater than fivefold dollar return on the cost of measles immunization, even in the early period when its effects were not yet fully felt.

Immunization against other childhood diseases, including rubella and whooping cough, has also been shown to be cost-saving. Fluoridation of the water supply saves very large sums of money, as a result of teeth that do not need filling or extraction. Testing for and then removing lead paint in urban neighborhoods where lead poisoning has been shown to be prevalent among children are also cost-saving. In other words, they save more money than would be used for treatment programs, if one waited for lead poisoning victims to come to the attention of the health authorities.

However, many people are surprised to learn that the cases cited are exceptional—that is, that most prevention programs whose economic costs have been examined don't save money. For example, programs designed to avoid the often life-threatening complications of high blood pressure cost more money than they save. Even in people with severe high blood pressure, the group that experiences the most impressive reduction in complications as a result of blood-pressure-lowering, only 20–25 percent of the cost of prevention programs is recovered in the form of savings from illnesses that are avoided. An important reason for this seeming paradox is that (fortunately) not every untreated person with high blood pressure suffers from complications or dies prematurely, or even has symptoms from the disease. But since no way is known to identify ahead of time those who will get sick, everybody with the condition should be treated. (This applies at least to those with diastolic blood pressure over 105; the evidence is still coming in with respect to people with elevations that are less marked.) That, in turn, means that the whole population should be screened to identify all persons at risk. Further, treatment of high blood pressure involves daily medication, often adherence to a diet, and periodic medical supervision. When a screening and prevention program is directed at a whole population and involves considerable cost, as is true in the case of high blood pressure and many other conditions, then that program may cost more money than is saved. In contrast, when the preventive measure in question is inexpensive, need be administered only once or a very few times, and requires little follow-up, as is the case for measles prevention and most other immunization programs, then the economic benefits may outweigh the costs, and often by far.

But even some forms of vaccination cost more than they save. For example, reference was made earlier to the importance of immunizing older people against pneumococcal pneumonia. If one restricted use of the pneumococcal vaccine to people over the age of sixty-five, the net cost (that is, the cost of immunizing the population involved minus the savings achieved by preventing pneumonia in that group) would be $1,000 per year of life saved, or even less. But suppose one immunized people between twenty-five and forty-four years of age, a group not at special risk and much better able to defend itself against the disease. Then, an enormous number of people would have to be vaccinated in order to save a life. Therefore, the cost per year of life saved would be much higher—$55,000 per year of life saved. Medicare does pay for immunization of people over sixty-five. On the other hand, such an investment would make little sense for the general population.

Periodic stool examination for traces of blood is useful as a means of detecting unsuspected cancer of the bowel. The test is simple and inexpensive. Nonetheless, it has been calculated that for every unknown cancer that turns up, $1,175 worth of examinations must be carried out. Infrequently, a cancer is found in an individual whose first stool examination is negative but whose second contains blood. The possibility of cancer becomes progressively less likely with each succeeding negative examination. Indeed, it has been calculated—largely as an exercise in cost-benefit measurement—that if one did repeated examinations on everybody in a population, then each cancer found as a result of a positive *sixth* test after *five* previous negative ones would cost $47 million. What is "worthwhile" thus becomes a question with an arbitrary answer. Most doctors recommend an examination of three stool samples annually for people over fifty years of age.

Intensive care units for newborns can save the lives of low-birth-weight babies. Their cost-effectiveness is sometimes measured by comparing their cost to the number of healthy years of life they salvage, that is, the number of babies who leave such units in good condition and who can look forward to a normal life expectancy. For newborns weighing between two and three pounds, such units have been calculated to cost $2,500 per year of life saved. Smaller babies are more difficult to treat and less likely to survive. Thus, the corresponding cost is $18,000 for newborns weighing between one and two pounds at birth. It has been shown, however, that every dollar spent on prenatal care would save more than $3 in remedial care after birth. This makes all the more shortsighted the cutbacks in the 1980s in government support of programs for maternal and child health care—programs that reduce the number of low-birth-weight babies, as well as decrease infant mortality and disabilities in children.

Programs in automobile safety involving mandatory air bags have cost-effectiveness ratios that are much more favorable—of the order of $2,000 per year of life. Many involving changes in the environment of the workplace are far more costly. For example, reducing by 90 percent the amount of benzene in the atmosphere of those places where the chemical is used would cost $6.6 million per year of life saved.

The elimination of cigarettes would save large sums of health care dollars in terms of averted illness and death. But these savings would be short term; the survival of former smokers and nonsmokers would soon mean an increased demand for care of the illnesses of the now larger population of elderly. The economic costs would also include revenues of about $6 billion lost to federal and state governments from tobacco taxes and the money required to retrain and place the large numbers of people who derive their incomes from tobacco growing and cigarette manufacture. Discussions of the economic consequences of removing cigarettes sometimes include reference to the greater demands on the Social Security system—estimated to be about $10 billion a year—that would result from the averted premature deaths. But this is not calculated as a cost of treatment with penicillin for what might otherwise be fatal pneumonia or of any other treatment program. It has no more relevance to discussions of the prevention of tobacco-related diseases or prevention of other health problems.

Cost-Effectiveness as a Criterion

Economic measurements, of course, do no more than tell us in very rough form what can be expected from specific investments. It is interesting that discussions of cost-effectiveness ratios are so often scrutinized when programs in prevention are considered. Our society does not ask that *treatment* programs save money as a condition of their adoption. Why apply different criteria in the evaluation of prevention programs? But in a time of growing resource constraints, when we cannot do all of both that is desirable, it will be useful to have as much information as possible about the costs and benefits of both.

For prevention, as well as for treatment and rehabilitation programs, we know how to do more than we are now doing. And for all three, we shall be able to do far more tomorrow than we can do today. For all three, resource constraints will force us to look more and more carefully at what we can expect in return for specific investments. It is important to have realistic projections. Estimates that as little as 4 percent of current health spending is for disease prevention and health promotion suggest that today's policymakers have not had recourse to such projections. In the prevention area, to take one example, such information may be one useful guide as to how much to commit to automobile safety and how much to protect against benzene in the workplace, if resources are not available to do as much of both as we might like.

With prevention programs, as with therapeutic, decisions will likely more often be made on the basis of a range of factors, including how the people affected look at investments. But here, as elsewhere, an increasingly important function of the health community will be to provide as much information as possible about effectiveness and costs. Then, at the very least, fewer surprises will result from the decisions that society takes.

If our hypothetical Jack Washington were a misanthrope, he would conceal the prevention story from as many of his acquaintances as possible. If he were diabolical, he would urge them to chain-smoke. Some preventive measures save health dollars, but more are costly, and all have demographic implications. The more Americans who survive to collect Social Security payments, the more insecure will be the Social Security system from which they will be paid. Nevertheless, the goal of the nation and its health care system is to keep all Americans in good health as long as possible. Our nation does not have the money to do all that it is capable of doing for the health of its people. Whenever choices must be made, effective prevention programs, including health education, will often prove better investments than more hospital facilities and the other expensive and imperfect technology used to treat lung cancer and other consequences of prevention failures.

10 Biomedical Research

Assume that you had been given a voice in three hypothetical budgetary decisions. The first was in England in 1880. You were asked to decide whether the very limited funds then available should be used to help feed malnourished children with advanced tuberculosis, or to support the research of a scientist interested in studying electrical current in the heart of a frog. The second setting was a small community in Germany about twenty years later. There the choice was whether to spend money to clean up the water supply at a time when large numbers of babies were dying of intestinal infections, or to finance research designed to develop a string galvanometer, an instrument for measuring electrical impulses generated by the human heart. Your third dilemma again occurred in Britain, but shortly after World War II. Then you were asked whether you would divert some of the funds needed for rebuilding war-damaged hospitals in favor of a research project to measure electrical currents in heart muscle cells with intracellular electrodes.

In those three situations, it would have been very difficult, and for some (me, for example) impossible, to have passed over the pressing social problems in favor of the research. But had those three projects (and many other basic inquiries without immediate or even likely relevance to health) been put aside, the development of open-heart surgery, treatment programs for hypertension, antibiotics, intensive care, and the prevention of poliomyelitis would have been at the least seriously delayed. That conclusion emerged from views expressed by a large number of experts consulted by Julius Comroe and Robert Dripps, two American physician-scientists, who, in 1976, traced the earlier research that led to those medical triumphs and five other major advances in the management of diseases that affect the heart or the lungs.

Kinds of Research: Distinctions and Overlaps

Among the questions asked by Comroe and Dripps was whether the research that was crucial to those developments was basic and whether it was clinical. They defined basic research as experimental or theoretical work undertaken not only to describe or measure natural events, but also to try to understand the mechanism of those events. Basic research is generally carried out without concern for the ultimate use to which the new information may be put. In contrast, applied research is also original research designed to obtain new knowledge, but directed at a specific practical objective. Development, which is often lumped together with research (as in R & D), is work that draws on research to produce or bring into use new or improved products or methods. Clinical research includes studies stimulated in any way by an interest in human disease on the part of the investigators. Biomedical research is concerned ultimately with the biological aspects of human health.

One example of basic research with a profound effect on medicine cited by Comroe and Dripps was the discovery by Roentgen of X rays, while he was studying a problem in physics. When Roentgen, a physicist, undertook his work, he had no reason to believe that it would ever have medical significance. But it has, of course, been among the most important contributions ever made to the diagnosis and treatment of disease. As an example of elegant applied, or mission-oriented, research (with, as it turned out, profound basic knowledge fallout), they cited the work of Pasteur, when he set out to learn how to prevent wine from turning to vinegar. In the process he discovered bacteria and started the science that established the relationship of germs to disease. Their example of development oriented to a medical need was the elaboration of methods for mass-producing penicillin.

More recent research that is simultaneously basic, applied, and clinical is that for which the 1985 Nobel Prize was awarded in medicine. As a result of a series of brilliant studies, Joseph Goldstein and Michael Brown have greatly increased understanding of how the body controls the production and disposal of cholesterol. Their work is an excellent example of *basic* research; it has probed many fundamental aspects of biochemistry, molecular biology, and genetics. It is *applied* research; it is directed specifically at cholesterol problems and particularly those involved in the development of atherosclerosis. And it is *clinical* research, for it was motivated in important measure by the researchers' concern for human disease, and much of it has been carried out on patients with various forms and degrees of atherosclerosis. Indeed, its clinical applications have been almost immediate. For example, it has led to methods for identifying in advance individuals who are at great risk for heart attacks and other complications of atherosclerosis.

Of the research projects that ultimately led to the ten major clinical advances studied by Comroe and Dripps, more than 60 percent were basic. Although all ultimately had important effects on clinical medicine, many were themselves not clinical in nature.

Applications

As well as demonstrating the crucial role of basic research, both clinical and nonclinical, in promoting the understanding and control of human disease, their survey points to the long delay that often occurs between a discovery and its application to problems in human health. For example, they traced the development of the electrocardiogram to many key research projects carried out in the eighteenth century. Similar observations were made in a 1968 study by others of the research that led to the development of the contraceptive pill, the electron microscope, and three other innovations. For each, much of the key work had been done thirty years before or earlier. Further, as in the study of the background work that made possible electrocardiography, most of the important path-breaking research was basic in nature, in these instances 70 percent.

But the speed with which recent developments in molecular biology and genetics have been translated into very practical terms, as in the case of the Goldstein and Brown work, indicates that the latent period is not invariably long. In fact, physicians with training in these fields now occupy faculty positions in clinical departments in the nation's leading medical schools and are using their combined backgrounds in medicine and science to seek greater understanding of the causes, treatment, and prevention of disease. Drs. Goldstein and Brown are notable examples of such medical researchers.

Biotechnology

The explosive growth of the field of biotechnology is additional evidence of the sometimes more rapid translation of biological theory into practical knowledge. Many of the concepts that underlie genetic engineering were developed in the 1960s, and some of the methods that are crucial in this field resulted from research in the 1970s.

Scientific publications almost regularly describe what biotechnology may bring to medicine (and to other fields, particularly agriculture). Consider a recent report about the ultimate fate of two children who had failed to grow because their own bodies did not make enough growth hormone. For several years they were among a group treated with human growth hormone prepared from pituitary glands, which are located in the brain. The glands were obtained at autopsy. The hormone treatment resulted in growth of the several people who received it, but it also proved, after a period of twenty years, fatal to two. They were found to have Creutzfeldt-Jakob disease, a degenerative disease that leads to progressive brain damage with dementia, similar in some ways to Alzheimer's disease. It is caused by a virus that is found in the brain and that may take twenty years to express itself. The virus must have been in the human brains from which the pituitary growth hormone was extracted. But since the cause of the disease was unknown when the hormone was prepared, no precautions could have been taken that would have avoided the eventual tragedy.

Today, pure growth hormone can be made by genetic engineering. It is completely free of viruses and similar contaminants, and one can say with confidence that it will not lead to such tragedies. Similar methods are in use to produce drugs that will be used in efforts to treat or prevent diseases ranging from the common cold to cancer. The products of biotechnology will be of growing importance not only to human health, but also to agriculture and many other commercial enterprises. A recent report from the Department of Commerce states that several hundred such firms now exist in the United States, and the worldwide market for their products could range from $40 billion to $100 billion by the end of the century.

Biotechnology rests on the results of basic research, much of which was carried out as recently as ten to twenty years ago and much without any notion of its potential commercial or clinical significance. Thus, the practical achievements of biotechnology are the more remarkable because it is so brief a time since the roots of the field were developing from a series of inquiries carried out in laboratories around the world primarily to address questions in fundamental biology. A primary goal of most of them was to help unlock the secrets of how the genetic material—DNA—reproduced itself and was translated in living cells.

Basic Science and Clinical Medicine

Basic science laboratories have served clinical medicine in more ways than providing knowledge that has had important clinical fallout. Since the end of World War II, they have trained many young physicians preparing for careers in academic medicine. There, aspiring medical researchers have steeped themselves in basic scientific theories and methods to apply to the study of human disease, after returning to their clinical departments. Simultaneously, they have been exposed to the rigorous discipline of scientific thinking. Perspectives obtained from such training have benefited medical practice and education, as well as research. In turn, interactions with medically trained people have stimulated many basic biologists to focus their thinking and often their research on medical problems brought to their attention by their clinical acquaintances. I am one of many medical scientists who profited greatly from such training.

In 1960, I took a leave of absence from my position in a department of medicine to spend a year in a laboratory of molecular biology. At that time my hospital responsibilities included the care of patients with cancer, and my research was directed at a search for differences between normal and cancer cells. Specifically, I was trying to learn more about the variations in growth patterns that distinguish normal from cancer cells. For example, when you cut yourself, the cells around the cut rapidly grow in to repair the defect. But when the area that has been cut is healed, the growth returns to its normal rate. Cancer cells, in contrast, seem unable to respect whatever the normal signals are; they multiply in uncontrolled fashion, and in the process grow over, around, or through normal cells, often destroying them. This is true of cancer cells growing in test tubes, as well as in patients. Along with many others, I thought that insights derived from such research might suggest ways to control cancer in patients.

Because there was so little information available about what caused normal cells to stop growing, I decided on a year in a research laboratory committed to questions of growth control. On the advice of B. L. Horecker, a distinguished biochemist who was my teacher and remains a close friend, I spent that year at the Pasteur Institute in Paris, where some of the work most seminal to molecular biology was going on.

It proved to be among the most exciting and intellectually rewarding years of my life. I was surrounded by a group of deeply committed, creative, and curious men and women who were asking of nature questions of fundamental importance. Almost all used bacteria as the subjects of their experiments. These single-celled organisms are among the simplest forms of life. They grow rapidly; under optimal growth conditions, many strains double their number in less than thirty minutes. Therefore, if one wants to determine whether, for example, a certain chemical will retard or speed growth, bacteria give answers overnight that in animals would take years. And since the machinery of life in bacteria is similar to that in higher forms, including humans, lessons learned from those simple cells are often broadly applicable. It was at once apparent that I was in an environment that might provide important leads to the cancer problem, and would surely give me new and invaluable ways of thinking about scientific questions of all kinds.

The ferment of the laboratory infused pure pleasure into the experiments that occupied every day and many evenings. My colleagues for the year were people as bright and imaginative and daring as any I had ever known. Their inquiries were directed at a vast unknown. A few years before, Watson and Crick had proved that genetic information is encoded in the DNA of living organisms. Now my new colleagues and others were asking in various ways how the genetic information is translated with almost perfect fidelity into the proteins of the cell, which include the cell's machinery. What controls the speed with which various life processes take place? How are those processes affected by environmental changes? Rarely, errors are made. How do they happen? What corrective steps are taken to compensate for them? The three senior scientists in the group, Jacques Monod, André Lwoff, and François Jacob were awarded the Nobel Prize in 1965 for work that was under way that year.

My immediate mentor was François Gros, an extraordinarily insightful scientist, whose brilliance was matched by his patience with my fumblings. (Several years later, after Monod's death, he would succeed him as head of Pasteur.) No laboratory bench was more than a few feet from a blackboard. And Monod's entry into our laboratory—at least once a day, sometimes more often—prompted everybody to put experiments on hold. First, a report, often from one of the younger scientists in the lab, of the results of yesterday's experiment. (I was more than slightly nervous, early in my third week, suddenly to be asked, *"Quoi de neuf, mon cher?"*) Monod's chalk recorded each crucial bit of new information on the blackboard, usually in a position that showed its place in the hierarchy of existing information. Then, a marvelous and often far-ranging discussion of how the new bit fit into current theory. Sometimes it didn't fit at all, and repetition of the experiment produced results that indicated error in the original observations. But sometimes it confirmed the original results; this led to reshaping the theory.

On occasion, in these forums, I would bring up certain aspects of the behavior of cancer cells. Those forays into the biology of cancer never failed to elicit fresh ways for me to think about the problem that had brought me to Pasteur. I found among my new colleagues what was often a shrewd sense of *what* questions to ask of nature and, equally important, an often uncanny instinct as to *when* to ask them. Trying to understand how to persuade a cancer cell to obey a stop-growth signal before identifying how normal cells respond to the signal, or even before knowing what that signal is, is like building the top floor of a house before the lower stories have been built or even planned. Motivation to find the answer to an important question is an essential part of good research. Knowing when to ask it is no less important.

My year at Pasteur Institute increased my respect for the role of basic science in the world of medical research. I returned confident that what was then called the New Biology would alter markedly the directions of my own research program and those of many others in the cancer field. But I had no idea that it would revolutionize biomedical (and other) science, and in a very few years.

New Knowledge and Knowledge Gaps

The research examined by Drs. Comroe and Dripps was restricted to work that led to major improvements in our ability to understand and treat diseases of the heart and lungs. Not surprisingly, parallel strides have taken place in other areas of medicine, as well. In 1980 Paul Beeson, who was for many years editor of one of the most widely used textbooks of medicine, compared the programs for treatment and prevention described for 362 conditions in the fourteenth edition of the book with those mentioned in the first edition, which had appeared almost fifty years earlier. These conditions include most of the frequently occurring and important illnesses for which a patient was then, or is now, likely to consult a doctor. They range from the common cold and bronchitis to diverse forms of cancer, gastrointestinal problems, and nervous ailments.

For only 3 percent of the 362 conditions did the 1927 edition describe prevention (examples: smallpox and scurvy) or cure (rickets and appendicitis). Appreciable help, but not cure, was available for another 3 percent. Beeson labeled useless or harmful the only measures, other than the physician's support to patient and family, then available for 60 percent of the conditions. By 1975, the time of the fourteenth edition, 22 percent of the same 362 conditions were curable or preventable. An additional 28 percent could be helped a great deal, while some useful steps were possible for an equal fraction. The fraction for which no specific medical measures existed was down to 22 percent.

These changes, the medical achievements of the past half-century, result from successful research. Among the most notable are the control of most of the infectious diseases of our country (but not most of those of the Third World), the treatment of diseases caused by too much or too little of the hormones of the body (for example, the thyroid, adrenal, and parathyroid glands), and the prevention or treatment of nutritional diseases. Many others have been mentioned elsewhere in this book. But they are only the barest beginnings of the job. Despite the promises of much that has been uncovered, the gaps are still very great in our understanding of virtually all of today's major diseases. Ways to treat more effectively or to prevent cancer, the complications of atherosclerosis, such as coronary heart disease and stroke, arthritis, emotional and mental diseases, mental deficiency, the many infirmities of aging, the neurological diseases—the list could be greatly lengthened, of course—do not merely await the assembling of the pieces of a set of puzzles. Far more pieces are missing than those that have been uncovered. Many that are missing will turn up in unexpected and unlikely places. Comroe and Dripps found this to be true of progress in heart and lung disease. History will surely have similar stories about progress in the control of diseases that now take the lives of many Americans and cause serious disability to so many more.

The best, perhaps the only, way to accelerate the appearance of missing pieces is to encourage the ablest people who are motivated and qualified to carry out basic research to pursue their interests and to help make it possible for them to do so. Fortunately, we are in a strong position to continue the basic research that is so necessary to the challenges before us, thanks in large part to the research enterprise built largely with enlightened federal support in the years following World War II. That support led to the growth of the National Institutes of Health (NIH) and the development of excellent biomedical research programs. Some of the scientists responsible for those programs were trained at the Bethesda, Maryland, campus of the NIH and at universities which derived financial support for their training programs from the NIH. Important research has been carried out both at the NIH and at universities around the country and around the world with NIH support. Viewed from any perspective, the NIH represents one of the great achievements of our own or any other nation.

Scientists now have insights into many fundamental areas that were mysteries just a few years ago. Most have emerged as a result of basic research and many with NIH support. These insights permit more informed questions about the serious diseases that surround us. For example, information uncovered concerning cell growth is used to guide scientists looking for disturbances in cancer cells that are responsible for their unrestrained growth. That, in turn, may ultimately help devise ways to control cancer.

Genes have already been moved experimentally from one animal to another. Thus, the prospect of replacing defective or absent genes in humans is no longer in the realm of science fiction. People with hemophilia, to take one example of a genetic disease, are subject to severe hemorrhages, which can be fatal in the absence of treatment. Bleeding occurs because their cells lack the information to make one of the plasma proteins that is essential for clotting of the blood. In principle, that information can be provided by inserting into the cells of the hemophilic patient the gene that contains instructions as to how to make the protein in question. Similarly, a number of other genetically transmitted diseases can be expected to be amenable one day to what is now termed gene therapy. Such approaches have raised ethical questions concerning manipulation of genes. Thoughtful people from many fields are now involved in considering those questions and a range of other ethical, legal, and philosophical issues raised by the powers of the "new medicine."

The study of the brain and the rest of the nervous system has in recent years attracted a growing number of creative scientists. As a result, an area that was very poorly understood just a few years ago is now giving up many of its secrets. Chemists, geneticists, molecular biologists, biophysicists, pharmacologists, and experts from many other disciplines have joined in these efforts. Some of the insights that are emerging already have clinical applications. For example, areas of the brain thought to be involved in Parkinson's disease were shown to have a deficiency of dopamine, a hormone in nervous tissue that is important in the transmission of nerve impulses. That was followed by the successful use of L-dopa, a dopamine compound, as treatment for patients with Parkinsonism. Many victims of depression and schizophrenia can be helped with drugs that have been recently developed. More scientists are turning to studies of the nature of Alzheimer's and other diseases of the nervous system.

Immunology is a field that has seen extraordinary advances. Here, perhaps even more than in other areas, the advance of knowledge has been accompanied by clinical applications. The transplantation of kidneys, bone marrow, hearts, livers, and other organs followed the elucidation of differences in tissues from one individual to another and the development of techniques for dealing with the barriers to transplantation that those differences create. In 1984, the Nobel Prize was awarded for the work that led to the production of monoclonal antibodies. Antibodies are the proteins that certain cells in each of us manufacture when they encounter foreign proteins. Techniques for the production of large quantities of each of these antibodies in pure form (monoclonal) may make possible the development of highly specific methods for diagnosing and possibly treating cancer and many other diseases.

Much of this work is now being carried out in universities. But in the future a substantial fraction, particularly that aimed at more immediate application, will be done by the growing number of private biotechnology and other companies. Unexpected benefits, as in Pasteur's work, emerge from applied research as well as from basic. Vincristine, an important cancer chemotherapy drug, is obtained from the periwinkle plant, and was first discovered because it was thought that extracts of the plant lowered blood sugar. Researchers looking for drugs to control the high blood sugar of diabetes found that it did not have the expected effect on sugar, but that it depressed white blood cell production. This suggested that it might be effective in patients with leukemia, a cancer of the blood characterized by the overproduction of white blood cells. The drug was found to benefit many patients with leukemia and with certain other cancers, like Hodgkin's disease, as well. Here is a situation where, as Pasteur put it, chance favored the prepared mind. What our society—the public sector, the private, and universities—must do is to continue to help those who wish to prepare their minds, and then provide them access to chance.

AIDS: Background for Progress

The unfolding story of the acquired immune deficiency syndrome (AIDS) epidemic, which is now sweeping much of the world, illustrates in several ways the importance of research to health. The advances in molecular biology and genetics of recent decades made possible the discovery that a virus causes the disease. A particularly important lead was provided by studies of a virus that causes leukemia in cats. Much of the cat work was carried out in the 1970s, before AIDS was even recognized. The scientists responsible could not have known then (or even now) of all the benefits their research would bring in terms of human health. They knew they were asking important questions about the mechanisms of an important problem. The agencies that provided financial support knew that the work was of high quality. They could not predict, however, where and when any new discoveries might be useful.

As it turned out, the cat leukemia virus and the virus that causes AIDS are similar. Knowledge and methods obtained from the cat research helped identify the AIDS virus and likely much sooner than would otherwise have been the case. It was hoped that isolating the AIDS virus would make possible the development of a vaccine. However, the AIDS virus frequently mutates, that is, makes subtle changes in certain of its components, including the proteins in its coat. In contrast, many viruses, such as those that cause measles and polio, are quite stable in their constituents. Therefore, a vaccine prepared with the virus that causes today's case of measles or polio will lead to the production of antibodies against certain proteins of the corresponding virus. These antibodies provide immunity against the proteins of that virus and thus against the virus itself and infection with the virus. In contrast, some viruses like influenza undergo changes from year to year in some of the proteins to which people develop antibodies. This means that a vaccine prepared from the flu virus that caused last year's epidemic would lead to the production of antibodies that will neutralize the proteins of that virus and, therefore, would protect against another infection with it. But the vaccine would likely be of limited effectiveness against the slightly transformed virus responsible for next year's epidemic.

Despite the rapid growth of knowledge about the AIDS virus and the disease it causes, scientists remain pessimistic about prospects for a vaccine or effective treatment in the near future. Meanwhile, AIDS continues to spread rapidly—more than 80,000 Americans had contracted the disease and more than half of those had died of it by the end of 1988. Between 1 and 2 million Americans, half as many Europeans, and perhaps 10 times as many Africans were infected with the virus. More than half, and perhaps all of them, were expected to get and die of the disease.

Clues that will lead to the development of a vaccine or of a drug against AIDS may come from the growing amount of research now going on in the AIDS field. But it may well come from seemingly unrelated basic research. The AIDS story, like many others, tells us that we must encourage the search to extend the horizons of knowledge in the biomedical sciences.

Health Problems and the Social Sciences

However important the continuation of a strong effort in basic biomedical research, it is clearly not sufficient to deal adequately with many of the health problems that confront the nation today. Control of the AIDS epidemic cannot await the development of vaccines and effective drugs. It is urgent that we use existing methods of prevention, while seeking new ones. We know that the principal methods of AIDS transmission are rectal intercourse among homosexual men and the use of contaminated syringes or needles by people taking intravenous drugs. The danger of AIDS transmission appears to have led to behavioral changes in some people. However, the limited success of this kind of health education is one more reflection of the need for rigorous programs of research in the social and behavioral sciences.

The diseases caused or aggravated by smoking are another obvious focus for considering the potential health benefits of more research in the social sciences. Many smokers are physically addicted to tobacco. Therefore, the biology of addiction is one important avenue for research on tobacco and health. But that doesn't tell us what effective measures might be taken to prevent children from beginning the habit and thereby from becoming addicted. Research on the social and behavioral aspects of the problem is also important for clinically useful information on many other of today's major threats to health. For example, success has been limited in persuading people who have high blood pressure, yet who feel well, that it is in their interest to take medication every day. The number of "easy" weight reduction schemes says that millions of overweight people are interested in losing weight, but are unable to translate that interest into effective and continuing weight control. Consider how poorly we now deal with such major health problems as many kinds of accidents, alcohol abuse, and drug addiction.

Research Priorities

I will mention only in passing the need for statisticians, economists, and other social scientists to work with physicians in evaluating the effectiveness of medical interventions. Chapter 11 takes up this major issue in detail. It is encouraging to note the attention now being given to medical research by large numbers of professionals from the statistical sciences. Medical practice is already profiting greatly from this trend. For example, cardiologists are working with statisticians and epidemiologists to sort out the factors responsible for the more than 30 percent drop in deaths from coronary artery disease in the past twenty years. As mentioned earlier, treatment programs have contributed to the improvement, but their role is less important than that of other factors, such as changes in smoking habits, diet, and exercise. Such information could provide guidance to decision makers obliged to divide scarce funds: How much should be put into epidemiologic research, how much into new coronary care facilities, and how much into attempting to extend the various preventive measures that can be shown to play a role? Other questions relating to the allocation of scarce health resources would also benefit greatly from more interdisciplinary research of this sort.

Research differently motivated and based to a considerable extent on engineering and the social sciences—designed to rehabilitate and to make life more comfortable—is required to help people with illnesses that cannot be cured or prevented. The number of people with such needs is increasing as our population grows older. Included are people with chronic illnesses, both physical and mental, and the mentally handicapped. Their needs range from better methods of pain relief, to better technology to compensate for difficulties in hearing, vision, and locomotion, to better ways to live alone when necessary or desired.

The Department of Health and Human Services now publishes periodic assessments of the nation's health needs and goals. They can be very useful guides to health research policies. Successful mission-oriented research also requires realistic appraisals of the state of basic knowledge, for they can help direct the application of relevant knowledge to health problems. For example, if information were recently uncovered that provided leads to the earlier diagnosis of diabetes or better treatment of kidney disease, it should be put to work promptly. Such appraisals are also important to help ensure that mission-oriented research is not begun prematurely—that is, before we have the basic guidelines that make application feasible. Some appraisals in the past may have been influenced by inappropriate optimism. For example, the "war on cancer" begun in the early 1970s was supported enthusiastically by American political leaders and private citizens. Many of them assumed that control of the disease would follow in a relatively few years the commitment of added funds. More than a decade and several billion dollars later, much important cancer research has been carried out, and some extraordinary insights have emerged. Most patients with cancer, however, still cannot be cured. Thus, some expectations have not been fulfilled. Perhaps partly as a result, a mood of skepticism with respect to research now exists among some Americans.

Possibly even more important, premature diversion of resources from basic research to applied can be harmful to the very field that one is attempting to favor. An example from the cancer field strengthens this point. One of the few truly new effective anticancer drugs since the beginning of the war on cancer is cisplatin. The drug was discovered by Barnett Rosenberg, a physicist who was interested in the effects of electrical currents on cell division in bacteria. Working in a department of biophysics—unconnected to any unit concerned with cancer or any other aspect of health—he found that bacteria were discouraged from dividing when he turned the current on. But he found that the inhibition was *not* the result of the current. Rather, he had been generating current with platinum electrodes, and the platinum had undergone a slight degree of decomposition. The products of the decomposed platinum included cisplatin, a seemingly new compound, which interfered with the ability of cells to reproduce themselves. That "new" compound, the physicist subsequently learned, had first been made in 1845. Pursuing his observations, he found that cisplatin inhibited not only bacteria but animal cells, as well. This, in turn, led to a series of tests against cancers in animals and finally human cancer, and the compound proved to be effective against several forms of cancer in people.

Cisplatin was discovered by a scientist who was not doing cancer research. Had the funds that made his first work possible been directed toward a search for anticancer drugs and away from the basic research on which he was engaged, cisplatin would likely not be among the drugs now available for cancer chemotherapy.

Support for Research

In today's climate of belt tightening, money for one research program often means less for others. For example, in 1985, the Reagan Administration committed more funds to AIDS research by reducing support for research in other areas. Additional money for AIDS was—and is—urgently needed, and most scientists endorsed the commitment of more funds to search for ways to control this disease. But one can name many conditions, including AIDS and cancer, whose long-term control would probably be set back if money were diverted from basic research to *premature* applied work.

This raises questions as to how the quality and direction of research are judged. Whatever its achievements, nobody would suggest that all basic research is first-rate or that all basic researchers are gifted. How was it known that the group of people who contributed so much to the development of the New Biology merited the generous support from government and private sector that made their work possible? Now, with ever more severe limits on resources and the growing number of important uses to which those resources could be put, it is the more important that they be used optimally. How does one measure excellence in science, basic and applied, clinical and nonclinical? How does one decide what fields to support? Who should get more, who less, and who none of a finite budget? To deal with those questions, our society has come to rely heavily on the peer-review system—distinguished scientists in each field are called upon to pass judgment on the quality and the promise of the work of their colleagues. They must be answerable to the society that supports them, of course. And they are obligated to share their findings and their thinking with their colleagues and with society. The peer-review system, like other systems in our democracy, has shortcomings. But nobody has as yet demonstrated anything better for judging scientific merit.

When money is in short supply, pressures are great to "economize" by reducing total support for research and often for basic research. From 1970 to 1980, inflation-adjusted figures indicate that funds for biomedical research in the United States increased at a rate of 3.3 percent per year. Throughout that period per capita support for biomedical research was greater in Switzerland and Sweden than in the United States. From 1980 to 1985 basic biomedical research funds in our nation increased from $5.5 billion to $7.8 billion, but overall spending for all nondefense-related research was held constant at about $16 billion. That means that the increase in basic biological research was at the expense of some other natural sciences and, even more, of social sciences and applied research and development programs. During the same period, funds for defense-related research and development activities were increased from $17.8 billion to $35 billion, and this before the huge commitment to research on Star Wars.

Limitations in our capacity to deal with most of today's most serious diseases constitute a compelling reason to preserve the biomedical research enterprise we now have and to strengthen our health-oriented social and engineering sciences capabilities. The fragility of such activities is hinted at when we read in the most authoritative scientific journal of the United Kingdom the editorial view that the British biomedical research enterprise, not so long ago comparable to our own, "is on its last legs." Sir Hans Kornberg, one of Britain's most distinguished scientists, ascribes in part the shrinkage of government support that is partly responsible to a "public disenchantment with science and the realization that basic support does not immediately lead to economic benefit."

How to Ensure Research Support

Will the United States learn from what is now going on in Britain? The public and the decision makers do turn frequently to science and health leaders for guidance with respect to policy issues. Those leaders have, as a result, obligations as well as privileges. The obligations include making the persuasive case for the importance to health of research—both applied and basic. They also involve, of course, presenting to the public and their representatives realistic appraisals as to what can reasonably be expected from various investments.

Let us return now to the hypothetical resource allocation questions of

Britain and Germany in earlier periods that were posed at the beginning of this chapter. Whatever the actual mechanisms, resources were then found to support research, despite the enormous existing social needs, and our generation is the healthier as a result. If we accept the fact that we owe to ourselves and to future generations continued support of basic research and of applied research, both biomedical and social, then how will *we* provide for it in a climate of increasingly constrained resources?

More and more difficult choices will be before us, particularly with expanding demands for funds. If the choices are made on an ad hoc basis and by those with immediate responsibility for meeting the pressing health needs of our citizens, the decisions will have to favor saving life and meeting immediate health needs. But the price could easily be neglect of research and particularly basic research. This is a price society cannot afford, in the long or even the short run.

Clearly, then, we must plan ahead for situations in which explicit choices have to be made in the presence of the pressing needs for medical care, which will continue to surround us and are likely to grow. Further, it is unfair to force those choices on the individuals with immediate responsibility—for example, the physician caring for a patient or the politician confronted by the parents of a sick or a hungry child—for addressing those immediate needs.

I believe that our advance planning process must provide *arbitrarily* for research. There is surely no magic formula that will satisfy all constituencies, or even any single one, all of the time. I see no better approach than to set aside—explicitly for health-related research—a constant fraction of the total resources we allocate for health. Then, just as the allocations for medical care can be apportioned among the areas of need—for the elderly, the children, the poor, and so on—so public research funds can be divided in the fashion thought to be most effective. It seems to me in the national interest, short-term and long, that a substantial fraction be set aside for basic research. It is also in our interest that the fraction be predictable and dependable. The starts and stops associated with grants that are not funded, or are funded late or after lapses, take many gifted scientists away from the work that they want to be doing and we should want them to do. In this country we are fortunate that private philanthropy can address unusual or unorthodox areas of research opportunity that may be passed over by public bodies. However, it is not reasonable to leave to the private sector responsibility for support of the major share of the nation's health research and development budget. In 1970, the federal share of our total R & D budget was 59 percent. By 1985 this fraction had fallen to 53 percent. A reversal of this trend should be given high priority.

In 1980 total funding in the United States for biomedical research was $19.95 per capita or about 1.9 percent of total health expenditures. If we were to add to that an additional 1 percent for biomedical research and health-related research in the social and engineering sciences, that would make a total of about 3 percent a year for research of all kinds in the health area. The formula might stipulate further that no less than one third be for basic research and no less than two thirds for overall biomedical research. The amount is large, but much less than what many industrial companies consider necessary to insure their future. We owe no less to the future of our health.

11 Technology Assessment: How to Improve Medical Care and Sometimes Save Money

Imagine the introduction of a drug that is believed by responsible doctors to help many patients with severe heart disease. It has major hazards; indeed, it is fatal to more than 5 percent of people. Further, the drug causes so much blood loss that every patient who takes it requires six to eight pints of transfused blood. In addition, a course of treatment with the new drug is extremely expensive—more than $10,000, including associated costs. Imagine also that the drug is widely disseminated; more than 35,000 people are treated with it each year at a total annual cost of $350 million. All this goes on for several years before the drug is approved—or even subjected to study—by a recognized authoritative organization.

The scenario is, of course, hard to visualize, because a drug is involved. Our drug laws are very stiff and require exhaustive testing under carefully prescribed conditions and approval by the Food and Drug Administration before any new one can be released for general use. No such legal restrictions exist, however, for operations or diagnostic procedures. As a result, the above state of affairs can and does exist in America when the innovation involves not a new drug or device, but an operation.

Coronary artery bypass graft surgery is the "drug" in the hypothetical situation described above. In fact, that situation is hypothetical only in that the intervention was a new surgical operation, not a new drug. In all other respects, the story is accurate.

It is estimated that over 250,000 Americans had undergone the operation in hundreds of hospitals throughout the country before the results of the first controlled study of its effectiveness were published in medical journals in 1977. As experience developed, the operation was shown to be effective in a large fraction—although by no means all—of the patients subjected to it. Further, as a result of the skills—both in judging who is suitable for the operation and who is not and in carrying out the operation—that evolve with experience with every new practice, the mortality rate has fallen dramatically to less than 1 percent. The need for blood transfusions has also dropped greatly—two pints are now used for most patients in many centers. But even now, great variations exist among hospitals and doctors in who is considered an appropriate candidate for the operation.

On many other occasions, however, widely used procedures have ultimately been shown to be completely ineffective and have been abandoned. For example, gastric freezing was used by many doctors as a treatment for people with ulcers of the stomach or small intestine. The technique involved the passage of chilled alcohol through a tube into a balloon placed in the stomach. Ulcer disease is noteworthy for its variability. It can light up—without apparent reason—and persist for weeks, months, or years. But it can also disappear for equally mysterious reasons and remain quiescent for shorter or longer periods, or permanently. After the first "successes" with gastric freezing were publicized, the procedure rapidly spread. More than 2,500 machines used for circulating the cold fluid through the stomach were sold, and many thousands of patients were subjected to the treatment. The cost was great in money. It was considerable in human terms as well, because complications did occur, for example, bleeding from the stomach. It soon became apparent that patients undergoing gastric freezing did improve, but about as often as other ulcer patients who were not treated. In fact, by the time that the results of the first controlled clinical trial showed the procedure to be without benefit, it had already been largely abandoned.

Had the new ulcer treatment been a drug, the event would probably never have happened. As stated, new drugs are subjected to a series of carefully controlled studies, the results of which must be approved by the federal government's Food and Drug Administration before the drugs can be marketed. Generally, only if the animal studies that precede human trials—if an animal model exists for the disease in question—are convincingly positive can clinical studies move forward. This process can be cumbersome (more so, some believe, than is necessary). It is considered by many to slow down the development of new drugs, but overall, its benefits—in terms of protection of the public—are thought by most people to be worth that disadvantage.

Stories similar to the gastric freezing experience continue to the present. A 1985 medical report concerned an operation that was thought to lessen the chance of strokes in people with atherosclerosis of the arteries that nourish the brain. It is called extracranial-intracranial arterial bypass and was introduced in 1967. It was carried out in the United States and in many other countries throughout the world before it had been carefully evaluated. Then, in 1977, a careful trial was begun involving more than 1,300 people who had previously experienced one or more minor strokes. Half of the patients were treated with the most effective medications and other nonsurgical measures known. The rest were given similar treatment and, in addition, underwent the operation. When the study was finished eight years later, it was clear that the patients who had been operated on did no better than those who received only medical treatment.

Unfortunately, the annals of medicine contain many such examples of interventions widely adopted before they were finally abandoned. These were not procedures overtaken by better ones. That is what one strives for in medicine. Rather, they were practices that were shown to be without any medical benefit, but only after they had been widely used. Bloodletting and the application of leeches are well-known examples from another era. But in this century we have seen equally ineffective interventions. Some involved relatively little risk, such as removal of all the teeth in a search for the hidden infections that were once thought to cause a variety of persistent problems, including sore arms in major league baseball pitchers and chronic arthritis. But many "treatments" were very dangerous and some life-threatening. Consider the treatment of epilepsy by removal of a part of the large intestine; the treatment of asthma by major neurosurgery in which fibers of the sympathetic nervous system were cut; treatment of the fluid that accumulates in the abdomen in certain diseases by creating small holes in the peritoneal membrane that covers the organs of the abdomen; x-ray treatment for enlargement of the thymus gland in infants and children and for acne; and removal of the adrenal glands as treatment for high blood pressure. All of these procedures carried great risks of death and serious disability.

Their advocates often included thoughtful and influential medical leaders. Recall that a Nobel Prize was awarded in 1949 for prefrontal lobotomy, which involved major brain surgery and which was widely used at the time to "treat" schizophrenia and other mental illnesses. What is now called psychosurgery is still practiced, but it is much more restricted than in the early years after its introduction. In this instance, as in the others, a new procedure was widely adopted without first having been rigorously evaluated. In general, the more resistant a disease to available treatments and the more spontaneous the changes in its manifestations, the easier it was to associate an intervention with the improvement that sometimes followed. Only later was the improvement shown to have been independent of the procedure in question.

Many of today's most common problems, both medical and surgical, are almost universally managed in ways that were inadequately evaluated at the time they were introduced. One such medical intervention is the treatment for patients with heart attacks. The custom twenty-five years ago was to keep such people on strict bed rest for six weeks. Comparative studies over the period since led to progressive reduction in the period of enforced bed rest to four weeks to three weeks to two weeks and then, in the late 1970s, to one week. Indeed, a study by English physicians showed no difference in survival for patients with uncomplicated heart attacks treated at home, as compared with a hospitalized group.

With respect to surgical treatments, radical mastectomy was the almost universal treatment for women with breast cancer from the time of its introduction at the turn of the century until a few years ago. Then, carefully controlled studies showed that removal of the breast alone cured as many women as did the much more destructive procedure of removing the breast and much of the underlying and surrounding tissue. Even more recent studies of early breast cancer suggest that cutting out the cancer alone, while preserving the surrounding normal breast, or radiation treatment after only a biopsy, may cure as many women as removal of the entire breast.

In contrast, some new technologies have been subjected to careful study at an early stage and then disseminated or restricted, depending on the findings. An example of the first was an investigation of antenatal screening by amniocentesis in several hospitals. This procedure involves sampling the fluid that nourishes the fetus while it is in the pregnant woman's uterus. Cells from the fluid can help identify serious abnormalities in the fetus, such as Down's syndrome, and may lead to decisions to interrupt the pregnancy or to take precautionary measures immediately after birth. Only after the benefits of amniocentesis were shown to outweigh its risks did it spread to other centers.

On the other hand, a scientific study of a proposed new and expensive method for treating patients with serious problems in breathing, so-called extracorporeal membrane oxygenation, showed it to save no more lives than existing, less costly methods of treatment. As a result, while it is still being studied, it has not been made generally available.

Why the Problem?

Few medical interventions are as decisive in their benefits and have as few side effects as penicillin and polio vaccine. It took little time to show that penicillin cured scarlet fever and syphilis and relatively rarely produced harmful side effects. One major trial (but one that was carefully planned and executed) demonstrated the wonders of the polio vaccine. In contrast, the effects of most new measures are not nearly so dramatic nor so much better than existing ones. As a result, most progress in medicine takes place in very small forward steps. Many of those steps require painstaking observation often over long periods of time in large numbers of people, in order to be certain that the direction is, in fact, forward, and that their benefits outweigh whatever complications may occur. Add to this the economic, ethical, legal, and other issues that often arise, and the complexities of evaluating medical interventions are apparent. Therefore, it is less surprising than may appear on the surface that so little comprehensive evaluation has been carried out.

Syphilis: Spontaneous Cures

High on the list of factors that make evaluation so difficult is the limitation in our understanding of the natural history of many diseases—that is, what happens in the absence of any treatment. For example, until thirty years ago it was almost universally assumed that a patient with untreated syphilis was doomed to a disastrous end as a result of such complications as severe mental disease, disabling disease of the nervous system, serious heart and vascular disease, or combinations of these and other effects. As a result, treatment was considered mandatory, even though in the preantibiotic era it entailed great risk. Then, in 1955, a Norwegian doctor named Gjestland published a follow-up study of a large number of patients with untreated syphilis. They had been hospitalized early in this century by another Norwegian doctor who believed that the benefits of the then-available drugs were not worth the great risks involved in their use. As a result, he kept patients with syphilis in the hospital during the contagious stage of their disease and then discharged them untreated. Of this group Dr. Gjestland found that 85 percent lived a normal life span and that 70 percent died without any residual evidence of the disease. (Think of the honors that medical investigators in the early part of the century might have won, had they described a treatment for syphilis that cured 70 percent of its victims, offered a normal life expectancy to an additional 15 percent, and produced absolutely no side effects!)

With the advent of penicillin and other antibiotics, the risks of syphilis treatment are now minimal, and antibiotic therapy is, of course, mandatory for everybody with active disease. However, many other illnesses for which treatments are risk-laden also have natural histories that are not fully appreciated. In the absence of such information, conclusions concerning the effectiveness of interventions are necessarily uncertain. Recall that failure to consider carefully the unpredictable aspects of the natural history of ulcer disease helps explain the gastric freezing story told earlier.

Records: Unreliable or Uncoordinated

Another factor that makes evaluation difficult is the discontinuity of medical care for many Americans. The resulting difficulties in accurate medical record keeping often confound efforts to establish cause and effect. For example, the prevention of recurrent bouts of sore throats in children is generally the goal of tonsillectomy. To be certain of the effects of the operation, however, one would have to follow and record carefully observations in large numbers of children before and after surgery, and in control groups of others treated only with antibiotics like penicillin for bacterial tonsillitis. But careful studies show that mothers of young children are often inaccurate in their recollections of, for example, the number of sore throats per year in the few years before and after tonsillectomy. As a result, inquiries that depend heavily on the mother's memory may show benefit from the operation when no such benefit actually occurs. Carefully controlled studies recently carried out indicate that in a few cases of very severe, recurrent tonsillitis tonsillectomy may have benefit. But in most cases, treatment with antibiotics is at least as effective, much less hazardous and painful, and less expensive. That conclusion, however, is still not universally accepted by physicians. As a result, several hundred thousand tonsillectomies continue to be carried out each year. In part this is also because most record systems are unsophisticated by the standards of modern data management and, therefore, inadequate for proper evaluation of medical technology.

Until recently most physicians have practiced alone or as part of relatively small groups. Even specialists see relatively few patients who have been treated in a variety of ways. Unless their experience with their patients is merged with that of others, it is lost to efforts to achieve an overview of a new (or an existing) approach to a medical problem. I have elsewhere mentioned the 250,000 Americans who were treated with coronary bypass graft surgery in multiple centers throughout the nation *before* the results of careful trials had been collected and published in medical journals. Suppose the records of those patients (with proper protection of privacy) had been part of a national data system and, as a result, available to doctors who were studying the results of the operation. Then an ongoing national analysis of all patients subjected to the then-new operation might have led to much earlier evaluation of bypass surgery.

Ethical and Legal Dilemmas

Another obstacle has been the ethical and legal problems that confront physicians who wish to act on their doubts about widely accepted modes of practice. Those who challenged the conventional wisdom that radical mastectomy was the best therapy for breast cancer, for example, had the ethical dilemma of exposing their patients to a form of treatment considered by a large majority of their colleagues to be inferior. And since the cure rate for breast cancer with any form of treatment is far less than 100 percent, they might have risked legal action if their patient had proved to be in the group not cured (and, as we now know, not curable by any available measure). Both of these considerations add further emphasis to the importance of careful evaluation *before* widespread acceptance.

Extra-Medical Input

It is apparent that comprehensive evaluation of medical technology requires not only physicians, but a range of other professionals as well. Statisticians, epidemiologists, economists, decision scientists, lawyers, ethicists, sociologists, managers—these are some of the experts who can contribute important information. Until recently, the health field attracted few such people. Happily, that situation is now changing, and highly trained professionals from many disciplines are turning their attention to health problems.

Patients' Personal Values

Lay persons too should become acquainted with the importance of evaluation of medical interventions. This is necessary, for many decisions that ultimately belong to the patient—examples: "Should my child be operated on for enlarged tonsils?" "Should I choose surgery or radiation as treatment for my breast cancer?"—involve summing up costs, risks, and benefits, but involve much more. What is often required after the scientific facts are in hand and fully discussed and understood are value judgments: "I am, or I am not, prepared to see what penicillin does this year for the tonsillitis attacks before turning to surgery." "I am willing to spend the six extra weeks of radiation treatment to keep my breast"; or "I would prefer to have the treatment phase behind me as soon as possible, even if it means having my breast removed."

These last are not judgments based on medical or scientific grounds. They are value judgments that doctor and patient, indeed two doctors or two patients, often make quite differently, even when provided identical information. This emerged in a study carried out in a group of normal volunteers who were interviewed about what form of treatment they would choose if they were found to have a certain kind of cancer of the larynx, or voice box. In about 60 percent of patients with that kind of cancer, surgery leads to long-term survival and the loss of normal speech. Only about half as many patients survive when x-ray treatment is used instead of surgery, but normal or nearly normal speech is preserved. About 20 percent of the volunteers indicated that they would prefer radiation—that is, they would accept the reduced chances for survival in order to preserve their voices. Although one's ultimate decision may differ when one is confronted with the problem itself, other evidence supports the view that emerged here—different people make very different choices, even when the tradeoff is in quality of life or life itself.

Funding Problems

Yet another barrier to technology assessment has been inadequate funding. One reason is that the costs of individual evaluations are often high. Another is that many groups—government and private—pay for medical care. Therefore, any resulting financial benefits are widely diffused. For example, the last major study of coronary bypass graft surgery, which was financed by the federal government, is estimated to have cost $26 million. That study indicated that more than 25,000 patients now undergoing such surgery each year have the kind of coronary disease that would do at least as well with medical measures. If that information were translated into medical practice, it is estimated that the savings to the nation could exceed $500 million annually. The financial beneficiaries would be many— the federal government (Medicare pays for many of the operations), for-profit and not-for-profit health insurance groups, industry, individuals, etc.

Because no single group considers itself primarily responsible, no group leads the way in funding the next such study, which might lead to even more savings. Meanwhile, the group primarily concerned, the patients who are unnecessarily operated on, lack the advocate they need.

Dissemination Lag

Finally, a few words on a closely related problem, that of translating the results of the evaluation process into medical practice. In the early 1970s cancer was first discovered in young women whose mothers had received diethylstilbestrol (DES) during pregnancy because it was believed to prevent miscarriages. Eighteen years earlier, a large study had demonstrated that the drug had no such preventive effect, but some physicians continued to prescribe it. Thus, some of the women who have developed vaginal cancer were exposed *after* the causative agent had been shown to lack the very action for which it had been prescribed.

Another example: For years after careful studies in medical journals reported criteria for safe discharge from the hospital of low-birth-weight infants, many doctors continued to keep them hospitalized for much longer than was warranted—until they reached an arbitrarily set weight. The resultant cost was huge in hospital days and therefore in both dollars and the risks associated with hospitalization. Many other instances can be cited of marked delays in adapting medical practice to lessons that the evaluation process had taught.

The Need Today

Medical reasons for comprehensive evaluation of both new and existing procedures continue to be compelling. Every intervention, no matter how seemingly small, entails risks. There is no such thing, for instance, as a "routine" test. Whether the benefits that the intervention may produce warrant the risks requires a judgment on the part of doctor and patient that can be rationally made only if the facts are fully laid out. Growing economic constraints in the health field make evaluation ever more important, for we confront a climate in which we can't afford all the useful things we know how to do. Therefore, information is needed to help eliminate practices that are of no value, and that displace worthwhile interventions. In addition, we are now at a point where we should know how to rank in order useful interventions, so as to help us make rational choices among them. This will be progressively more important as budgets get tighter. Let us assume, for example, that the Congress were to set the Medicare budget for next year at a level just below that for the current one. In deciding what to cut, policymakers, doctors, and the public would find it useful to know the returns—in lives saved and in lives improved—on the various investments that might be made with the last available dollars: heart transplants, cataract operations, nursing home care, or others. Such information is sought in the relatively new area of research in the health field called medical technology assessment.

"Technology" Defined

Used in this context, "technology" refers to the broad range of equipment, drugs, and procedures employed in the care of people. It includes the facilities and personnel required for medical interventions, as well as the interventions themselves. The assessment process refers to evaluations not only of the effectiveness and safety of the intervention, but also of its costs, research value, effects on medical care in general, as well as of its ethical, legal, and social implications. Thus, comprehensive technology assessments of heart transplantation, a heart disease prevention program, and an approach to more effective management of low-birth-weight infants, just to mention three important activities, would lay out in as much detail as possible the costs, risks, and benefits that could be anticipated from each investment. They would tell us of the problems—ethical, legal, and social— that each might entail. Finally, they would guide us in rationally dividing resources among them, if we could not afford to do them all, or to do them all in the measure that we might like.

How Much Is Enough?

We are urgently in need of such information not only for proposed new health programs, but for a very large number of practices that are widely used today. Let us consider three: first, the use of a specialized and expensive hospital facility; second, a surgical procedure that has long been practiced; and third, the uses to which recently introduced high technology is now being put. All are of great medical importance. All are surely overused. The first is the use of beds in hospital coronary care units for patients with chest pain. The second relates to the controversy that currently surrounds the question of what is the "appropriate" rate of removal of the uterus in our nation. The third is the issue of how many computed tomography (CT) scanners and subsequent-generation technology we need in the United States.

Hospitalization for Chest Pain

Dr. Lee Goldman and his colleagues at a Boston teaching hospital have recently studied patients over thirty years of age who come to the emergency room of the hospital because of chest pain. The first order of business for such patients and their doctors in hospital ERs is generally to determine whether the cause of the pain is a heart attack. Whether the doctor recommends hospitalization in the coronary care unit or sends the patient home rests on the outcome of the various tests carried out. The decision is crucial, for the technology of the unit can be life-saving for the patient in the early stages of a coronary attack. At the other extreme, if the chest pain is the result of a relatively innocent condition, say, a muscle strain, it is in the patient's interest to be kept out of the hospital—it is poor medical practice to expose a person needlessly to the risks of hospitalization. In addition, in this time of limited resources, it is important that doctors be sparing in the use of coronary care unit beds wherever there are not enough to accommodate all patients suspected of having heart attacks; this means most doctors in most hospitals. In Dr. Goldman's hospital, one day in the coronary care unit now costs $850.

Dr. Goldman has found that one group of patients with chest pain have certain characteristic abnormalities in their electrocardiograms. Three quarters of them prove to have heart attacks. Of a second group, patients with chest pain and normal electrocardiograms, 95 percent have a reason for their chest pain other than a heart condition. Only 1 percent have real heart attacks, while another 4 percent have heart disease but less severe than a full-blown heart attack. But most patients who come to emergency rooms with chest pain fall into a third—intermediate—group: they have equivocal or early electrocardiographic signs of trouble. Depending on the nature of those signs, their chances of developing heart attacks over a period of twenty-four to seventy-two hours range from 3 to 25 percent.

The practice in most hospitals has been to hospitalize not only all the patients in the first and third groups, but most in the second. Dr. Goldman's work has been directed at distinguishing those patients who should be hospitalized from those who should not be and, within the group who are hospitalized, those who may need the special personnel and equipment of the coronary care unit. His work shows that most patients in the second group, those with normal electrocardiograms, can safely go home, with instructions to return, or to call the doctor, if the pain returns or if other symptoms appear. The patients in the third group need hospitalization, but they do as well in a facility with some but much less intensive supervision than the coronary care unit. The saving in hospitalizing patients in such "intermediate" facilities is $300 per day per patient. Dr. Goldman calculates that if the lessons of his work were applied around the nation, the total savings would be more than $300 million a year.

Elective Hysterectomy

Hysterectomy is the major operation most frequently performed in the United States. In 1978 more than 700,000 women underwent the procedure. At that rate, it has been calculated that more than half of American women will have the operation before they are sixty-five. But the frequency with which the operation is carried out from one area in the country to another, or even within the same state, varies by as much as 3.6 times. Some researchers have found that the larger the number of surgeons in the area being studied, the more frequent the operation. That is true within this country and from one country to another, as well. Thus, Britain, which has half as many surgeons as we do on a per capita basis, carries out about half as many hysterectomies. On the other hand, Canada and Australia, which have about as many surgeons as we, do about as many operations.

What can be concluded from such differences? Are we doing too many hysterectomies in some areas of the nation or too few in others? Should the British be doing more, or the Canadians, Australians, and Americans all be doing fewer? Can we generalize about all the operations for which area variations have been found or are different conclusions warranted for different operations?

The issue of how to translate important research results into medical practice is another question that is now receiving much attention. Before publishing his findings in medical journals, one investigator shares them with doctors in the areas he studies. On occasion this has led to changes in practice. For example, the rate of tonsillectomy among children in some areas of Vermont fell from 65 percent to 8 percent after the Vermont Medical Society gave local physicians data on variations within that state. In the belief of many physicians, the reduction in that operation suggests (but only suggests) that too many tonsillectomies were being performed in some parts of the state. But if the "proper" rate for, let us say, hysterectomy were the higher one, then such conformity downward would be deleterious to the health of the community. Thus, while the study of areawide differences in the frequency of various medical practices contributes a great deal to technology assessment, it serves mainly to signal a pressing need for additional information of other kinds.

Nobody disputes the importance of removing a seriously diseased uterus. But much controversy surrounds the estimated 30 percent of hysterectomies that are done in the United States for what are termed elective reasons, such as sterilization and/or prevention of cancer. As mentioned elsewhere (Chapter 2), when objections to interventions can be raised on economic grounds, medical problems often coexist. That is true in this situation.

With respect to the risks, a study at Stanford University showed that more than 7 percent of women undergoing hysterectomy had complications that varied from moderate to life threatening. Several reports in medical journals indicate that death occurs in from 0.1 to 0.4 percent of cases. If 30 percent of the 700,000 operations carried out in 1978 were elective, that means that between 210 and 840 women died as a result of an operation that was carried out for reasons that were not life threatening. (The psychological costs are more difficult to calculate; I mention them here only in passing.) This does not in itself argue against elective hysterectomy, of course. Complications and deaths may result from the cancers that the procedure is intended to prevent, as well as from unwanted pregnancies. The question in medical terms is whether elective hysterectomy is the safest way to achieve contraception or protection against serious illness and death from cancer of the uterus.

The cost of an uncomplicated hysterectomy in 1978 was estimated to vary from $1,700 to $2,600. That means that the cost to the nation was between $357 and $546 million for the care of the uncomplicated cases alone. The costs of the complications would add greatly to the bill, and the so-called indirect costs, such as lost wages, would be more yet.

Other considerations arise when a doctor is confronted with the matter of whether to recommend elective hysterectomy. In recent years physicians have been particularly conscious of the legal implications of their behavior. Many people seem unaware of the fact that every operation entails some risk of complications and even death, even when the professionals and the facilities are the best available. If a doctor recommends elective hysterectomy and the patient dies or suffers a serious complication as a result, can that doctor be found culpable in a malpractice suit? What if the recommendation is against the procedure, and the patient subsequently dies in childbirth or from cancer of the uterus?

I cite these issues in part to demonstrate the complexities of technology assessment (and of medical practice!). Specialists from many fields are required to help anticipate and deal with the kinds of questions that will increasingly arise. Ultimately, decisions must be made by the patient in consultation with the physician. But the quality of these decisions will rest on the quality of information that has been collected, the quality of the analysis to which it has been subjected, and the quality of its communication to the patient, as well as the technical quality of the medical performance.

An expert committee of the Institute of Medicine of the National Academy of Medicine recently considered the general problem of technology assessment. Its conclusion was that hysterectomy is often carried out for reasons that can be questioned. The committee stated further that additional data are required to reach a firm conclusion. Few would argue with either statement.

CT and MRI Scans

The CT scanner is a machine that combines x-ray equipment with computers and makes possible visualization of normal and abnormal body structures in unprecedented detail. For example, it permits rapid and precise detection of diseases within the skull—clots, hemorrhages, tumors—with minimal discomfort and risk to the patient. As such, it has in some instances replaced procedures that were far less accurate and that often involved considerable discomfort and some risk. It is extremely expensive—the current price of one machine is almost $1 million. The estimated 2,000 machines throughout the country have operating costs of almost $1 billion annually.

In the United States millions of CT head scans are now done each year, many on patients with headaches. Some doctors order the procedure to be certain that a brain tumor or other serious disease within the head is not overlooked. In many patients the scan makes unnecessary other procedures that involve discomfort and risk. But the expense of the CT technology has led to probing questions concerning its overall significance in terms of patient benefit. Take the problem of brain tumors as an example. They are relatively uncommon, occurring in fewer than 13,000 Americans each year, or less than 1.5 percent of all cancers. More than 80 percent are incurable. Although CT scans make possible earlier diagnosis and treatment, the outcome is no better—that is, no more patients are cured. Similar observations have been made in other countries; in the major teaching hospital in Glasgow, Scotland, no decrease occurred in deaths or duration or degree of illness among all patients with diseases within the skull following the installation of a CT scanner.

The CT scanner was invented in Great Britain. Yet, the British have 10 percent as many scanners for the body and 30 percent as many head scanners as we do (numbers adjusted for population differences). They are, of course, concerned with questions of what more of the technology could mean in terms of patient welfare. With constraints on their health resources far greater than in the United States, however, they are also forced to confront more explicitly than we what they would have to give up if more resources were committed to scanners.

Arguments can be marshaled for the United States also to insist on such information for all new technology *before* it is widely disseminated. It is the more important at this time, and for this kind of technology, for the nuclear magnetic resonance (NMR) scanner—or its newer name, the magnetic resonance imaging (MRI) scanner—a new, even more powerful, and even more expensive technology for probing the structures of the body, is now in production. The spread of CT scanners has been justified by some on grounds that, even where it has not made a difference in terms of the outcome of a disease, it has replaced unpleasant and more dangerous tests.

One argument used for the newer technology is that whereas the CT scanners expose the patient to very small amounts of radiation, the MRI machines produce none. In addition, the latter sometimes give different information from the former. Like the CT scanner, the MRI machines, in academic centers, are yielding important research information; for example, they can define with great precision the affected areas in the brain and spinal cord of patients with multiple sclerosis. What remains to be determined, however, is what benefits the MRI scanner would bring in terms of patient outcome. Until that information is available from studies now in progress, it is impossible to say to what extent they will merit the very great additional investment they would require for widespread use. With technology of such enormous expense, it is particularly important that we consider the programs that the new undertaking would force us to forgo.

Practical Measures

The hysterectomy and the CT scan examples make clear that uncertainty surrounds questions of both safety and effectiveness of many technologies now in widespread use, as well as all new ones. The implications to the nation in terms of lives, suffering, and dollars can only be guessed at. The reasons are many and complex, and no single measure designed to deal with the problem can be expected to do more than touch on a part of it. While some centers, both government and private, are addressing aspects of it, much more can and needs to be done. Many people have offered constructive suggestions in a variety of areas.

The Council on Health Care Technology

Following a proposal made by the Institute of Medicine committee on technology assessment, the Congress mandated the formation of a Council on Health Care Technology. It was placed in the private sector to "maximize its resources and credibility." Its statutory purposes are to promote the development and application of appropriate health care technology assessments and to review existing health care technologies in order to identify those that are obsolete or inappropriately used. The Institute of Medicine established such a council in early 1986. The council will catalog existing information on the subject, develop assessment methods and criteria, identify areas in need of study, both carry out such studies and provide support for them in other centers, disseminate the results of studies, and promote education, training, and technical assistance in the use of assessment methods and results. The council will receive financial support from both public and private sectors.

Improved Record Keeping

Another change—in the way in which medical data are recorded and stored—could contribute much to technology assessment and to patient care. Medical records, which are now kept by individual doctors and institutions, could be kept in compatible fashion throughout the nation. Data would be made generally available, with proper safeguards for patient privacy, of course.

New procedures would be regarded by physicians and patients in the same way as new drugs and would not be carried out except on an experimental basis, until their usefulness had been validated. The objection is sometimes raised that this would delay the diffusion of new procedures, and that would likely be the case. But some argue that the benefits of protecting the public from the many procedures that are ultimately proved to be without value would make this price worth paying.

The organizations that might supervise the testing of new procedures could include universities and widely respected professional organizations. Assume, for example, that the American College of Surgeons maintained a registry of all new and unproved operations. Surgeons wishing to use an "untested" procedure would, as at present, need the approval of the supervisory body within the hospital in which they practice. In addition, they would follow a protocol developed for the college by its members, the nation's surgical leaders, and maintained by it. Information would be collected according to that protocol and stored, analyzed, and made available to others by the college. As mentioned earlier, had coronary bypass surgery been so "regulated" from the time it was introduced in such a voluntary fashion, information concerning its usefulness and its limitations would probably have been made widely available at a much earlier time.

The involvement of prestigious groups like the American College of Surgery and the Institute of Medicine would have additional advantages. For example, had either stated many years ago that technology assessment was required to establish the best form of management of breast cancer, those surgeons who were then uncomfortable with radical mastectomy would have felt freer to try other approaches. Those who are still using radical mastectomy now that it has been shown to be no more useful than simpler procedures would be more likely to change their behavior. In addition, such involvement might help discourage unjustified malpractice suits.

Sanctions Imposed by Insurers

Many third-party insurers, including Medicare and Medicaid and private companies, now withhold compensation for procedures that are regarded as outmoded or experimental. Such an arrangement, which builds appropriate incentives into payment systems, could be used as a means of helping ensure the use of technology assessment as a part of medical practice. For example, let's assume that compensation to surgeons and institutions for coronary bypass graft surgery had been conditional from the start on patient and doctor involvement in a trial supervised by a recognized authority, such as the IOM or the American College of Surgeons. Then, comprehensive and compatible data could have been collected on every patient subjected to the procedure from the start and made widely available. That could have speeded greatly the development of useful and reliable guidelines for other patients and doctors.

The needed activities in technology assessment will require a great deal of additional financial support, particularly at the start. The IOM committee proposed that public and private health insurance organizations set aside 0.2 percent of their expenditures for this purpose. While this fraction is small as compared with those that most industries set aside for development purposes, the contribution from the federal agency concerned with paying for medical services for 1984 would have approximated $177 million, as compared with an actual allocation for this purpose of $33 million. The Congress set aside a total of $2 million for the first three years of the new council's activities, contingent on the availability of matching funds from the private sector. These are small sums if looked at in the light of the IOM committee's estimate that the nation's overall expenditures for useless and unproved medical technologies amount to tens of billions of dollars annually.

We may not find large, immediate economic returns on investments in technology assessment, for the process itself will entail new costs. Further, as I pointed out, translation of the results of assessment are often slow. Therefore, at least some of the benefit will accrue only over a period of years. But important savings in human terms, which, after all, would be a major objective of the effort, would begin at once.

12 Health Services Research: Health 2000, an Experiment in Health Care Delivery

The United States needs new delivery systems for health care. *New,* because existing ones do not serve many millions of Americans, and they cost more than they should for those they do serve. *Systems,* because it would be futile to expect to find *one* nationwide solution to the problem of providing all citizens with health services at affordable cost. The great differences in needs and tastes in different parts of the country mean that no single, all-inclusive program could ever be effectively designed or managed in Washington. But flexible and responsive systems could be developed on a regional basis. They could provide the variety of options that our tradition of individualism requires. If, say, two programs (of several) on trial in different parts of the nation were found to work, they might then be adopted by other areas, with variations arranged to conform with local circumstances.

The nation's health care access and cost problems, then, offer a strong case for change. A strong case can also be made for making such change on a pilot basis. Every social change represents an experiment. Even those that succeed brilliantly almost always need modifications along the way. And those that fail should be permitted to disappear without an excessive commitment of the nation's resources and hopes. Every experiment in the natural sciences is preceded by pilot studies. Those in the social sciences deserve no less.

This chapter proposes a pilot experiment in health care delivery. Its setting is a hypothetical city in a hypothetical state, but it could be tried in any of many real settings in the nation. It is based on a plan devised in

1977, by a committee* that set out to develop a model system for the delivery of health services. Its goal was to ensure care for all citizens in a community and to control costs with positive incentives and with minimal regulation. We called the plan Health 2000, because the committee believed that if it were tried, it should be phased in slowly, and, therefore, would likely not be operational before the twenty-first century. I have modified the original plan to allow for some of the changes in health care delivery that have taken place in recent years, and to reflect my own prejudices. However, nothing has happened to alter my belief that, to meet the needs of the entire population at an affordable cost, every plan requires a single source of funding. That important feature is retained in what follows.

It should be emphasized that the plan has never been tested and is therefore still only a model. But in order to consider it in some detail, let us assume that Health 2000 is, in fact, operational in the year 2000, and let us examine how it came to be and how it is working.

The Scope of the Plan

The imaginary scene is Northville, U.S.A., in the year 2000. Northville, with 800,000 residents, is the largest city in the state of Westland, whose population is just under 3 million people. Thirteen years ago, the governor of Westland and the mayor of Northville convened a group of citizens concerned with the growing costs of medical care and even more with the gaps in medical coverage in the state. The mandate to the committee was to propose a plan that would lead as rapidly as possible to comprehensive health services for all citizens of Westland at a cost of no more than $1,200 (in 1987 dollars) per capita, which was less than two thirds of the total amount the nation was then spending for its medical programs. The services were to include primary care, ambulatory care facilities, secondary hospitals for the care of less complicated problems like pneumonia and hernia surgery, tertiary hospitals for more complex problems, such as heart surgery and high voltage radiation treatments, home care programs, ambulatory

---

* The committee was chaired by Thomas O. Pyle, president of the Harvard Community Health Plan, Inc., and myself, and included the following working group members: Daniel Creasey, president of the Risk Management Foundation of the Harvard Medical Institutions; Richard C. Killin, counsel, Harvard Community Health Plan; Martin S. Klein, president, Institutional Strategy Associates, Inc.; H. Richard Nesson, president, Brigham and Women's Hospital; Marc Roberts, professor of Political Economy, Harvard School of Public Health; the late Herbert Sherman, associate director for technology, Institute for Health Research, Harvard Community Health Plan and Harvard University; and Jay Winsten, assistant dean, Harvard School of Public Health. The project staff consisted of Sharon Kaufman and Kathy Hughes, then students at the Harvard School of Public Health.

and hospital care for the mentally ill, and long-term care facilities for the chronically ill. Certain services, like cosmetic surgery and private hospital rooms, were not included, but they were to be available to those wishing to pay out-of-pocket for them.

Regional Size

The committee soon learned that candidate areas for experiments in the delivery of comprehensive health services must be large enough to be self-sufficient; that is, a population of much less than 500,000 people could not keep busy on a full-time basis all of the medical specialists and highly complicated and expensive technology of 1987. On the other hand, with few exceptions, regions with more than 3 or 4 million people are too large to permit adequate supervision and coordination. This meant that to achieve the "right" population, some areas would have to cover more than one state, while others would be restricted to parts of very large cities, like New York and Los Angeles.

The state of Westland was in many ways a very good setting for an experiment in reorganizing the health care system. It had an appropriate number of residents. Its capital city, Northville, was the largest population center and within easy commuting distance of the rest of the state. Perhaps most important, Westland had a large number of lay and professional groups willing to work hard to bring about improvements in its health care arrangements. They recognized that the problems in the delivery system were deep-seated and would not be resolved with simple measures. They were determined not to change what were in some ways great strengths except where essential to the achievement of their principal goals. On the other hand, they knew that major changes would be necessary and that many would be controversial. They were aware that some of the people who would be affected recognized the need for change in the long term, but hoped to be able to defer it until they were no longer active. Therefore, the committee decided to phase in all broad changes gradually over several years.

With the help of Westland's congressional delegation and of the federal administration, the health planning committee enlisted representatives of the U.S. Department of Health and Human Services. A plan was developed, discussed at length by citizen groups, the state medical and nursing societies, and various committees of the state legislative and executive branches. Federal action was also required; for example, in place of Medicare and

Medicaid funds for the residents of the state, the federal government agreed to match the state's contribution to the program. The final blueprint was approved in late 1988. A series of complicated negotiations then began—with the state medical society, the nursing association, the trustees and staffs of nonprofit hospitals, the corporations that run the for-profit hospitals and nursing homes, and others. The first steps in implementing the program were taken the following year, and the fully developed program that now, in the year 2000, serves the area was operational ten years later, that is, in 1999. Here is how it works.

Administrative Structure

Within the state there is a federally chartered, not-for-profit Regional Health Corporation (RHC). The Westland RHC has a policy-making board of five people, including two presidential and three gubernatorial appointees, all of whom are familiar with the state's health needs. One must be a member of the business council of the area, and another must be from a regional union. Each member serves for five years, and the terms are staggered. The RHC has a chief executive officer, who is chosen by the board on the basis of expertise in the health field and management skills, and whose salary is competitive with other top executives in the health field. The structure is designed to provide the RHC with political independence and public credibility, as well as with the knowledge and power needed to deal effectively with a complex health system involving an annual budget of $3.5 billion. With advice from its several constituencies, the RHC has developed an overall plan to meet the health care needs of its region. Now that plans similar to Health 2000 are being developed in nearby regions, the RHC coordinates its plan with those of surrounding RHCs and with national policy.

When the Health 2000 idea was being worked out, it was decided to make no more changes in the existing health services delivery system than were necessary to meet the major new goals. But no way could be found to retain the multiple payment mechanisms of the 1980s and simultaneously set priorities. For example, if a decision was made to shift more resources into care of the elderly and less into certain other health programs, mechanisms had to be available to translate the decision into action. As long as multiple payers—government, private insurance companies, individuals, and others—were on the scene, such decisions could not be implemented. The Canadian experience was consistent with this view. Only after each provincial government became the sole funding source for health for its residents did Canada achieve both control of costs and universal access to health services.

Funding

Against that background, it was decided to make the RHC the single funnel for all health care funds used in Westland—from federal, state, and local governments, and from private sources. This feature is essential to the workings of the program. All residents of the state are insured on a capitation basis—that is, all health care needs are covered by premiums paid periodically. The RHC is responsible for making certain that all residents are covered. Government agencies pay the RHC premiums for the elderly and the poor. The state's large industries pay insurance premiums for their employees to the RHC. Self-employed individuals pay their premiums directly to the RHC. The RHC negotiates with the state and federal governments to set benefit levels. To formulate its annual and longer-range plans, the RHC must, of course, know the total amount of money available within the periods in question. Further, to use financial incentives to implement the plan, the RHC must control the distribution of *all* resources. The RHC can borrow for capital investment against future capitation payments.

At the beginning of each year the RHC negotiates contracts with hospitals, nursing homes, and all other institutions in the region, and with representatives of the doctors, nurses, social workers, and other providers. Those contracts set levels of payment and describe specific expectations in terms of services. Payments are based on capitation—that is, the number of people whose health needs are met, rather than on, for example, procedures performed or number of days in hospital. (Many experiments in this country comparing people whose health needs are covered by capitation with those on fee-for-service arrangements indicate that capitation discourages the overprovision of services and the provision of more costly services, when less costly ones will do as well.) High priority is given to disease prevention and health promotion programs. These involve consumer education activities emphasizing prevention measures and how to use the health care system most effectively.

Health 2000 was designed to encourage competition among its constituent institutions and groups. Every family is free at defined intervals to switch from one doctor in an IPA (independent practice arrangement) or HMO (health maintenance organization) to another doctor in the same or another IPA or HMO, from one hospital to another, and from any other health facility to another. Competition presents an incentive for each organization to achieve economies without compromising services, indeed, to use the money saved to provide new or better services and thereby attract more people.

The architects of the Health 2000 plan recognized that every innovation would carry a price. For example, they were aware that centralizing health planning risked repressing individual initiative. However, they felt that such planning could reduce costly duplication and lead to better integration of services. Because they could find no other way that seemed as likely to achieve that important goal, they decided that the risk was warranted.

They discussed the issue of cost control at length. Many who had studied Canada's success in controlling health costs believed that it was crucial that the provincial governments be responsible not only for negotiating with providers, but also for finding a sizable fraction of any additional money they contract to provide. The Health 2000 committee felt that the RHC would also have strong incentives to keep costs down. First, it would be aware of regional liability for a large part of any increase in costs. They also knew that the presence on the RHC of people from the business and union communities would keep the cost issue in focus.

Those who developed Health 2000 were aware that several experiments suggest that health costs are kept down when people share in the expenses—that is, in so-called copayment or coinsurance arrangements. After considerable debate, they decided against the option, despite its attractive features. The compelling arguments against it related to equity and efficiency. If it were applied across the board, it would put undue hardship on low-income people. If it were adjusted for income, its administration would be cumbersome, and the administrative costs would be high. Further, the experience of others with a variety of copayment arrangements indicated that it is often very confusing, particularly to elderly people. For these reasons, then, the degree of cost control that might have been achieved with coinsurance was decided not to be worth the tradeoffs, and it has not been a part of the Health 2000 program. The exceptions to the sole-source coverage of health care are the supplemental payments that are collected from the individual for amenities like private rooms and noncovered services like cosmetic surgery.

The RHC pays special attention to the collection of data concerning the health of people in the region. It has developed a series of techniques for evaluating the performance of the participating institutions and individuals, as well as of the system as a whole.

Research Commitments

The RHC commits almost 2 percent of its total receipts to research. A part of that money is used to support technology assessment, because the RHC recognizes that that process is essential to its function. It does not, for example, cover new medical or surgical procedures until they have been approved by its expert committee on new technology. Emphasis is also given to other kinds of health services research, including that designed to develop more effective methods of health promotion. Ten percent of the research money is committed to fundamental biomedical research, for the RHC recognizes its crucial importance to the health of today's and tomorrow's citizens. The RHC also provides support for the state medical society's program for the early detection and treatment of illness and alcohol and substance abuse among physicians.

Distribution of Services

Hospitals and nursing homes within the state continue to be owned and operated by both nonprofit groups and for-profit corporations. They all are under contract to the RHC, which attempts to ensure that all are operated efficiently and in coordinated fashion, and that the needs of all citizens are met. Thus, the RHC arranges that facilities for emergency care are appropriately distributed, that adequate but not excessive facilities and personnel are available for heart surgery and radiation therapy, that the needs for custodial care are met for those with chronic illness, both physical and mental, that patients are readily transferred from one institution to another or home, as their condition dictates.

As a result, Health 2000 is arranged as a unified system in which community needs are met without costly duplication. Thus, the term "system" is broadly defined and includes hospitals, centers where simple procedures, like some hernia and cataract operations, are performed without hospitalization, home care programs, nursing homes, and other facilities. This helps avoid the rather common situation of an earlier era in which a patient sometimes remained for days or longer in a $500 per day acute hospital bed only because a bed that cost less than half that amount in a long-term care facility was not available. It also helps avoid another familiar problem of the past in which that same expensive hospital bed was used because finances could not be arranged for the home care that would have been vastly preferred by patient and doctor.

The RHC recognizes the added expense involved in patient care in the hospitals, nursing homes, and ambulatory care centers that are attached to the state medical school. Their missions are crucial to today's health care and tomorrow's. Therefore, supplemental payments are negotiated with each to cover the costs associated with teaching medical students and residents. Because the federal government believes it to be in the nation's interest to encourage this kind of activity in the states (many years, more than half of the medical students and residents in the Westland Medical School are from out of state), 50 percent of these added costs are paid for by the federal government.

Range of Facilities

To create the system, extensive changes were necessary when Health 2000 was set up. For example, a hospital in Beltsville, a community of 50,000 thirty-five miles from Northville, had been doing heart surgery and other forms of tertiary care work. In the case of many of the complicated operations it carried out, such as heart valve replacements and complex cancer surgery, fewer than 10 to 20 percent as many were done as at Northville General Hospital. Both complication rates and costs were much higher in Beltsville than in Northville. As a result, the Beltsville Hospital was converted to a community hospital, where doctors now hospitalize patients with problems like less complicated heart attacks and appendicitis. It functions, of course, as part of the overall Westland health care system. Patients in the Beltsville Hospital who develop conditions that require more specialized treatment are readily transferred by ambulance or helicopter to Northville General, which is now used as the referral hospital for the state. St. James Hospital, a mixed secondary and tertiary care hospital in Northville, had an obsolescent plant and was seeking money to rebuild. When it was determined that Northville General could meet the area's tertiary care needs, St. James was rebuilt as a secondary hospital for the area. Northville Memorial, a third hospital in the community, which had had an occupancy rate of less than 50 percent, was converted to a rehabilitation center and nursing home and is now used primarily for the elderly. Northville State Hospital, which was run by the state for the care of the mentally ill, had a reputation—unfortunately deserved—of poor care. It has been brought up to the standards of the acute care hospitals and is now much more attractive.

About 30 percent of doctors, nurses, and other professionals who provide health services outside the hospital are now affiliated with one of

Westland's four health maintenance organizations, two of which are of the closed panel type. Two are part of national firms, and the others are incorporated locally. The HMO offers comprehensive medical services for an annual fee. The closed panel variety has a group of doctors who work within a single organization and from whom the consumer picks a primary-care doctor (generally, an internist, a family physician, or a pediatrician), who then acts as the gatekeeper. Any medical problem for which the individual seeks advice or other help—recurrent headaches, back pain, immunizations, etc.—is brought to the primary-care doctor, who is responsible for seeing that all problems are properly dealt with and for maintaining the medical record. The primary-care team includes skilled nurses who work closely with the doctors. Complex problems are referred by the primary-care doctor to specialists, who are members of the closed panel.

An important part of developing Health 2000 was strengthening community health programs. The West Side HMO, for example, has comprehensive home care services in the area of Northville in which it is located. It has organized medical, nursing, homekeeping, occupational and recreational therapy, and other programs. Had Philip McCormick, whose hospitalization for radiation treatment of lung cancer and subsequent problems were mentioned in Chapter 5, been a member of WSHMO, his doctor would have easily arranged for him to be cared for at home. Nurses would have been in attendance to help make him as comfortable as possible. Fortunately, he had no financial problems, and his wife saw that the household was well looked after. But if he had been poor or not had close relatives who cared, a WSHMO social worker could have arranged to have a housekeeper come in at intervals to shop and prepare meals.

The HMO provides a basic benefit package to all members, as specified by the RHC. It receives payment from the RHC on a capitation basis for the care of its members. It strives for efficiency in its operations to permit it to offer the kind of service that attracts and retains patients. To do so, it emphasizes not only the quantity of services available, but also their quality and sensitivity to patients' wishes. Once a year, during open enrollment, patients are free to renew their membership in WSHMO or to move to a competing group that also offers complete ambulatory health services.

Independent Medical Practice

Although one third of Westland's residents have joined HMOs, most people, both patients like the Carlyles and doctors like Daniel Beck, described first in Chapter 2, have continued with more traditional independent practice arrangements. In order for these so-called IPAs to receive money from the RHC, physicians agreed to a new payment mechanism. Primary-care doctors like Dr. Beck inform the RHC about the scope of care (the range of diagnoses and procedures) they plan to provide their patients. For example, they might say that they will assume total care of all of their patients with uncomplicated heart attacks. At the other extreme, others might indicate that they will routinely call on a cardiologist as a consultant for such patients. They also give the RHC a list of their consultants. The RHC provides capitation funds to the primary-care providers in the IPAs based on the number of patients who select them and the scope of practice they indicate they offer. The consultants designated by the primary-care providers are also capitated in accordance with the number of people for whom they are listed as potential specialists.

Here is how that arrangement might have worked for Dr. Beck. Let's assume that he estimated that, on average, he is responsible for 80 percent of the medical care needs of his patients. Assume also that 1,600 patients have asked him to serve as their primary-care doctor and that the RHC has allocated a total of $200 per year for medical fees for each person. Dr. Beck, then, would receive $256,000 (0.8 × 1600 × $200) per year to cover his practice expenses, including his own salary, and those of his nurse, his secretary, and his office. Let's assume now that the surgeon who operated on Mr. Carlyle was listed as the referring surgeon by fifteen internists like Dr. Beck. Their total patient population numbered 20,000. Let's also assume that a surgeon's compensation is $15 per year for every patient for whom he is the consultant in surgery. Then the RMC would give Mr. Carlyle's surgeon a total of $300,000 per year. These incomes are calculated in advance each year and are not tied to the number of procedures the doctors carry out. Thus, there is no financial incentive for a doctor to do more procedures. (These remarks do not apply to payments received by medical personnel for their time spent carrying out noncovered procedures like cosmetic surgery.) The size of doctors' lists is determined by the limits set by the doctors and the preferences expressed by patients.

If during a given year doctors refer more or less than the predicted 20 percent (or other fraction set in advance) of their patients' needs to other doctors, then the RMC negotiates compensation for them for the next year at a correspondingly lower or higher level. The same applies to specialists— that is, if primary-care physicians refer more patients to specialists for more services than were anticipated, the specialists can expect a larger fraction of the capitation fund. To return to the example of medical care for patients with heart disease, let's consider the doctor who originally planned to assume total care for all patients with uncomplicated heart attacks. In fact, it turns out that she calls in consultants half the time. She is thus doing less work, and her cardiologist consultant more, than predicted. Appropriate adjustments in the compensation of both are therefore made.

If patients receive what they or their primary-care doctors consider inadequate or insensitive care from specialists, the primary-care physicians will choose different specialists for referral. Thus, again, the incentives are structured so as to encourage good medical care, patient satisfaction, and sound economics.

The architects of Westland's Health 2000 plan undertook to bring under better control certain problems that were of great concern in the 1980s. One was medical malpractice litigation. A second was the uncontrolled increase in the number of medical specialists setting up practice in the state. Progress has taken place with respect to both.

Controlling the Malpractice Problem

Medical malpractice settlements accounted for 1–2 percent of the nation's health bill in the early 1980s. Some suggested that an additional 5–10 percent of the bill, that is, as much as $35 billion, was the result of "defensive" medicine—for example, extra tests or exploratory operations carried out because doctors felt obliged to protect themselves against possible lawsuits, and not because they felt them necessary to patient health. (In fact, procedures that are really unnecessary expose patients to needless risk, as well as to expense. Thus, they represent bad, as well as expensive, medicine.) From the start, one feature of Health 2000 has been an important deterrent to malpractice suits—its universal coverage. Patients who know that they are covered for all additional medical expenses and for lost income that may result from, say, an unpredictable complication of a drug or an operation have less incentive to sue to protect themselves against unexpected (and unmanageable) costs.

Another feature of Health 2000 that makes malpractice suits less likely is its emphasis on the quality of medical care. Doctors working together in HMOs or in IPAs are in a position to question, consult with, and otherwise supervise each other. Recently developed methods for measuring quality of care are applied by each group to assess its own performance on a continuing basis. This information is fed back to the doctors. It is also used by the RHC as part of its continuing efforts to assure quality in the system. It has been particularly useful in reducing, although it has not eliminated, a problem that was severe in the 1980s: the patient neglect that resulted from cutting costs.

Finally, during the period when the Health 2000 plan was being discussed, Westland's government passed no-fault legislation for medical malpractice suits. The combination of changes has been followed by many fewer suits and an increase in the fraction of each award going to the plaintiff from about 30 cents on the premium dollar in the 1980s to 80 cents now.

Health 2000 was structured so as to encourage freedom and closeness in doctor-patient relations and simultaneously to ensure that the more vulnerable citizens of society were not left out. In the 1950s and early 1960s, doctors were criticized because so many of the elderly and the poor had no access to medical care. Then, after the Medicare and Medicaid legislation was in force, newspaper headlines sometimes reported the function of "Medicaid mills"—typically, storefront operations where large numbers of poor people were subjected to inappropriate tests and treatments, for which unscrupulous doctors were collecting huge sums of public money.

As investigations have shown, these operations were the exceptions. Unscrupulous doctors did and do exist, but they are few. In proportion to decent and caring doctors, their numbers are probably as small as the comparable ratios of unscrupulous to decent and caring journalists, lawyers, taxi drivers, business leaders, and trade union members and officials. Most doctors respect the laws and the customs. Those laws and customs at one time permitted, and sometimes encouraged, practices that made no sense economically. Medical incomes rose steeply at a time when health insurance, both government and private, provided financial incentives to do "everything" for the patient, with no penalty felt by the patient, at least in the short term. Often, the incentives led to uneconomic practices. If Blue Shield–Blue Cross would pay both hospital and doctor bills for the patient hospitalized to investigate the basis for abdominal pain, but not for expenses incurred outside the hospital, was it not in the patient's interest to hospitalize? If Medicare paid for the CT scan for the patient with headaches, even though the outcome of the scan would have no effect on treatment, the temptation to do the scan was very great.

When doctors benefit financially from decisions they make, how does one deal with the conflict of interest issue? This received a great deal of publicity in 1985, after President Reagan was found to have cancer of the bowel on colonoscopy, an examination of the large bowel with a flexible tube containing lenses and mirrors. Immediately, Americans in large numbers were reported to have approached doctors seeking the same examination. At that time some asked how one could expect an objective answer, since the doctor consulted was often the doctor who would do the examination. The fee for the examination, which requires less than thirty minutes, was often more than $700. When the bill was paid by a third party—the government or a private insurance company—the patient had no financial reason to suggest restraint. This led critics of the fee-for-service system to argue more strongly for a salaried arrangement for doctors, with salary levels unrelated to the number of procedures carried out.

Many inside and out of medical practice are unhappy with a salaried arrangement for doctors. They say that in some HMOs, Veterans Hospitals, and other institutions where salaries are fixed, doctors don't make the extra effort that is seen in the fee-for-service setting. In what may be a slight variation on the theme that American doctors by and large represent a cross section of Americans with other skills, they say that doctors' motives are similar to those in other callings, and that, not surprisingly, they respond similarly to incentives.

Clearly, the doctors convicted of criminal activities with respect to Medicaid funds are typical only of themselves. Similarly, nobody would suggest that Daniel Beck, the internist practicing independently, and Joan Rubin, the HMO doctor, who were described in Chapters 2 and 3, are the prototypes of all doctors. Many doctors on salary will work as many hours as necessary to provide the best medical care for their patients, just as many fee-for-service doctors will carry out no more procedures than they think their patients require, independent of who pays whom how much. But there must be many doctors in the middle ground. The question confronting the Health 2000 architects was how to recognize the variations in personality and taste among doctors and patients and still protect those who have been neglected in the past.

Canadians did this one way, retaining the fee-for-service system, the British another, using a salaried arrangement for all doctors. Both systems have strengths and weaknesses. Health 2000 attempts to capture the best of both worlds. While it has eliminated the fee for service, it does provide both the independent practice and the HMO arrangements to the public and to doctors.

In the 1970s and 1980s for-profit hospitals promised to offer the health care system the efficiencies of better management techniques and the advantages of sound financial incentives. Whatever their virtues, those organizations were not designed to, and did not, meet the needs of the members of our society who could not pay for medical services, no matter how desperate their health problems. This deficiency has been repaired by making all such organizations answerable to the RHC, a governing authority with responsibility and the resources to see that the health needs of all citizens are met.

Controlling Physician Supply

The problem of doctor and particularly specialist oversupply confronted several countries, including the United States, when discussions concerning Health 2000 began. In 1980 a committee appointed by the U.S. Secretary of Health and Human Services predicted that the country would have an excess of 150,000 physicians in the year 2000. Another report suggested that as many as 90 percent of doctors would be specialists. This was of special concern because more doctors generally means more tests, more operations, and more costs. For example, several studies showed that variations in the number of certain kinds of surgical operations from one country or area to another were often related to the number of surgeons practicing in the places compared. Other countries dealt with physician supply in a variety of ways. In the United Kingdom, for example, the number of salaried posts for doctors was strictly limited. Since with few exceptions a doctor could not get along without a salaried position, this served as an effective control. Canada prohibited the immigration of doctors. In the Netherlands many physicians were unemployed in the 1980s.

The Health 2000 committee wanted to ensure that Westland attracted as many good primary-care doctors and as many specialists as the state needed, but no more. The heavy concentration of HMOs helped with the problem, for each HMO took on only as many primary-care doctors, orthopedic surgeons, obstetricians, cardiologists, and others as its patient population needed and could support. The RHC's payment mechanism helped prevent more specialists than needed coming into the state in independent roles. Recall that specialists in IPAs were paid according to the number of patients for whom they had been designated consultants. In the early years of Health 2000, extensive "grandparenting" arrangements were set up, so as to make minimal disturbances in existing doctor-patient arrangements. But new doctors entering the Health 2000 area were governed by the new regulations. These led to a fairly rapid entry into the state of primary-care doctors, who had previously been in short supply, and much more limited entry of specialists.

Special Populations: The Old and the Mentally Ill

As is true for the rest of the nation, the Westland Health 2000 finds itself confronted with a growing number of elderly people and all the health problems that means. For example, about 14 percent of Westland's population is over sixty-five and 7 percent over seventy-five. About one fifth of the over-seventy-five-year-olds—that is, more than 40,000 people—need help with their home management activities. That number includes two fifths, or 25,000, of the over-eighty-fives. About 20,000 of the over-sixty-five-year-olds, and 20 percent, or 12,000, of the over-eighty-fives suffer from dementia. These changes in the number of elderly were anticipated, of course, and plans for their care received a great deal of attention during the Health 2000 planning process.

Westland now has a total of 23,000 of its residents in nursing home beds, an increase of more than 40 percent since 1987. Even more attention has been given to day care programs and home care programs to keep the elderly of all economic groups at home. These have permitted both the families of older citizens and volunteers to make life more attractive for the elderly and to hold costs within limits for Westland. But all of this has had a price, and the amount and fraction of total health money allocated to care of the elderly has climbed year by year.

In the Health 2000 planning process Westland also gave high priority to the care of the mentally ill, both in and out of hospital. In the state 3,500 long-term hospital beds are devoted to the care of those people who cannot function outside. Community mental health centers provide medical and social services to the people with mental illness who don't require hospitalization. The centers ensure the quality of hospices and private homes in the community accommodating ambulatory patients who do not live with their families.

An Overview

Let's consider now how Health 2000 might have benefited some of the people whom the American health system failed in the early 1980s. The Janice Brown story (Chapter 5) would have been different in several ways. First, when her husband lost his job, the responsibility for maintaining the family's health insurance would have passed automatically from his employer to the state. Second, when she developed abdominal pain, she would have called her primary-care doctor. He would have arranged to see her at once or would have suggested that she go to the nearest hospital with emergency facilities. A surgical specialist would have been called and arranged for the operation that was necessary. Finally, at the end of the illness, the family would not have been left with unpaid hospital bills hanging over them.

Assume that Oakland, California, were in a Health 2000 region. Then the 458 people whose transfer to a public hospital was mentioned in Chapter 5 would have been cared for by their doctors or, in such acute situations as the automobile accident, in the nearest facility with provision for emergency care. All would, of course, have been insured. Transfers might have been arranged for several, but only if their medical needs had been for an institution with more or less sophisticated facilities than the one to which they first went or were taken. All of the institutions would receive an annual allocation, calculated in advance on the basis of expectations, for their activities during the year.

If Barbara Wallace, the woman described in Chapter 5, who referred herself for headaches to a succession of specialists, had been a member of the WSHMO, she would have first reported her headaches to her primary-care doctor. The doctor, in turn, after hearing her story, reviewing her record, and examining her, would have decided whether she needed to be seen by a specialist.

If, under Health 2000, Mrs. Wallace had been a member of an IPA, she would have consulted her primary-care physician about her headaches. As in the HMO arrangement, this physician would have seen Mrs. Wallace before (or, more likely in this instance, instead of) her access to specialists.

Insisting that the primary-care physician serve as gatekeeper is good practice in medical as well as economic terms. That doctor is in the position to insure that care is coordinated and comprehensive, which was surely not true of Mrs. Wallace's experience with her arrangement of the 1980s. It would also likely save considerable money, for the financial incentives of Health 2000 are structured so as to reduce the likelihood of overprovision of services.

While Health 2000 and similar or related programs are being adopted around the nation, an umbrella organization is also needed at a national level. It would articulate a national health policy, formulated at least in part on the basis of inputs from regions. It would monitor performance at the regional level. It would serve as a conduit through which federal health care funds would flow to regions on a capitation basis. It would serve as a mechanism for coordinating data collected from the various regions on different medical practices. It could, for example, help assure adequate evaluation of technology before its widespread dissemination.

No illusions should accompany the proposal for a trial of Health 2000. Indeed, we should beware of any changes offered as *the* answer to national health problems. But we can do much better than at present. For example, we can provide medical services much more efficiently. We can make those services available to all, or almost all, of our people. The fact that even one country—Canada—that was only a short time ago beset with problems similar to our own has seen dramatic change should induce us to ask how it managed its difficulties and to what extent its experience is applicable to our situation.

Improving access to medical services is, or should be, an important goal for the entire nation. Those without any access at present have the most to gain. But those unable to find appropriate care also have much at stake. As we come closer to the goal, resources will be used more efficiently. Therefore, it should be high on every list of health priorities.

As different experiments are pursued to improve the current situation, certain common guidelines are important. First, let's be certain to hold on to those many aspects of American medicine that are serving us well. In that category is the excellence of tertiary medical care in many parts of the nation. Second, every change in the system should preserve the privileged relationship between doctor and patient. Continuity of medical care is crucial to maintain its quality and sometimes to contain its costs. Walk-in clinics seem to be responding to a need that many people feel, but they cannot offer the kind of informed and continuous care that most people need. Third, the sectional differences from one part of the country to another reflect at least in part cultural differences that must be respected. And services that are administered at a local or regional basis are likely to be more responsive to important needs than are those that are managed from a distance. On the other hand, ample experience tells us that federal guarantees are required to assure the filling of gaps caused by local problems.

Just as much of what exists should be kept, some should be discarded. Faulty incentives in the administration of health services and in payment mechanisms encourage both high costs and poor quality of care. Duplication of facilities and inadequate coordination of services do the same. Deficiencies in primary care have similar effects; everybody needs a gatekeeper, and any new system should have that as one prerequisite.

Health 2000: Some Reservations

When word of the Health 2000 experiment spread through the country, beginning in late 1987, some knowledgeable observers worried about the tradeoffs that Westland made in order to set up its plan. For example, some were suspicious of vesting so much authority in a Regional Health Corporation. In an age of widespread distrust of institutions, such a group might not, these critics felt, have public credibility. Indeed, these same people questioned whether an RHC would be responsive to the wishes of the public. Further, they were skeptical that it could maintain political independence. Others felt that it was important to retain the fee-for-service arrangement, that in the long term a capitation arrangement would lead to patient neglect. Some were concerned that the bureaucracies created would disenfranchise physicians. Others took issue with the proposition that the risk of suppressing individual initiative was worth taking; they felt that other ways could be found to achieve the same goals, including the elimination of duplication and better integration of services. Several people opposed the decision not to build cost sharing into payment arrangements. They argued that income tax data could serve as the basis for a workable sliding scale, thereby protecting poor people, while discouraging those who could afford to pay from overusing medical resources. Some physicians were skeptical about the compensation arrangements for doctors in the IPAs. They urged careful testing for feasibility, acceptability, and unexpected adverse outcomes. Others expressed doubt that Health 2000 would temper the malpractice problem.

But virtually all of these critics shared with Westland residents at least one deeply felt belief: The "system" of health services of the pre-1987 era had not worked, at least with respect to its costs and access for all citizens. Happily, news of Health 2000 stimulated them to do more than offer criticisms; many developed alternative schemes directed at the same goals, but with features that addressed *their* concerns. Some were successful in persuading other health regions of the nation to undertake their programs on an experimental basis.

Built into every arrangement, Westland's and the others, are methods for evaluation and for exchanging information. As a result, in the year 2000, the nation is taking advantage of its size, in that it has several separate health experiments under way, each with differences and similarities. In response to its own experiences and those elsewhere, Health 2000 has already been modified. It will be subjected to continuing evaluation and to comprehensive review at ten-year intervals.

A continuing health contest is under way nationwide. The participants are the country's 110 health regions, with populations ranging from 800,000 to 3.5 million, of which Westland is one. Leadership is determined at intervals, and points are given for the lowest infant mortality rates, the highest life expectancy, the lowest number of days people miss work for illness, the highest quality of nursing homes, the lowest costs of medical care, the lowest number of people with heart attacks, the lowest number of smokers, the largest amount of money committed to research, the lowest number of hospital days, the highest fraction of over-eighty-five-year-olds able to manage at home, the lowest number of automobile accidents and the highest fraction of accident victims who survive in condition to function normally in society, the lowest number of teenage pregnancies, suicides, and homicides, and a range of other measures, including the degree of citizen satisfaction as determined by periodic surveys. I predict that the Westland of my fantasy will be close to the top of the list.

IV

PRIORITIES

13 Health Care Tomorrow: Rationing by Design?

Rationing: What word more accurately describes offering the best emergency care in the world to Americans who are acutely ill or injured, like John LeGrand, whose severed arm was restored, and refusing that care to other Americans with similarly desperate problems, but without health insurance? Any discussion of redistributing health resources must be prefaced by emphasizing the message presented early in this book: Our first order of business should be to protect the more than 37 million Americans now uninsured. By recovering money now wasted in the system, we could, for the present, provide universal coverage for basic health care. We could not do it, however, unless two conditions were met: first, that we reach a consensus about what is "basic," and second, that funding for such coverage flow through a single channel. Then, policymakers, after seeking advice from experts and citizen groups, could decide what fraction of the total would be committed for acute care hospitals, how much for primary care, how much for care for the elderly, how much for research, and so on. They could also make decisions concerning areas of the nation in need of special allocations.

Britain put itself in position to implement its policies in the 1940s when it created the National Health Service, because the latter controls almost all health funds. Canada's health services payment system was similar to ours until 1971, and the delivery system remains so. Until 1971, like the United States, it found that because of its diverse payment mechanisms, it could not translate its health goals into policy. But then, laws were enacted that gave each provincial government authority over *all* health funds. As a result, popularly supported health policies are now being implemented. The Canadian experience is the most relevant I know. Their approach is worth a trial. However, given the success of pluralistic approaches to problems in our country, that trial should be limited to a few states or areas. Meanwhile, other approaches might be tried elsewhere. Their common goal would be to make health spending more responsive to our needs and wishes while preserving our tradition of multiple pathways.

Mandating Access to Medical Care

The growing presence of for-profit medical care corporations makes it more urgent that we develop a policy and mechanisms to translate that policy into action. Some for-profit corporations may turn out to be more efficient than existing institutions in delivering medical services, although that has yet to be proved. However, their activities must be subject ultimately to policies that are set in the interest of the communities in which they are located. That does not mean that they should assume financial responsibility for the medical care of, for example, poor children, any more than that society asks food companies to feed them; both are the duties of the community. If, however, for-profit corporations control all or most of the health facilities in their community, they must participate fully in such publicly supervised and financed programs as Medicare and Medicaid. For only if they do so can care be assured for the children, the poor, the elderly, the mentally ill—those groups in our society with the greatest medical needs and often the feeblest voices. Similarly, if private companies have a monopoly on hospitals and other patient care institutions in a community, *they* must agree to provide access to them for the clinical teaching and research activities of local medical schools. Again, it is the responsibility of society to ensure that such programs are adequately financed. Since good teaching programs generally mean improved patient care (practice in a goldfish bowl is the way it is sometimes described), enlightened corporations will welcome the privilege of liaisons with medical schools.

If health care funds flowed in the United States as they do in Canada— that is, through regional government—consider what might have happened in Massachusetts in the spring of 1984, when the question arose as to whether the state would support a program in liver transplantation. A liver transplant and the first year of care (about 60 percent of patients survive a year or longer) cost about $200,000. At that time it had just become known that infant mortality rates had risen in poor areas of Boston; about twenty more babies had died per year where annual maternal and child health funds had been cut back by $600,000. If our principal objective had been to do the most good for the most people with our health money, we would have voted to defer the liver program at least until funding had been restored for maternal and child health.

But deferring the liver program would have meant death sentences for the patients with liver failure. Thus, if our principal objective had been to make best use of *all* our money, we would have found funds for both the maternal and child health program and for the patients with liver failure. As long as waste exists in the system of health services or outside, it will be difficult for us to accept decisions that lead to death sentences. This is not to say that we can evade tough tradeoff decisions. Rather, before we confront them, we should exhaust all possible mechanisms that could make them unnecessary.

Two conditions are necessary if we want policies on resource allocation that are widely known and accepted. The first is consensus concerning society's responsibilities in the health field. If we can't do everything that we would like to do, what programs take priority? Second, when we can't provide everything to all who are in need, who decides who gets what, and how?

What Is "Basic"?

In examining the first issue, that of societal responsibilities, it is useful to lay out certain principles on which perhaps all but extreme partisans might agree. Society has a responsibility to see that emergency care is available to all, independent of income, social status, or geography. The highway injury victim is an example. Another responsibility is to ensure the application of those preventive services needed to protect society as a whole, such as immunization against communicable diseases, as well as basic public health measures (water, sanitation, and so on) and environmental safety. A third responsibility, most Americans seem to feel, is protection of the whole population against economic devastation as a result of catastrophic illness. Another is the provision of basic health services of good quality for the poor, particularly children, the elderly, the mentally ill, and the mentally or physically handicapped. A fifth is for government (as well as the private sector) to give high priority to funding sound basic and clinical research, including research on the effectiveness of unproved medical interventions.

On the other hand, government does not have the responsibility to provide certain kinds of care that some people might wish to buy. Procedures that are not fully validated (but subject, of course, to protection of citizens from fraud), cosmetic surgery, and such amenities as private hospital rooms are cases in point.

Which health services are basic and should be available to all? Let me list some programs and activities to which I would give high priority:

- Health insurance for all citizens.
- Emergency medical services arranged geographically to ensure availability for all.
- A system of primary care for all Americans, so that every citizen who wants one has a gatekeeper.
- Acute hospital care, both secondary (for childbirth, for example, and for relatively straightforward problems, such as appendicitis and pneumonia, when the latter are too complicated for home management) and tertiary (for more complex problems like heart and brain surgery, and certain kinds of cancer chemotherapy).
- Community care programs for the poor, with special emphasis on the needs of pregnant women, infants, and children.
- Comprehensive care programs for the elderly, including home care programs, day care centers, and nursing homes.
- Hospitals, day care centers, and proper custodial facilities for the mentally ill and the mentally handicapped.
- More extensive preventive programs directed at cigarettes, alcohol, diet, and drugs.
- Support on a continuing basis and at predictable levels for biomedical research and for health services research.
- Support to make medical education available to meritorious students independent of family income.

But we are spending more for health than many countries that do not have the gaps that we do. As we have seen, Canada has gone far toward achieving *its* (similar) goals at an affordable price; indeed, the Canadians made care universally available and kept costs lower than ours. As in Canada, general guidelines might be set nationally and more specific ones at state or more regional levels in recognition of local variations in needs and preferences.

Consider how this might work if the Regional Health Corporations, as postulated in the previous chapter, were in place. Let's assume further that for a given year 10 percent of health funds flowing into the regions were designated for nursing home care, 25 percent for acute secondary and tertiary care hospitals, and 10 percent in the flexible category. Area 1, with a higher proportion of elderly residents, might use half of its "flexible" money to build and maintain more nursing home facilities, while Area 2 might choose to use a similar fraction to increase and modernize its intensive care capacity. In both situations, every proposal for the use of available funds would be examined in the context of the total health needs of the community.

Who Gets Priority?

So much for setting priorities for the allocation of health resources to various program areas. When a society decides to commit to a given program less money than is needed to make it available to all who would benefit, as is now the case for treatment for kidney failure in the United Kingdom or maternal and child health care here, that raises another issue about which we need consensus: When there isn't enough to go around, who should be given preference? In fact, independent of the amount of money a society is prepared to spend, that question arises with respect to human organs for transplantation, because the demand exceeds the supply.

The criteria are limited for deciding who will receive a given medical benefit and who will not. Need, ability and willingness to pay, likelihood of benefit, value to the community, and a lottery are more prominent possibilities. But all have serious defects. Ability to pay as a requirement for access to medical care was rejected in principle by Americans when the Medicaid and Medicare legislation was adopted. With government cutbacks in support for health programs for the poor in the 1980s, however, means has become an increasingly frequent determinant of who gets medical care in many parts of the country.

Value to the community has also been used as a criterion for selection. This was the yardstick often used by community "God committees" to assign the limited number of places in kidney dialysis programs in the days before legislation made available government funds for that life-saving treatment to all Americans with kidney failure. That yardstick did lead to discrimination—in favor of, for example, not only the young, but also males and the mentally fit. The implications of making judgments on an arbitrary basis—let us say, of age—are put into focus by the story of William Berry, whose medical history was summarized in Chapter 4. As a philanthropist and community leader, he has certainly been "socially useful" in the sixteen years since modern medicine saved his life at a time when he was already seventy years old. And yet, he would not have been a candidate for an expensive procedure if society had rationed on the basis of age.

At least 10 percent of the more than 70,000 Americans on dialysis are on a waiting list for kidneys. However, each year enough kidneys are found for only about 6,000 transplant operations. This has contributed to recent protests about the number of wealthy foreigners who come for kidneys to some transplant centers in the United States. Some are said to pay as much as four times what the Social Security insurance reimburses for the operation. Others are reported to be given "inferior" kidneys. I would—reluctantly—subscribe to a policy that restricted the distribution of such scarce resources as kidneys and other organs to foreigners until after we had met the needs of our own people. But as difficult as it is, the issue of who will get a scarce kidney is tempered by the fact that dialysis offers a life-preserving alternative treatment. Those in need of heart and liver transplants have no such recourse; they will die, in months or weeks, sometimes in days, unless they receive a transplant.

Seven Americans received heart transplants in 1970 and 440 in 1984. The lives of as many as 50,000 Americans who die each year of heart disease might be prolonged if heart transplants were available. But the operation requires a healthy heart obtained within a few hours of death of the donor. In effect, this limits donors largely to young accident victims whose hearts can be obtained at the instant of death. Therefore, it is unlikely that more than 2,000 of the 50,000 people in need each year could be so treated.

Candidates for heart transplants in most hospitals that carry out the operation must be able to pay the present cost of about $150,000. Thus, for this procedure, ability to pay is one criterion that determines eligibility. (Some patients, like the gospel singer described in Chapter 1, are given access to public funds.) Because of the strictly limited number of donor hearts, candidates for the operation are also very carefully screened on medical grounds. Thus, a second criterion—likelihood of benefit—is generally applied. Status is a third—for example, people over the age of fifty years are usually excluded.

The heart transplant operation is still sufficiently uncommon so that the criteria used to select recipients are not widely discussed. But as the demand grows, the fairness issue will be increasingly raised, as it has been for other medical interventions in short supply. And then we shall likely hear voices urging a lottery as the fairest way to allocate one of the scarcest resources of all—healthy hearts.

This approach, however, also has defects. Would it be acceptable to society if the single heart available today were given to, say, a seventy-five-year-old person who is unlikely to survive long because he has other serious diseases, or a criminal (the convicted rapist-murderer is the person often conjured up in discussions of this sort) who entered and won a lottery, while the losers include men and women in the community who are in their twenties and thirties and who have young children? Or, let us return to the matter of kidney transplants in an even more extreme hypothetical situation. We know that a kidney from some close relatives is less likely to be rejected by a recipient's normal immune mechanisms. As a result, some people with kidney failure receive transplants donated by living family members. Suppose that a parent of a person whose own kidneys had failed decided to donate a kidney, so that his son or daughter could come off dialysis. Should we exert moral pressure on such a parent to enter that kidney in a lottery involving others whose tissues are compatible? (And what parent would agree?)

Questions of *who* belongs on a priority list for a scarce medical intervention, as well as of *what* programs merit higher priority, have answers that will differ from person to person and even from the same person, depending on time and circumstance. It is no accident that two of the most thoughtful books on this subject are entitled *Tragic Choices* and *Who Shall Live?* In fact, no entirely satisfactory answers will ever be found, for there are none. That is true for the question of who will receive the scarce organ or other kind of medical care that is in short supply. It is equally true for the question of which programs we commit resources to when we can't do them all. Ultimately, our choices must be arbitrary, but we can choose.

Of the several possible ways to allocate scarce organs or other resources, I would—at the time I write this—pick the "God committee" approach. It strikes me as less evil than the others, but evil nonetheless. And even more evil as I consider how the committee should be picked. I make and state a choice, because it would be unseemly to dodge the issue after offering so many gratuitous comments on the need to make choices. Further, making the choice gives me an opportunity to stress that after living with this, or any other, approach for a time, I would want the right to change my mind. Thus, the fact that there is no "right" way is tempered by knowing that no decision need be rigid. In all likelihood, the process of today's allocation decisions will be modified tomorrow, as new technologies make old rules unsuitable, and as constituencies that are slighted today assert themselves or are otherwise recognized.

Not to Choose Is a Choice; No Choice Is Perfect

Two conclusions emerge from an examination of *how* to set priorities. First, not to choose often produces outcomes that prove less acceptable than those we might have opted for. Second, no matter how the process is carried out, it cannot be satisfactory. Therefore, the case is the more compelling to minimize both the number of decisions that must be made and the number that are made under pressure of time, of anxiety and emotion, and of media attention.

In the absence of an overall policy, most doctors will seek as much in the way of resources as they can get to serve their patients—that is, for all programs that address a medical need, and for all patients with that need. If society decides to defer for the time being, for example, an artificial heart program, doctors can live with the decision, even if unhappily. If they are provided a budget for, let's say, ten patients a year, they can—working with others, according to guidelines that are explicitly set forth—select the ten patients to be done. When they exhaust their resources before all patients in need have been cared for, they will at least be secure in the knowledge that they did all that *they* could.

But until now we have functioned without an overarching health policy, and we are in trouble. The problem can only grow as our population ages and as our medical capabilities increase.

Health Policy Is Social Policy

It is possible, indeed mandatory, for officials and the public in general to become sufficiently informed about medical and other technical issues, as well as the social, so that they can reach reasonable and defensible conclusions. Not so long ago most health issues were left largely to professionals for decisions. It is now widely recognized, however, that they belong to society as a whole. It is also clear that the quality and acceptability of the outcome rest upon the degree of public participation not only in the decisions themselves, but in the details that lead to those decisions.

One way to address the decisions would be through the creation of a national commission to lay out the problem, to define its components, to analyze how each has come to pass, to propose changes, and finally to suggest how to carry out trials of those changes. That commission's ultimate charge would be to propose health policies that would lead to first-class medical care and improved opportunity for first-class health for the entire nation, and then to recommend ways in which those policies could be carried out. At least of equal usefulness would be a series of regional commissions with mandates from various regions of the country—a medium-sized state here, a large city there, a group of neighboring small states elsewhere—to examine the health needs of their areas and to recommend remedies. It is important to recall that Canada's changes began at the provincial level. The federal government has provided baseline standards for the entire nation and helped with funding, but wisely left to the provinces planning that reflected local conditions.

Competing National Needs

The fraction of resources committed to health has been rising steadily for several decades, for a range of reasons but generally not because policymakers decided that the health sector merited more resources than others. Now, the emphasis is on stopping the rate of rise, or cost containment in today's vernacular. It may well be that medical costs should not rise further, because other demands for the same money are more pressing. But that, too, is a question sufficiently important to warrant considerable public discussion and then resolution.

Many economists point out that the 10.6 percent of our gross national product now spent on medical services is not necessarily a ceiling. Why not spend 13 percent or 15 percent of GNP on health? Indeed, opinion polls have shown that Americans generally support more health coverage. The principal argument for *not* committing more money to health is that it would mean less for other things. To deal sensibly with the question of whether to allocate more for health, then, requires our knowing what we would have to give up. This is particularly important at a time when so many other sectors of our life also have pressing needs. Consider, as examples, the proposed federal government share of $30 billion for a fifteen-year national plan for sewage treatment to meet minimum Clean Water Act standards. Or the $100 billion estimated cost of cleaning 10,000 toxic waste dumps that threaten to poison much of the nation's water supply. Or the ten-year plan offered by New York's mayor to rebuild the city's infrastructure over ten years at a cost of more than $40 billion, at a time of similar needs in other cities and towns throughout the country. Or the $90 billion that could be consumed in a ten-year period for research on President Reagan's Strategic Defense Initiative program (Star Wars), or the $1 trillion that former Secretary of Defense James Schlesinger estimates it would cost to produce and deploy such a system.

In recent years I have worked with physicians from around the world who have come together to talk with our fellow citizens about the medical consequences of nuclear war. The medical people have been unanimous in the view that the world as we know it could not survive a nuclear war. They have heard the opinions of highly placed military officers and diplomats from West and East that the use of even one nuclear weapon would likely lead to an all-out exchange (a view that may be wrong but the world can't afford to test). General James Abrahamson, who directs the Star Wars program at the Pentagon, has said that "a perfect astrodome defense is not a realistic thing." In other words, we cannot achieve absolute military security, no matter what we spend. Doctors have asked whether there has ever been a time in the nuclear era when a decision to stop testing and building nuclear devices would have left *any* people or nation worse off. Nobody has suggested that there was. Therefore, they have urged an immediate stop to the building of more nuclear arms systems. Soviet doctors have been as outspoken on this issue as Americans and those of other nations. It is possible that they know about zero-sum games—that resources are finite. They must know, for example, that the medical needs of the Soviet people dwarf ours; theirs is said to be the only country in Europe where life expectancy has been *falling* and infant mortality *rising* in recent years. If the Soviets stopped building nuclear arms, the money would not necessarily be diverted to health programs for their people. But the chances of more money for health would certainly be greater.

Parallel Problems: Health and Military Security

I focus on the nuclear arms race, not only because it competes with health care for resources, but also because, like health, it has been relatively shielded from public inspection. As with health, decisions are generally left to experts. As with health, more investment is not necessarily better.

Some of these lessons were brought home to me a few years ago when I was invited to testify on the medical consequences of nuclear war before a committee of the U.S. Senate. In a private conversation in advance, I mentioned my apprehensions to a senator who is very knowledgeable about military matters. I must be missing something, I said, in this area so far removed from my own field. Nobody disputed the fact that the world's nuclear arsenal had a total explosive force equivalent to 16 *billion* tons of TNT, more than 2,700 times the 6 *million* tons used by all sides in World

War II. It is estimated that this grotesque force, 97 percent of which is held by the Soviets and us, is sufficient to kill every man, woman, and child twelve times over. I had heard some experts say that 200 or 300, another that twenty or thirty, of today's bombs and delivery systems could virtually destroy any nation. But we already possessed a total of 30,000 nuclear bombs, of which more than 10,000 were intercontinental, and the Soviet Union had almost as many.* Surely, I said to the senator, there must be facets of the problem—very likely classified—that I was overlooking. Those facets would explain this seemingly irrational spending policy, at a time when American citizens were in desperate need of health and other social programs. Or, is it possible, I asked the senator, that the emperor has no clothes?

You cannot imagine, he replied, how naked the emperor really is. He went on to comment about our nuclear arms policy and about other defense issues. His remarks were strikingly similar to some of the generalizations that apply to the health field:

- Capabilities have far outstripped resources. It is essential that methods be found to set priorities.
- Better methods are needed for measuring returns on various investments so that choices can be made rationally.
- Existing resources can be used far more efficiently.
- Many systems now being built on a large scale have not been adequately evaluated. Indeed, people in and out of government are not paying enough attention to the purposes of various nuclear systems. Do they successfully address those purposes?
- Inadequate attention is given *all* possible forms of prevention. A strong military force is necessary to protect ourselves in this troubled world. But what of other approaches?
- The military professional is a crucial source of technical information, but should not be the final court of appeal.
- The nation urgently needs an informed public to help set priorities. Most issues before us are not only technical, but also questions of values and of common sense judgment.

---

* The argument for redundancy is, of course, that our opponents must realize that even if their first strike were to destroy most of our nuclear capability (itself a highly dubious assumption; everybody seems to acknowledge that at least the one third of our nuclear arsenal carried by submarines would be immune to a first strike), we would still have enough to retaliate in kind. This would make a grisly sort of sense, if one were to ignore the widely accepted "nuclear winter" view that a massive strike by only one side could destroy both nations and most others. But no one, apparently, knows where to draw the line.

Some object to my raising the issue of the nuclear arms race in discussing the nation's health needs. They point out that the fraction of the defense budget used for nuclear arms is small—no more than 15–20 percent. ("Small" is a relative word; 20 percent of an annual defense budget that now exceeds $300 billion could do wonders for the nation's needs in maternal and child health services, research, and many other neglected health areas.) Others say that the waste in the health field consumes precious resources, perhaps even more than that spent on nuclear arms. Both statements are accurate. Both are irrelevant to my point, so long as money that could save lives or protect health is used for purposes that most people would agree—once all the facts were laid out—are of lesser or *no* merit and can even be harmful.

A Question of Values

Each of us is as qualified as the experts to evaluate the argument that an enemy is more deterred by the prospect of being obliterated 1,000 times over than twelve times or merely once. Just as every citizen is as qualified as health professionals to understand tradeoffs like forty newborn babies saved in a two-year period versus three patients with liver failure.

We don't have to be expert in foreign affairs to have an opinion as to how much security the industrialized nations of the world bought with the $300 million they spent over ten years to eradicate smallpox, as compared with what was achieved with the $28 billion spent in 1983 alone for arms exports to Third World countries. Perhaps a few million dollars given to improve the health of the children of Central America would bring more security to the area than the billions we have spent to arm the parents—and often the children.

We need the "doctor" in every field to give us the facts. But the facts are not at issue—it's our values. Decisions on where to spend our money will depend on the views of the majority of citizens about which needs are most important to fill. We cannot achieve perfect health for all any more than we can achieve a "perfect astrodome defense." But every American child who grows up healthy and competent is a tangible asset. And those who do not can be expected to be costly to taxpayers, whether because of poor health or retarded intellectual or social development. Every possible spending decision in our world has to be evaluated and compared with all others.

Dr. Brian Jarman, one of England's leading general practitioners, believes that however acute the need for additional money for health care in his country, the need is even greater in some other areas of British life. He recently did extensive research on the factors that influence the workload of his colleagues throughout Britain. He found that from one general practice to another, the problems confronted by doctors are not, as one might expect, primarily determined by factors like hazardous work conditions for the people in the area or the number of doctors in practice, although those do make a big difference. Far more important is a range of social conditions, including the number of elderly and particularly elderly living alone, the number of children under five years of age, the quality of housing, the degree of poverty, and the extent of unemployment.

I asked Dr. Jarman what he thought would be the results of a proposed severe cut in the health budget in his area of London. It won't have nearly so much effect, he said, as an even larger reduction projected for the education budget. Education, he continued, is the field that is suffering most from government cuts. In the long run, it will have the most profound effect on the physical and emotional health of the next generation, as well as on the overall well-being of the nation.

We don't know how soon we will face the kind of dilemma that confronts British patients and doctors who don't have enough kidney dialysis facilities to go around. The timing will be determined by a range of factors, including the speed of development of new medical technology. But it seems likely that we shall more and more often face decisions whose outcome will determine who shall live. That inevitably sharpens the question as to whether more resources should be directed at medical care.

The answer to that question is in part dependent on our knowing what factors, in addition to medical care, affect health. Since poverty, ignorance, unemployment, and homelessness are important contributors to poor health, dealing with these problems might do as much or more for health as putting more money into medical services. Thus, economic, as well as humanitarian, reasons may exist for giving priority to such areas in deciding where to spend money.

But even with major changes in the health care system, the pressures for rationing will grow with advances in medical technology and because tomorrow's population will be older and their medical needs larger than today's.

Epilogue:
What Do We Want?

You could not step twice into the same river,
for other waters are ever flowing on to you.

—Heraclitus, *The Universe*

The health of the people is really the foundation
upon which all their happiness and all their powers
as a state depend.

—Benjamin Disraeli, 1877

Many approaches to medical education and medical care that were acceptable a generation ago are inadequate today; the same thing must be said about medical judgments and even ethical and moral decision making. My medical school class, 1948, was Harvard's last for men only. The only two sessions we had on family planning were given "unofficially" outside of the classroom, because the sale of contraceptive devices was then illegal in Massachusetts. When I was an intern, I was told by professors that most patients with cancer "can't deal with the diagnosis and don't want to know it." Things are changing far more rapidly now; much of what physicians and the public agree is appropriate for the 1980s will likely be inadequate for the conditions of the 1990s and beyond.

Books like this one risk being outdated before they are even published. Some problems I have described, such as huge sums spent for unnecessary hospitalization, may have been controlled in part by the time this book is read. Regrettably, however, there seems little chance that most of the serious defects in our health care system will be blown away by today's brisk winds of change. Indeed, many changes now going on risk making things worse. In part, this is because we have not set priorities. And even if we were to, our fragmented payment system would make it difficult for us to translate them. In part, it is because we still don't keep in mind that every change in the system may have not only its desired consequences, but unexpected and unwelcome side effects. That, in turn, makes it important to try out any radical departures on a pilot basis before making total commitments, as was done in Canada, whose present health care system grew out of an experimental program developed by the province of Saskatchewan. As is true of Canada, the vastness and heterogeneity of our country present a challenge—a challenge because health problems differ from one area to another. Solutions will differ as well. Past experience tells us that Washington is not capable of diagnosing and preventing or treating all local problems. Regional needs and regional conditions can be visualized as the horizontal woof of our ever-changing social fabric, and the national state of mind as the longitudinal warp. We conceived of this nation as a democracy centuries before civil rights legislation guaranteed a vote to every citizen, regardless of gender, race, or means. Indeed, long before the franchise, universal literacy was perceived as a right. As now we recognize that a citizen illiterate or disenfranchised is a citizen disabled, I believe that a national awareness must dawn that to deny people access to health care is, similarly, to disable and even to dehumanize and to destroy them.

What is defined as "basic" health care from region to region and from decade to decade may vary (as does the definition of "basic" education). I have provided my own definition in Chapter 13, and I acknowledge that it is subject to change in the future, if only because our capabilities will develop with our technology.

What will not change, however, are two indispensable elements of a decent health care system: (1) the prevention of illness, which involves social as well as medical intervention, and (2) caring for the patient. So my final words will be concerned with these two.

Prevention and the Pump Handle

A cholera epidemic broke out in the Golden Square district of London in the summer of 1854. At that time Londoners took their drinking water from neighborhood wells. While the cause of cholera was not then known, Dr. John Snow, a very astute London doctor, believed that whatever was responsible was transmitted in drinking water. Snow observed that most of the cases occurred in the area where the residents took water from a pump on Broad (now Broadwick) Street. The picture was at first confused by two seemingly conflicting observations. First, he noted a smaller outbreak in a neighboring area near a pump on Great Marlborough Street. Second, workers in a brewery on Broad Street were free of cholera. Careful detective work—involving a survey and a map, tools of the epidemiologist's trade— led him to discover that the water of the Great Marlborough Street pump was so foul that many people in the area walked the extra distance to the Broad Street pump. As for the brewery workers, Dr. Snow was told by the proprietor, Mr. Huggins, that the workers took water from a deep well within the brewery and not from the Broad Street pump. Armed with this evidence, Dr. Snow felt he had an ironclad case. He persuaded the local government officials to remove the handle of the pump, and the epidemic ended shortly thereafter.

Note that discovering the source of the problem was necessary, but not sufficient to control the cholera outbreak. Snow also had the "political" tasks of educating people and persuading the authorities to remove the pump handle. Only then was his work complete—spread of the cholera had been prevented.

As I have pointed out throughout this book, prospects are remote for treating successfully all, or even most, of today's health problems. Even if widely effective cures were found, like the remarkable and very expensive feats of medicine and surgery that save the lives of some of today's victims of cancer and heart disease, the costs could be prohibitive. In contrast, many disease prevention programs have been less expensive, risky, or un- comfortable. Examples include those carried out by design, like the elim- ination of smallpox around the world and the control of polio in the United States and in many other countries, and others which have resulted from still unexplained mechanisms, like the recent marked decrease in stomach cancer. Such events suggest that we are surrounded by "pumps" that could be controlled to prevent today's major health problems. We need to follow Dr. Snow's example: Identify the pump that is responsible and then take the handle off. Health professionals have identified the "pump" responsible for lung cancer, emphysema, and much of today's heart disease: cigarettes. What remains is to do what Snow did next to stop the spread of cholera— people must be educated about the relationship, and government officials must be induced to take off the handle.

We now see festering the problems of millions whom our society has virtually abandoned. What do we do, for instance, about epidemics of teenage pregnancy, drug addiction, suicide, and homicide? We feel frus- trated because we are unable to find medical "cures" for these problems. As for prevention, we don't have John Snow–type evidence, but it is likely that our neglect of maternal and child health programs, housing, nutrition, education, and employment in the inner cities plays a role. Even though we cannot now prove a causal relationship, humanitarian considerations alone should provoke us to raise the level of living for Americans now enduring conditions worse than in many Third World countries. If, as we do so, we record carefully what transpires, we may be able to determine whether there is in fact a cause-and-effect relationship. If a relationship is found, the experiment will have been worth running, if only for reasons of economy. It costs the community twice as much to keep someone in jail for a year, at least in New York, as it does to send him to Harvard. And if—by remote chance—no relationship emerges, removing the blight will by itself have been well worth the effort and cost.

Some day, perhaps all of today's major diseases will have been prevented by the removal of a variety of pump handles. Meanwhile, individual Americans need their physician to help in preventing disease, as well as in curing, caring, and rehabilitating. Therefore, another principle for our healthier tomorrow should be to ensure that our medical care system makes available to all citizens skills, caring, and continuity.

Caring: Sarah Cohn's Lesson to Me

This occurred in the pre-Medicaid days when poor people were patients of institutions like hospitals or clinics, when they were patients at all. Mrs. Cohn was a patient at the tumor clinic of the Boston hospital where I worked. She was divorced and without living relatives. Life had treated her harshly, starting with her imprisonment in a Nazi concentration camp, long before she was found to have a cancer that had spread to her bones and her lungs. During the time that I knew her, she was in and out of the inpatient service of the hospital several times for treatments that failed to arrest the spread of her cancer. She required progressively stronger medication for the pain that racked her body.

Mrs. Cohn knew of her diagnosis. She knew that we were having little success in treating her. But I was able to promise her that ways would be found to alleviate her symptoms, including her severe pain. With respect to her cancer and her future prospects, she made clear that she wanted me to answer only the questions she posed, and she posed very few. Rather, she complained bitterly about the humdrum events of her bleak life: the bus that was late, the landlord who was rude, the neighbor whose dog was not leashed. At first, I found it hard to summon the patience to hear her out. As I came to know of her first husband and her children who were murdered by the Nazis, of the abuses of her alcoholic second husband, and of more, I developed greater insight into what she was suppressing by complaining about trivia. She was a remarkable woman, and she knew that I respected her and admired her extraordinary courage. Even in her sickest days, even in a hospital bed, she was scrupulously neat. I never saw her, for instance, when she was not carefully made up. Though she could not or would not find words for her deep fears, she realized, I think, that I knew how she felt. As we came to know each other, the flow of complaints slackened. We would talk about books and music, but not her past and not her future.

Three years after her cancer had been discovered, its spread was so extensive that she could no longer take care of herself. She had no savings, and the facilities then available for patients with her medical problems, particularly poor patients, were far more limited than today's. My social worker colleague found a place for her on the "charity ward" of a chronic disease hospital several miles away. I was not on its staff, but I talked about her illness and her background with the doctor in charge. He assured me that she would be well looked after, and I promised her that I would visit in a few days.

Two days later Mrs. Cohn reappeared in my clinic. She looked distraught—her eyes swollen and her face pale, drawn, and fatigued. Her hair was tangled and dirty. Clearly, she was now indifferent to the way she looked. In the examining room she wept inconsolably, as she told me what had happened. Carrying the few belongings she had been instructed to bring, she had arrived at the chronic disease hospital in severe pain and feeling even more depressed than usual. No medication was offered her, and after three hours she asked to see the doctor. He was slow in coming. When at last he did and she told him just how displeased she was, he was abrupt. (Unless people were fully aware of how abominable her life had been, Mrs. Cohn did not readily evoke sympathy.) She said that the doctor was short with her and, she said, cruel. "He told me that I had a few months to live. He didn't need to tell me that. He said not to make myself and everyone else miserable. He said I should try to *enjoy* the time left to me!" She gave a despairing shrug. "There is nobody to hear me now, and I have no reason to live. I walked out of the hospital last night after he left, and I won't go back. I want you to give me a prescription for enough sleeping pills so that I can kill myself."

That I couldn't do. I could only find her a bed in a different hospital where I alerted the staff to what had happened and to her needs. She died within a few weeks, and I reflected on my failure. During the time she had been a clinic patient, she had regarded me as her personal physician, and I encouraged her to do so. When I gave up her care, it was my responsibility to see that someone else took charge who was fully aware of all of her needs, who would have regard for her well-being, and who would listen with attention and respect to what she was saying and what she didn't or couldn't say. When illness strikes people like Sarah Cohn, of whom the world is oblivious—and they are legion—the only reliable human contact may be with physicians or other health professionals.

I want to share the lesson Mrs. Cohn taught me with today's architects of new health care systems. I am particularly anxious to reach those who are so callous as to accept the prospect of two-class medicine in America. Surely, they don't realize how degrading second-class medical care can be. None would want it for themselves or their families. Few, surely, would defend our fobbing it off on the more than 37 million Americans now without health insurance and the uncounted millions who are insured but have no primary-care doctor. Doctors, not institutions, care for people.

The failures of our health care system stigmatize us as a nation. Those who doubt me might speak to English or French or Swedish friends, who will listen with disbelief to stories about Americans who have been refused hospitalization for cancer surgery because they were unable to deposit several thousand dollars cash in advance. For a state government to make funds available for organ transplants for all citizens while thousands of preschoolers are not immunized against the common childhood diseases, as is true in Illinois, is indefensible. So is the fact that the federal government permits millions of American children, and poor, elderly, and mentally ill citizens without access to medical services, to fall through what the Reagan Administration has called a "safety net." And our nation's expenditures of tens of billions of dollars for nuclear arms systems that contribute nothing to our security, while it is unable to find much smaller sums to provide food and medicines for hungry babies is not only inhuman, but short-sighted—the harvest we reap will cost us more than we save by denying them nutrition and medical care.

The future of America's health is far more a social than a medical or a technical question. Does the health of our nation mean as much to us as the health of his did to Disraeli? If so, what actions will we take to improve and preserve it? What are we prepared to give up? Who shall die and who shall live and be well? Wrenching questions. I believe that they will be among the most crucial of the next decade. If we leave the answers to chance as we have in the past, there is no reason to expect outcomes any better than what we have had. On the other hand, if we recognize that their control rests in our hands, we can choose to shape them to our values. Sorting out the questions and making changes will require determination and wisdom, and resolving them, fairness, generosity, courage, and integrity. They will require political leaders prepared to make unpopular decisions.

The answers will do much to determine what kind of a society ours will be. I believe it will be a society that gives priority to ensuring the health of all its citizens, the weakest as well as the strongest. I believe it will be a society that sees as one of its primary concerns the state of health of other nations around the world. Such a society, but no other, will, in my view, have the foundation to make possible the happiness and the security of our children and of theirs.

Notes

1. Rationing by Default

Page
5 **growing demand:** These projections, though generally accepted, are estimates. Not to overstate, I have generally given conservative figures. Much of the statistical information throughout the book is from invaluable publications from the National Center for Health Statistics, such as K. R. Levit, H. Lazenby, D. R. Waldo, and L. M. Davidoff, "National Health Expenditures, 1984," *Health Care Financing Review* 7, no. 1 (1985): 1–35; D. P. Rice, T. A. Hodgson, and A. N. Kopstein, "The economic costs of illness: a replication and update," *Health Care Financing Review* 7, no. 1 (1985): 61–80; and D. P. Rice and J. J. Feldman, "Living longer in the United States: demographic changes and health needs of the elderly," *Milbank Memorial Fund Quarterly; Health and Society* 61, no. 3 (1983): 362–396.

2. Caring

13 **caring:** F. W. Peabody, "The care of the patient" in *Doctor and Patient* (New York: Macmillan Co., 1930), pp. 27–57.

25 **disappointment, anger, and degradation:** K. Wrenn, "No insurance, no admission," *New England Journal of Medicine* 312, no. 16 (1985): 373–374.

29 **negligence by hospital personnel:** California Medical Association and California Hospital Association, *Report on the Medical Insurance Feasibility Study* (San Francisco: Sutter Publications, 1977).

30 **the vicious cycle of commitment:** B. Jennett, *High technology medicine: benefits and burdens* (New York: Oxford University Press, 1986), p. 65.

31 **do not resuscitate:** S. E. Bedell and T. L. Delbanco, Choices about cardiopulmonary resuscitation in the hospital. When do physicians talk with patients? *New England Journal of Medicine* 310(17): 1089–1093.

32 **withholding treatment:** J. J. Paris and F. E. Reardon, "Court responses to withholding or withdrawing artificial nutrition and fluids," *Journal of the American Medical Association* 253, no. 15 (1985): 2243–2245.

3. Finding Care

39 **place of residence:** J. Wennberg and A. Gittelsohn, "Variations in medical care among small areas," *Scientific American* 246, no. 4 (1982): 120–134.

40 **unnecessary procedures:** J. P. Bunker, "When doctors disagree," *New York Review of Books,* April 25, 1985, pp. 7–8, 10–11.

4. Advances in Medical Technology

58 **Stanford heart transplants:** R. W. Evans, D. L. Manninen, L. P. Garrison, Jr., and A. M. Maier, "Donor availability as the primary determinant of the future of heart transplantation," *Journal of the American Medical Association* 255, no. 14 (1986): 1892–1898.

66 **cost of care:** B. S. Bloom, R. S. Knorr, and A. E. Evans, "The epidemiology of disease expenses: the costs of caring for children with cancer," *Journal of the American Medical Association* 253, no. 16 (1985): 2393–2397.

67 **halfway technology:** L. Thomas, "The technology of medicine," *New England Journal of Medicine* 285, no. 24 (1971): 1366–1368.

5. Money, Time, and Lives: Costs of 'The System'

69 An especially useful source for this chapter was "The Aging Society," in *Daedalus*, vol. 115, no. 1, Winter 1986. It is a well-planned, well-documented, comprehensive symposium, which I recommend to all concerned readers.

70 **inefficiency:** D. U. Himmelstein and S. Woolhandler, "Cost without benefit: administrative waste in U.S. health care," *New England Journal of Medicine* 314, no. 7 (1986): 441–445.

70 **historical development:** P. Starr, *The social transformation of American medicine* (New York: Basic Books, 1982).

70 **unnecessary care:** J. A. Califano, Jr., *America's health care revolution: Who lives? Who dies? Who pays?* (New York: Random House, 1986).

74 **health insurance:** R. M. Gibson, K. R. Levit, H. Lazenby, and D. R. Waldo, "National health expenditures, 1983," *Health Care Financing Review* 6, no. 2 (1984): 1–29.

77 **Medicare-Medicaid legislation:** President's Commission for the Study of Ethical Problems in Medicine and Biomedical and Behavioral Research, *Securing access to health care: a report on the ethical implications of differences in the availability of health services,* vol. I (Washington, D.C.: U.S. Government Printing Office, 1983), pp. 16–17.

80 **nursing home expenditures:** A. Stein, "Medicare's broken promises," *The New York Times Magazine,* February 10, 1985.

81 **incomes of physicians:** U. E. Reinhardt, "Health manpower forecasting: current methodology and its impact on health manpower policy" in *Manpower for Health Care* (Washington, D.C.: National Academy of Sciences Press, 1974), pp. 19–58.

88 **vagrant population and mental illness:** E. L. Bassuk, "The Homelessness Problem," *Scientific American* 251, no. 1 (1984): 40–45.

88 **psychotropic drugs:** N. Andreasen, *The broken brain: the biological revolution in psychiatry* (New York: Harper & Row, 1983).

88 **California Medicaid:** D. U. Himmelstein et al., "Patient transfers: medical practice as social triage," *American Journal of Public Health* 74, no. 5 (1984): 494–497.

90 **Cook County Hospital:** R. L. Schiff et al., "Transfers to a public hospital: a prospective study of 467 patients," *New England Journal of Medicine* 314, no. 9 (1986): 552–557.

91 **economic pressures on hospitals:** A. S. Relman, "Economic consideration in emergency care: What are hospitals for?" (editorial), *New England Journal of Medicine* 312, no. 6 (1985): 372–373.

92 **ethical obligation to ensure access:** President's Commission (1983), op. cit.

93 **the elderly will be healthier:** J. F. Fries, "The compression of morbidity," *Milbank Memorial Fund Quarterly; Health and Society* 61 (1983): 397–419.

95 **one-hoss shay:** O. W. Holmes, "The Deacon's Masterpiece."

6. Lessons from Britain

101 **the quality of patients' lives:** D. Stetten, Jr., "Coping with blindness," *New England Journal of Medicine* 305, no. 8 (1981): 458–460.

103   **neurological skills sharpened:** T. J. Murray, "Neurology manpower, Canada, the United Kingdom and the United States." Presentation at annual meeting of the American Academy of Neurology, New Orleans, La., April 27, 1986.
105   **no chronic dialysis:** A. J. Wing, "Why don't the British treat more patients with kidney failure?" *British Medical Journal (Clinical Research)* 287, no. 6400 (1983): 1157-1158.

7. Lessons from Canada

111   **health care cost inflation:** R. G. Evans, "Health care in Canada: patterns of funding and regulation," *Journal of Health Politics, Policy and Law* 8, no. 1 (1983): 1-43.
117   **provincial governments:** Ibid..
118   **fees for common procedures:** U. E. Reinhardt, "The compensation of physicians: approaches used in other countries," *Quality Review Bulletin* 11, no. 12 (1985): 366-377.

8. Third World Health Problems: Lessons and Opportunities

122   **Third World medicine:** J. R. Evans, K. L. Hall, and J. Warford, "Shattuck Lecture— Health care in the developing world: problems of scarcity and choice," *New England Journal of Medicine* 305, no. 19 (1981): 1117-1127.
129   **common pasture:** H. H. Hiatt, "Protecting the medical commons: who is responsible?" *New England Journal of Medicine* 293, no. 5 (1975): 235-241.
129   **ruin to all:** G. Hardin, "The tragedy of the commons. The population problem has no technical solution; it requires a fundamental extension in mortality," *Science* 162, no. 859 (1968): 1243-1248.

9. Prevention: Its Value and Its Cost

137   **environmental factors:** R. Doll and R. Peto, *The causes of cancer: quantitative estimates of available risks of cancer in the United States today* (New York: Oxford University Press, 1981).
149   **inner city hospitals:** J. L. McKnight, "Politicizing health care," *Social Policy* 9, no. 3 (1978): 36-39.
149   **health of impoverished Indians:** W. McDermott, K. W. Deuschle, and C. R. Barnett, "Health care experiment at many farms," *Science* 175, no. 17 (1972): 23-31.
150   **Centers for Disease Control:** N. W. Axnick, S. M. Shavell, and J. J. Witte, "Benefits due to immunization against measles," *Public Health Reports* 84, no. 8 (1969): 673-680.

10. Biomedical Research

155   **medical triumphs:** J. H. Comroe, Jr., and R. D. Dripps, "Scientific basis for the support of biomedical science," *Science* 192, no. 4235 (1976): 105-111.
156   **disposal of cholesterol:** M. S. Brown and J. C. Goldstein, "A receptor-mediated pathway for cholesterol homeostasis," *Science* 232, no. 4746 (1986): 34-47.
158   **hormone treatment:** T. K. Koch, B. O. Berg, S. J. DeArmond, and R. F. Gravina, "Crentzfeldt-Jakob Disease in a young adult with idiopathic hypopituitarism," *New England Journal of Medicine* 313, no. 12 (1985): 731-733.
161   **programs of treatment and prevention:** P. B. Beeson, "Changes in medical therapy during the past half century," *Medicine* (Baltimore) 59, no. 2 (1980): 79-99.
167   **effective anticancer drugs:** B. Rosenberg, "The fascinating story of cisplatin," *Your Patient & Cancer* 1, no. 3 (1981): 49-56.

169   **British biomedical research:** "Dead-end for British research," *Nature* 310, no. 26 (1984): 261–262.

169   **public disenchantment with science:** Sir Hans Kornberg, "Balancing pure and applied research" in W. A. W. Neilson and C. Garfield, eds., *Universities in crisis: a mediaeval institution in the 21st century* (Quebec: The Institute for Research on Public Policy, 1986), pp. 87–109.

11. Technology Assessment: How to Improve Medical Care and Sometimes Save Money

172   **over 250,000 operations:** H. H. Hiatt, "Lessons of the coronary-bypass debate," *New England Journal of Medicine* 297, no. 26 (1977): 1462.

173   **first controlled clinical trial:** L. L. Miao, "Gastric freezing" in J. P. Bunker, B. A. Barnes, and F. Mosteller, eds., *Costs, risks, and benefits of surgery* (New York: Oxford University Press, 1977), pp. 198–211.

174   **atherosclerosis of the arteries:** EC/IC Bypass Study Group, "Failure of extracranial-intracranial arterial bypass to reduce the risk of ischemic stroke. Results of an international randomized trial," *New England Journal of Medicine* 313, no. 19 (1985): 1191–1200.

175   **heart attacks treated at home:** H. D. Mather et al., "Myocardial infarction: a comparison between home and hospital care for patients," *British Medical Journal* 1 (1976): 925–929.

175   **carefully controlled studies of breast cancer:** B. Fisher et al., "Ten-year results of a randomized clinical trial comparing radical mastectomy and total mastectomy with or without radiation," *New England Journal of Medicine* 312, no. 11 (1985): 674–681; "Limited surgery and radiotherapy for early breast cancer," *New England Journal of Medicine* 313, no. 21 (1985): 1365–1368.

175   **antenatal screening by amniocentesis:** G. S. Omenn, "Prenatal diagnosis of genetic disorders," *Science* 200 (1978): 952–958.

175   **extracorporeal membrane oxygenation:** L. H. Edmunds, Jr., *Extracorporeal support for respiratory insufficiency* (Springfield, Va.: Technical Information Service, 1976).

176   **wonders of the polio vaccine:** P. Meier, "The biggest public health experiment ever: the 1954 field trial of the Salk poliomyelitis vaccine" in M. Tanur et al., eds., *Statistics: a guide to the unknown,* 2nd ed. (San Francisco: Holden Day, 1978), pp. 3–15.

176   **untreated syphilis:** T. Gjestland, "The Oslo study of untreated syphilis: an epidemiologic investigation of the natural course of the syphilitic infection based on a restudy of the Boeck-Bruusgaard material," *Acta Dermato-Venereologica* (Stockholm), Vol. 35, Supplement 34 (1955): 3–368, Annexes I–IX.

177   **tonsillectomy:** J. L. Paradise et al., "Efficacy of tonsillectomy for recurrent throat infection in severely affected children. Results of parallel randomized and nonrandomized clinical trials," *New England Journal of Medicine* 310, no. 11 (1984): 674–683.

179   **cancer of the larynx:** B. J. McNeil, R. Weichselbaum, and S. G. Pauker, "Speech and survival: tradeoff between quality and quantity of life in laryngeal cancer," *New England Journal of Medicine* 305, no. 17 (1981): 982–987.

179   **quality of life or life itself:** B. J. McNeil, S. G. Pauker, H. C. Sox, Jr., and A. Tversky, "The elicitation of preferences for alternative therapies," *New England Journal of Medicine* 306, no. 21 (1982): 1259–1262.

179   **major study of coronary surgery:** "Myocardial infarction and mortality in the Coronary Artery Surgery Study (CASS) randomized trial," *New England Journal of Medicine* 310, no. 12 (1984): 750–758.

180 **no such preventive effect:** W. J. Dieckmann, M. E. Davis, and S. M. Rynkiewicz, "Does the administration of diethylstilbestrol during pregnancy have therapeutic value?" *American Journal of Obstetrics and Gynecology* 66 (1953): 1062–1081.

180 **arbitrarily set weight:** R. B. Berg and A. J. Salisbury, "Discharging infants of low birth weight: reconsideration of current practice," *American Journal of Diseases of Children* 121 (1971): 414–417.

182 **chest pain:** H. V. Fineberg, D. Scadden, and L. Goldman,, "Care of patients with a low probability of acute myocardial infarction," *New England Journal of Medicine* 310, no. 20 (1984): 1301–1307.

184 **women undergoing hysterectomy:** Institute of Medicine (U.S.) Committee for Evaluating Medical Technologies in Clinical Use, *Assessing medical technologies* (Washington, D.C.: National Academy Press, 1985), pp. 22–23.

185 **technology assessment:** Ibid, pp. 22–23.

187 **Council on Health Care Technology:** Ibid, pp. 252–253.

189 **additional financial support:** Ibid, pp. 14, 221–224.

12. Health Services Research: Health 2000, An Experiment in Health Care Delivery

203 **specialist oversupply:** A. Tarlov, "The increasing supply of physicians, the changing structure of the health-services system, and the future practice of medicine," *New England Journal of Medicine* 308, no. 20 (1983): 1235–1244.

13. Health Care Tomorrow: Rationing by Design?

216 **wealthy foreigners:** L. Gruson, "Center for transplants aids Pittsburgh ascent," *The New York Times,* September 16, 1985.

217 **scarce medical intervention:** G. Calabresi and P. Bobbitt, *Tragic choices* (New York: W. W. Norton, 1978); V. R. Fuchs, *Who shall live? Health, economics, and social choice* (New York: Basic Books, 1974).

219 **more health coverage:** R. J. Blendon and D. E. Altman, "Public attitudes about health care costs: a lesson in national schizophrenia," *New England Journal of Medicine* 311, no. 9 (1984): 613–616.

222 **additional money for health care:** B. Jarman, "Identification of underprivileged areas," *British Medical Journal (Clinical Research)* 286, no. 6379 (1983): 1705–1709.

Epilogue: *What Do We Want?*

225 **cholera epidemic:** J. Snow, "Cholera" in L. Clendening, comp., *Source Book of Medical History* (New York: Dover, 1942), pp. 468–473.

Further Reading

Aaron, H. J., and Schwartz, W. B. (1984). The painful prescription: rationing hospital care. The Brookings Institution, Washington, D.C.

Angell, M. (1985). Cost containment and the physician. *Journal of the American Medical Association* 254(1):1203–1207.

Andreasen, Nancy (1983). *The broken brain: the biological revolution in psychiatry.* New York: Harper & Row.

Axnick, N. W., Shavell, S. M., and Witte, J. J. (1969). Benefits due to immunization against measles. *Public Health Reports* 84(8):673–680.

Bailar, J. C. III, and Smith, E. M. (1986). Progress against cancer: *New England Journal of Medicine* 314(19):1225–1232.

Bedell, S. E., and Delbanco, T. L. (1984). Choices about cardiopulmonary resuscitation in the hospital. When do physicians talk with patients? *New England Journal of Medicine* 310(17):1089–1093.

Beeson, P. B. (1980). Changes in medical therapy during the past half century. *Medicine* (Baltimore) 59(2):79–99.

Bernard, B. P. (1985). Private hospitals' dumping of patients. *New York Times,* October 28, 1985.

Black and white children in America: key facts (1985). Children's Defense Fund, New York.

Blendon, R. J., Rogers, D. E. (1983). Cutting medical care costs: primum non nocere. *Journal of the American Medical Association* 250(14):1880–1885.

Blendon, R. J. (1986). Health policy choices for the 1990's. *Issues in Science and Technology* II(4):65–73.

Bloom, B. S., Knorr, R. S., and Evans, A. E. (1985). The epidemiology of disease expenses: the costs of caring for children with cancer. *Journal of the American Medical Association* 253(16):2393–2397.

Blumenthal, D., Schlesinger, M., and Drumheller, P. B. (1986). The future of Medicare. *New England Journal of Medicine* 314(11):722–728.

Boyle, M. H., Torrance, G. W., Sinclair, J. C., and Horwood, S. P. (1983). Economic evaluation of neonatal intensive care of very-low-birth-weight infants. *New England Journal of Medicine* 308(22):1330–1337.

Braunwald, E. (1983). Effects of coronary-artery bypass grafting on survival. Implications of the randomized coronary-artery surgery study. *New England Journal of Medicine* 309(19):1181–1184.

Brown, M. S., and Goldstein, J. C. (1986). A receptor-mediated pathway for cholesterol homeostasis. *Science* 232(4746):34–47.

Bunker, J. P. (1985). When doctors disagree. *New York Review of Books,* April 25, 1985, pp. 7–8; 10–11.

Cairns, J. (1978). *Cancer: science and society.* San Francisco: Freeman..

Cairns, J. (1985). The treatment of diseases and the war against cancer. *Scientific American* 253(5):51–59.

Calabresi, G., and Bobbitt, P. (1978). *Tragic choices.* New York: Norton.

Califano, J. A., Jr. (1986). *America's health care revolution: Who lives? Who dies? Who pays?* New York: Random House.

Canada. Department of National Health and Welfare (1975). A new perspective on the health of Canadians: a working document. Information Canada, Ottawa.

Caplan, A. L. (1985). Ethical issues raised by research involving xenografts. *Journal of the American Medical Association* 254(23):3339–3343.

Cecil Textbook of Medicine, 17th edition (1985). Edited by J. B. Wyngaarden and L. H. Smith, Jr. Philadelphia: Saunders.

Centerwall, B. S. (1984). Race, socioeconomic status, and domestic homicide: Atlanta, 1971–72. *American Journal of Public Health* 74(8):813–815.

Changing mortality patterns, health services utilization, and health care expenditures, United States, 1978–2003 (1983). U.S. National Center for Health Statistics, Vital and health statistics, series 3, analytical and epidemiological studies no. 23; PHS-83-1407. U.S. Government Printing Office, Hyattsville, Md.

Chassin, M. R., Brook, R. H., Park, R. E., Keesey, J., Fink, A., Kosecoff, J., Kahn, K., Merrick, N., and Solomon, D. H. (1986). Variations in the use of medical and surgical services by the Medicare population. *New England Journal of Medicine* 314(5):285–290.

Comroe, J. H., Jr., and Dripps, R. D. (1976). Scientific basis for the support of biomedical science. *Science* 192(4235):105–111.

Coronary artery surgery study (CASS): a randomized trial of coronary artery bypass surgery. Quality of life in patients randomly assigned to treatment groups. (1983). *Circulation* 68(5):951–960.

Costs, risks, and benefits of surgery. (1977). Edited by Bunker, J. P., Barnes, B. A., and Mosteller, F. New York: Oxford University Press.

Detsky, A. S., Stacey, S. R., and Bombardier, C. (1983). The effectiveness of a regulatory strategy in containing hospital costs. The Ontario experience 1967–1981. *New England Journal of Medicine* 309(3):151–159.

Dickman, R. L., and Bukowski, S. (1982). Epidemiology and ethics of coronary artery bypass surgery in an eastern county. *Journal of Family Practice* 14(2): 233–239.

Doing better and feeling worse: health in the United States (1977). *Daedalus,* proceedings of the American Academy of Arts and Sciences 106(1).

Doll, R. (1983). Prospects for prevention. *British Medical Journal (Clinical Research)* 286(6363):445–453.

Doll, R., and Peto, R. (1981). *The causes of cancer: quantitative estimates of available risks of cancer in the United States today.* New York: Oxford University Press.

Enthoven, A. C. (1980). *Health plan: the only practical solution to the soaring cost of medical care.* Addison-Wesley, Reading, Mass.

Enthoven, A. C., and Noll, R. G. (1984). Prospective payment: will it solve Medicare's financial problem? *Issues in Science and Technology* 1:101–116.

Evans, J. R., Hall, K. L., and Warford, J. (1981). Shattuck Lecture—health care in the developing world: problems of scarcity and choice. *New England*

Journal of Medicine 305(19):1117–1127.

Evans, R. G. (1983). Health care in Canada: patterns of funding and regulation. *Journal of Health Politics, Policy and Law* 8(1):1–43.

Evans, R. W. (1983). Health care technology and the inevitability of resource allocation and rationing decisions (parts I and II). *Journal of the American Medical Association* 249(15):2047–2053; 249(16):2208–2219.

Evans, R. W. (1986). The heart transplant dilemma. *Issues in Science and Technology* II(3):91–101.

Failure of extracranial-intracranial arterial bypass to reduce the risk of ischemic stroke. Results of an international randomized trial (1985). The EC/IC Bypass Study Group. *New England Journal of Medicine* 313(19):1191–1200.

Fein, R. (1986). *Medical care, medical costs: the search for a health insurance policy.* Cambridge: Harvard University Press.

Feshbach, M. (1984). Soviet health problems. *Transactions in Social Science and Modern Society* 21(3):79–89.

Fineberg, H. V., and Pearlman, L. A. (1982). Low-cost medical practices. *Annual Review of Public Health* 3:225–248.

Fingerhut, L. A. (1982). Changes in mortality among the elderly, United States, 1940–78. U.S. National Center for Health Statistics (vital and health statistics, series 3, Analytical Studies no. 22; PHS 82-1406), Hyattsville, Md.

Fisher, B., Redmond, C., Fisher, E. R., et al. (1985). Ten-year results of a randomized clinical trial comparing radical mastectomy and total mastectomy with or without radiation. *New England Journal of Medicine* 312(11):674–681.

Freeland, M. S., and Schendler, C. E. (1983). National health expenditure growth in the 1980's: an aging population, new technologies, and increasing competition. *Health Care Financing Review* 4(3):1–58.

Freidson, E. (1970). *Professional dominance: the social structure of medical care.* New York: Atherton Press.

Fuchs, V. R. (1986). *The health economy.* Cambridge: Harvard University Press.

Fuchs, V. R. (1984). The "rationing" of medical care. *New England Journal of Medicine* 311(24):1572–1573.

Fuchs, V. R. (1974). *Who shall live? Health, economics, and social choice.* New York: Basic Books.

Gibson, R. M., Levit, K. R., Lazenby, H., and Waldo, D. R. (1984). National health expenditures, 1983. *Health Care Financing Review* 6(2):1–29.

Gibson, R. M., Waldo, D. R., and Levit, K. R. (1983). National health expenditures, 1982. *Health Care Financing Review* 5(1):1–31.

Ginzberg, E., with Ostow, M. (1969). *Men, money, and medicine.* New York: Columbia University Press.

Gjestland, T. (1955). The Oslo study of untreated syphilis: an epidemiologic investigation of the natural course of the syphilitic infection based on a restudy of the Boeck-Bruusgaard material. *Acta Dermato-Venereologica* (Stockholm) (suppl 34):3–368 (annex I–LVI).

Goldman, L., and Cook, E. F. (1984). The decline in ischemic heart disease mortality rates: an analysis of the comparative effects of medical interventions and changes in lifestyles. *Annals of Internal Medicine* 101(6):825–836.

Gorovitz, S. (1982). *Doctors' dilemmas: moral conflict and medical care.* New York: Oxford University Press.

Graham, J. D., and Vaupel, J. W. (1981). Value of a life: what difference does it make? *Risk Analysis* 1(1):89–95.

Grant, J. P. (1985). The state of the world's children, 1986. Oxford University Press, Oxford, New York.

Gray, B. H., and McNerney, W. J. (1986). For-profit enterprise in health care. The Institute of Medicine Study *New England Journal of Medicine* 314(23): 1523–1528.

Gruson, L. (1985). Some doctors move to bar transplants to foreign patients. *New York Times,* August 10, 1985.

Hack, M., and Fanaroff, A. A. (1986). Changes in the delivery room care of the extremely small infant (less than 750 g). Effects on morbidity and outcome. *New England Journal of Medicine* 314(10):660–664.

Hadley, J. (1982). *More medical care, better health?: an economic analysis of mortality rates.* Washington, D.C.: The Urban Institute Press.

Hardin, G. (1968). The tragedy of the commons. The population problem has no technical solution; it requires a fundamental extension in mortality. *Science* 162(859):1243–1248.

Hiatt, H. H. (1975). Protecting the medical commons: who is responsible? *New England Journal of Medicine* 293(5):235–241.

Himmelstein, D. U., and Woolhandler, S. (1986). Cost without benefit: administrative waste in U.S. health care. *New England Journal of Medicine* 314(7): 441–445.

Himmelstein, D. U., Woolhandler, S., Harnly, M., Bader, M. B., Silber, R., Backer, H. D., and Jones, A. A. (1984). Patient transfers: medical practice as social triage. *American Journal of Public Health* 74(5):494–497.

Institute of Medicine (U.S.) Committee for Evaluating Medical Technologies in Clinical Use (1985). *Assessing medical technologies.* National Academy Press, Washington, D.C.

Jarman, B. (1983). Identification of underprivileged areas. *British Medical Journal (Clinical Research)* 286(6379):1705–1709.

Jarman, B. (1984). Underprivileged areas: validation and distribution of scores. *British Medical Journal (Clinical Research)* 289(6458):1587–1592.

Jennett, B. (1986). High technology medicine: benefits and burdens. New York: Oxford University Press.

Jennett, B. (1984). Inappropriate use of intensive care (editorial). *British Medical Journal (Clinical Research)* 289(6460):1709–1711.

Kane, R. A., and Kane, R. L. (1985). The feasibility of universal long-term-care benefits: ideas from Canada. *New England Journal of Medicine* 312(21): 1357–1364.

Levit, K. R., Lazenby, H., Waldo, D. R., and Davidoff, L. M. (1985). *National health expenditures, 1984, Health Care Financing Review* 7(1):1–35.

Loehrer, P. J., and Einhorn, L. H. (1984). Drugs five years later: cisplatin. *Annals of Internal Medicine* 100(5):704–713.

Lister, J. (1984). Private medical practice and the National Health Service. *New England Journal of Medicine* 311(16):1057–1061.

Lurie, N., Ward, N. B., Shapiro, M. F., et al. (1986). Termination of Medi-Cal benefits. A follow-up study one year later. *New England Journal of Medicine* 314(19):1266–1268.

Manning, W. G., Leibowitz, A., Goldberg, G. A., Rogers, W. H., et al. (1985). A controlled trial of the effect of a prepaid group practice on use of services. *New England Journal of Medicine* 310(23):1505–1510.

McCormick, M. C. (1985). The contribution of low birth weight to infant mortality and childhood morbidity. *New England Journal of Medicine* 312(2):82–90.

McDermott, W. (1978). Medicine: the public good and one's own. *Perspectives in Biology and Medicine* 21(2):167–187.

McDermott, W., Deuschle, K. W., and Barnett, C. R. (1972). Health care experiment at many farms. *Science* 175(17):23–31.

McKeown, T., and Lowe, C. R. (1974). An introduction to social medicine, 2d edition. Oxford: Blackwell Scientific Publications.

McNeil, B. J., Pauker, S. G., Sox, H. C., Jr., and Tversky, A. (1982). The elicitation of preferences for alternative therapies. *New England Journal of Medicine* 306(21):1259–1262.

McNeil, B. J., Weichselbaum, R., and Pauker, S. G. (1981). Speech and survival: tradeoff between quality and quantity of life in laryngeal cancer. *New England Journal of Medicine* 305(17):982–987.

Mechanic, D. (1985). Cost containment and the quality of medical care: rationing strategies in an era of constrained resources. *Milbank Memorial Fund Quarterly; Health and Society* 63(3):453–475.

Meisel, P., and Kendrick, W., eds. James Strachey to his wife, Alix, 1924 (1985). *Bloomsbury/Freud: the letters of James & Alix Strachey, 1924–1925.* New York, Basic Books.

Murray, T. J. Neurology manpower, Canada, the United Kingdom and the United States. UK/US/Canada. Presentation at annual meeting of the American Academy of Neurology, New Orleans, La. April 27, 1986.

Myocardial infarction and mortality in the coronary artery surgery study (CASS) randomized trial (1984). *New England Journal of Medicine* 310(12):750–758.

Nichols, E. K. (1986). *Mobilizing against AIDS: the unfinished story of a virus.* Institute of Medicine/National Academy of Medicine. Cambridge, Mass.: Harvard University Press.

Otten, A. L. (1985). Slowing drop in infant death rate fuels debate on U.S. spending for child, maternal programs. *Wall Street Journal,* July 23, 1985.

Palmer, J. L., and Gould, S. G. (1986). The economic consequences of an aging society. *Daedalus,* Journal of the American Academy of Arts and Sciences. 115(I):295–323.

Paradise, J. L., Bluestone, C. D., Bachman, R. Z., et al. (1984). Efficacy of tonsillectomy for recurrent throat infection in severely affected children. Results of parallel randomized and nonrandomized clinical trials. *New England Journal of Medicine* 310(11):674–683.

Paris, J. J., Reardon, F. E. (1985). Court responses to withholding or withdrawing artificial nutrition and fluids. *Journal of the American Medical Association* 253(15):2243–2245.

President's Commission for the Study of Ethical Problems in Medicine and Biomedical and Behavioral Research (1983). Securing access to health care: a report on the ethical implications of differences in the availability of health services, vol. I. Washington, D.C.: U.S. Government Printing Office.

Relman, A. S. (1985). Economic consideration in emergency care. What are hospitals for? (editorial) *New England Journal of Medicine* 312(6):372–373.

Relman, A. S. (1980). The new medical-industrial complex? *New England Journal of Medicine* 303(17):963–970.

Rice, D. P., Hodgson, T. A., and Kopstein, A. N. (1985). The economic costs of illness: a replication and update. *Health Care Financing Review* 7(1):61–80.

Rice, D. P., and Feldman, J. J. (1983). Living longer in the United States: demographic changes and health needs of the elderly. *Milbank Memorial Fund Quarterly; Health and Society* 61(3):362–396.

Rosenberg, B. (1981). The fascinating story of cisplatin. *Your Patient & Cancer* 1(3):49–56.

Roueché, B. (1980). The Medical Detectives. New York: Times Books.

Russell, L. (1986). Is prevention better than cure? Washington, D.C.: Brookings Institution.

Sai, F. T. (1984). The population factor in Africa's development dilemma. *Science* 226(4676):801–805.

Sandhu, B., Stevenson, R. C., Cooke, R. W., Pharoah, P. O. (1986). Cost of neonatal intensive care for very-low-birthweight infant. *Lancet* 1(8481):600–603.

Scitovsky, A. A. (1985). Changes in the costs of treatment of selected illnesses, 1971–1981. *Medical Care* 23(12):1345–1357.

Sivard, R. L. (1985). *World Military and Social Expenditures* 1985. Washington, D.C.: World Priorities.

Schiff, R. L., Ansell, D. A., Schlosser, J. E., et al. (1986). Transfers to a public hospital: a prospective study of 467 patients. *New England Journal of Medicine* 314(9):552–557.

Starr, P. (1982). The social transformation of American medicine. New York: Basic Books.

Stein, A. Medicare's broken promises (1985). *New York Times Magazine,* February 10, 1985.

Stern, M. P. (1979). The recent decline in ischemic heart disease mortality. *Annals of Internal Medicine* 91(4):630–640.

Stetten, D., Jr. (1981). Coping with blindness. *New England Journal of Medicine* 305(8):458–460.

Thomas, L. (1971). The technology of medicine. *New England Journal of Medicine* 285(24):1366–1368.

Thurow, L. C. (1984). Learning to say "no." *New England Journal of Medicine* 311(24):1569–1572.

Thurow, L. C. (1985). Medicine versus economics. *New England Journal of Medicine* 313(10):611–614.

United States General Accounting Office (1985). *Constraining national health care expenditures, achieving quality care at an affordable cost.* GAO/HRD-85-105, Washington, D.C.: U.S. Government Printing Office.

The value of preventive medicine (1985). CIBA Foundation Symposium 110:1–258.

Verbeek, A. L., Hendriks, J. H., Holland, R., et al. (1984). Reduction of breast cancer mortality through mass screening with modern mammography: first results of the Nijmegen project, 1975–1981. *Lancet* 1(8388):1222–1224.

Vital statistics of the United States: vol. I, *Natality;* vol. II, *Mortality;* vol. III, *Marriage and divorce.* Hyattsville, Md.: U.S. National Center for Health Statistics.

Waitzkin, H. (1984). Two-class medicine returns to the United States: impact of Medi-Cal reform. *Lancet* 2(8412):1144–1146.

Weinstein, M. C. (1983). Cost-effective priorities for cancer prevention. *Science* 221(4605):17–23.

Weinstein, M. C., and Stason, W. B. (1977). Foundations of cost-effectiveness analysis for health and medical practices. *New England Journal of Medicine* 296(13):716–721.

Wennberg, J., and Gittelsohn, A. (1982). Variations in medical care among small areas. *Scientific American* 246(4):120–134.

Wessell, D. (1984). Medical quandary: transplants increase, and so do disputes over who pays bills. *Wall Street Journal,* April 12, 1984.

Wing, A. J. (1983). Why don't the British treat more patients with kidney failure? *British Medical Journal (Clinical Research)* 287(6400):1157–1158.

Wolinsky, H. (1984). Organ transplant aid bill signed. *Chicago Sun Times.*

Wrenn, K. (1985). No insurance, no admission. *New England Journal of Medicine* 312(16):373–374.

Index

About the Author

Dr. Hiatt did his undergraduate work at Harvard College and received his M.D. from the Harvard Medical School. Trained in clinical medicine, biochemistry, and molecular biology, he joined the Harvard University faculty in 1955 and has been there since. From 1963 to 1972 he was Herrman L. Blumgart Professor of Medicine at Harvard Medical School and Physician-in-Chief at Beth Israel Hospital. From 1972 to 1984 he was dean of the Harvard School of Public Health. Since that time he has been Professor of Medicine in both the Medical School and the School of Public Health, and Senior Physician at the Brigham and Women's Hospital.

Dr. Hiatt is the author of over seventy scientific papers and has written for the lay press in areas of disease prevention and health services. In addition, in recent years he has written and spoken about the health implications of the nuclear arms race.

He is a member of the Association of American Physicians, the Institute of Medicine of the National Academy of Sciences, the American Academy of Arts and Sciences, and the American Society for Clinical Investigation, as well as several other organizations.